Southern Literary Studies

Louis D. Rubin, Jr., EDITOR

The Southern Mandarins

The Southern Mandarins

Letters of Caroline Gordon to

Sally Wood, 1924–1937

Edited by Sally Wood

FOREWORD BY ANDREW LYTLE

Louisiana State University Press

Baton Rouge and London

Manufactured in the United States of America
Designer: Barbara Werden
Typeface: Linotron Galliard
Typesetter: G&S Typesetters, Inc.
Printer and Binder: Vail-Ballou Press

LIBRARY OF CONGRESS CATALOGING IN PUBLICATION DATA

Gordon, Caroline, 1895–
    The Southern mandarins.

    (Southern literary studies)
    1. Gordon, Caroline, 1895–   —Correspondence.
2. Wood, Sally—Correspondence.   3. Tate, Allen,
1899–   —Biography—Marriage.   4. Authors, American—
20th century—Correspondence.   I. Wood, Sally.   II. Title.
III. Series.
PS3513.05765Z497 1984   813'.52   [B]   83-16229
ISBN 0-8071-1137-6

Frontispiece: Caroline Gordon, Allen Tate, and Sally Wood in Toulon, 1932.
Courtesy of Papers of Caroline Gordon, Princeton University Library.

*For Allen, with whom Caroline
spent her happiest years, and
Larry, with whom I spent mine*

Contents

Acknowledgments

These letters could not have been published without a great deal of help. The recipient wishes especially, among many others, to thank Ashley Brown of Columbia, South Carolina, who has worked closely with the letters and Caroline Gordon's fiction.

Anne Boyle, formerly a graduate student at the University of Rochester, Rochester, New York, did most of the typing, looked up references and transcribed the photocopies of the letters supplied by the Princeton University Library. Her treating them as a constant discovery revealed them as new to the present generation.

And we also thank Howard C. Horsford of the University of Rochester who took over a large share of the correspondence and academic details.

Brief selections of the letters have appeared before in the *Southern Review*, XVI (April, 1980), and in the *Visionary Company: A Magazine of the Twenties*, I (Summer, 1981).

Biographical Notes

CAROLINE GORDON was born in 1895 at her Meriwether grandmother's plantation, "Merry Mont" (Todd County, Kentucky, on the Tennessee line). Meriwethers were originally among the first Virginia settlers—the famous explorer, Meriwether Lewis, was a collateral descendant—and in later western migration, relatives remained in close association, occupying many thousands of adjacent acres in southern Kentucky. Her Virginian father, educated as a minister, had come to tutor Meriwether children, becoming the first outsider married by a daughter of the densely knit "connection" of family cousins.

Caroline's father educated her at home, especially in the Classics, while he conducted a boys' school in Clarksville, just across the state line. After she graduated from Bethany College, West Virginia, in 1916 she too taught high school, then tried journalism before coming north to Greenwich Village where she first met Sally Wood. And shortly, late in 1924, she there married the young poet Allen Tate who had introduced himself to her earlier when he and Robert Penn Warren, a near neighbor in Kentucky, came calling at her parents' home.

Living as they did on the sharp edge of poverty, the Tates had to leave their infant daughter, Nancy, born the next year, in the care of the elder Gordons while they and, for a while, Hart Crane lived in an isolated farm house in Putnam County, New York, near Sherman, Connecticut. But winters proved too difficult, and they returned to the city. There Caroline first picked up work as a part-time secretary to Ford Madox Ford, the beginning of the long-time association so greatly important to her.

In 1928 Allen was awarded a Guggenheim Fellowship on which they spent much of the next two years in France, much of it near Ford. From there, her first short story was published in Yvor Winters' *Gyroscope*. After she returned to Tennessee, the enthusiasm of Scribner's notable editor, Maxwell Perkins, led to the publication of a long string of her novels and short stories by that firm.

In Tennessee she and Allen had taken over a farmhouse on a bluff above the Cumberland River, just outside of Clarksville, calling it "Benfolly" after Allen's wealthy brother, Ben, who had helped them buy it. Then, on another Guggenheim, this time awarded to Caroline (1932), they again spent several months in France, and still later, they lived two winters (1934–1936) in Memphis while Allen taught at Southwestern University. But the center of their strenuously creative and hospitable life was Benfolly, where she completed several of her best stories and four novels, including *Aleck Maury, Sportsman* (1934), which memorialized her father's passion for fishing. A still later novel, *The Strange Children* (1951), draws on those Benfolly years and the many friends famous or soon to become so who shared that hospitality.

In the fall of 1938 the Tates left Benfolly—permanently as it turned out—to take up a joint academic appointment at the Women's College of the University of North Carolina, Greensboro. In the following years they were in Princeton, Washington, or New York, sometimes teaching and always writing. But strains led to a divorce, granted in 1946, though quickly followed by remarriage. (In that year, also, Bethany College bestowed a Litt.D. on its distinguished alumna.) In the late 1940s the Tates became communicants of the Catholic church, but a further long separation ended in a second divorce in 1959. In these years, Caroline's teaching of creative writing took her to many universities across the country, ending at the University of Dallas when she was eighty. Finally, in ill-health and too frail to continue, she went with her daughter and son-in-law, Nancy and Percy Wood, to their home in San Cristóbal, Mexico, where she died in 1981 and is buried.

SALLY CALKINS WOOD was born in 1897 into a comfortably prosperous family in Rochester, New York. She attended Wellesley College, where she had family connections, and graduated from there in 1918 into the fervor of World War I. As secretary to the chief nurse of the Red Cross, she learned of the need for nursing help in army camp hospitals and returned to Massachusetts to help with the wounded and ill at Camp Devens. Deeply affected by this experience, she returned to Rochester, completed nurse's training, and worked as a public health nurse among the desperately impoverished. Her first marriage was to an investigator of labor conditions in Pennsylvania coal mines; later they settled in Greenwich Village (1924) where she resumed an old habit of writing.

Caroline Gordon, too, had come north from Kentucky and Tennessee to write; with a relative married and living near Rochester who knew the Woods, she introduced herself to Sally Wood, and they became immediate friends. Underneath all the differences between North and South were similarities—a strong sense of family, an education in Latin and Greek, familiarity with the psychic injuries both of wars and the struggles of poverty, black or white, together with a devotion to fiction—maintained in the midst of the many poets and friends of Caroline's new husband, Allen Tate.

But almost immediately after standing by at the birth of the Tates' daughter, Sally Wood left for France where a brother was seriously ill, the separation that occasioned the first letters. Remsen Wood's illness meant a protracted recovery in Switzerland and France, and then just as Sally returned to the States, Allen's Guggenheim award took the Tates to France. Still later her marriage into the absorbing life of Dr. Lawrence Kohn, first resident physician in the Medical School in Rochester, made reunions with the Tates shorter, but after this, though the friendship did not wane, later letters have regrettably disappeared. Mrs. Kohn still lives in Rochester.

Published Works

By Caroline Gordon

Novels

Penhally (1931)
Aleck Maury, Sportsman (1934)
 Reissued with an afterword in 1980. Published in Great Britain as *The
 Pastimes of Aleck Maury: The Life of a True Sportsman*
None Shall Look Back (1937)
The Garden of Adonis (1937)
Green Centuries (1941)
The Women on the Porch (1944)
The Strange Children (1951)
The Malefactors (1956)
The Glory of Hera (1972)

Short Story Collections

The Forest of the South (1945)
Old Red and Other Stories (1963)
The Collected Stories of Caroline Gordon (1981)

Other Works

The House of Fiction: An Anthology of the Short Story (1950)
 With Allen Tate. Revised edition, 1960.
How to Read a Novel (1957)
A Good Soldier: A Key to the Novels of Ford Madox Ford (1957)

By Sally Wood

The Murder of a Novelist (1941)
Death in Lord Byron's Room (1948)
Translations of Louis Aragon's war poetry in *Poetry, Kenyon Review,* and
    Sewanee Review, and in *Aragon, Poet of the French Resistance*
Short stories in the *Magazine, Sewanee Review,* and *Hudson Review*
Book reviews in *Kenyon Review* and *Sewanee Review*

A Note on Editorial Principles

Caroline Gordon hastily typed all her letters to Sally Wood, excepting only an occasional postscript and two or three letters of any length. Transcription has presented no difficulties. Simple typing errors and misspellings have been corrected; punctuation has largely been left as Caroline Gordon dashed it off, except where sense demanded clarification; the casual syntax and handling of foreign words are her own, as are the inconsistencies in the way she spelled her name and in her use of salutation and complimentary close.

The conventional signs of ellipsis—three or four periods—indicate short abridgments made for editorial reasons. Where passages of some length have been excised, a line of ellipses so indicates. Caroline also used a variable number of periods as a loose form of run-on punctuation, and to distinguish her practice from the editor's, we have used a series of five periods wherever this punctuation is Caroline's.

Apart from one sentence of impatience with a still-living friend, the editorial abridgments are of two kinds. By far the larger but relatively less important class are passages concerned with matters purely personal to Sally Wood—her health, her family, her friends. Though in part occasioned by personal reticence, these abridgments are primarily intended to concentrate attention on the life and affairs of Caroline Gordon. A scattered group of acerbically critical sentences, though of some interest, have been deleted on the advice of several knowledgeable people to avoid causing needless distress to the persons most concerned.

No attempt has been made to "pretty up" these letters, however. Caroline did not write them for publication but as private communications to a close friend. They reveal weaknesses as well as strengths, dislikes as well as likes. The opinions in these letters are uninhibitedly frank; they are the views of an outspoken woman who could be as impatient with her friends as she was generous toward them. Nor has any attempt been made to disguise Caroline's dated view on blacks. A woman of her time and place, she largely shared the southern notions about blacks that were prevalent in the first half of this century. While she felt responsible for all of the blacks in the county, she looked on them as recalcitrant children. Yet she trusted them, enjoyed their society, and recognized differences among them in talent and intelligence. Although we can repudiate some of her views from the vantage point of the late twentieth century, we did not think it proper to pretend that Caroline Gordon was more advanced in her thinking about race than most of her contemporaries.

Almost never did Caroline date her letters; the dates supplied here usually come from the postmarks of surviving envelopes, or sometimes from the context of the letter. Out of her own intimate knowledge, Sally Wood has written the continuity accompanying the letters and much of the annotation, which has intentionally been kept to a minimum.

The originals of the letters are now with the other Tate and Gordon papers in the Princeton University Library.

The Southern Mandarins

Foreword

This collection of letters from Caroline Gordon to Sally Wood is of great value to the Republic of Letters. The letters are intimate without being confessional. They move at the pace of fiction. The anecdotes and small scenes are almost as good as those found in Caroline Gordon's stories and novels. They are written at a gallop; the affectionate appeals and hopes for visits with her friend Sally Wood are urgent when fatigue or the turgid boil in the mind fails to cast up the true word. To have a confidant becomes almost a necessary convention for the artist.

But throughout the letters there is a restraint, the instinctive and cultivated truing of form. Caroline Gordon worked for the discipline that would surmount the particular signs of sex. Nobody would mistake the sex of a writer like Katherine Anne Porter; with Caroline one could not tell whether her work was written by a man or woman. This is evidence of a pure elevation of her style. If she writes at a gallop, it is the gait of the typewriter putting down sentences already made in the head. And that is rarely done at a gallop. By and large the visits between these two women, either in this country or abroad, were infrequent. It was the same with Caroline's husband, Allen Tate, in his correspondence with John Peale Bishop. They likewise rarely met. One cannot help speculating how fortunate such friendships are for those condemned to suffer the *cacoëthes scribendi*. In times of stress the letters may have been a comfort and reassurance.

It is clear that Sally Wood not only has a sound understanding of what an art is about, but also what it is: that power in the imagination that through craftsmanship delivers the artifact, the thing made. I'm afraid she feels this view of it is more commonly accepted than it is. In spite of the disorder in the publishing world she tried to get these letters published in the Northeast and was refused. The editors of the Louisiana State University Press understood their worth.

Friendship for Caroline Gordon and respect for her as an artist is the impelling interest, but also Sally Wood sees in the Tate-Gordon household a refuge almost, a place where writers could foregather. There is a continuous reference on Caroline's part, sometimes a bitter one, to her role as hostess. This was not the simple matter of bed and bread common to southern life, so long as the communities of families held together. It was that, too; but Sally Wood distinctly had in mind the community of artists, for which the Tates kept almost open house. In the twenties workers in the arts had cause to feel their calling fairly esoteric. Materialism through its intrument, industrialism, had already isolated the arts. The machine is a tool, and when the tool is automatic or served by craftsmen as attendants, the artists become embattled. A painter has a palette, a dancer a rhythm, the writer a pen or its equivalent; and each renders his subject according to his vision and skill. But it is the habit of the craft which brings them together, to talk around technical matters. Certainly for the storyteller he must never, oh never, as Henry James would say, talk out the action itself. This prevents the doing of it somehow. It must be kept secret and private in the working head and eye until it is finished.

I would say, not to underestimate other qualities, that the most moving effect of this book (and it is indeed a book) is its display of the strain, the sacrifices, at times the sorrows Caroline Gordon undergoes in keeping faith with her work. To understand this in its total context requires some attention to the climate offered to those who live by writing, dancing, or painting. I stop here, for there are still those others, if few and unknown, who follow the ancient commitment to the work their genius selects for them. Perhaps for clarity I should say guardian angel. No man is a genius; he has a genius. From the twenties on many poets and other writers, to further restrict the subject, gathered in New York City, particularly in Greenwich Village, which was still a village with its obvious advantages. It was also cheap; and, during prohibition, after peeping through a hole in the door, you could eat your meal with a red wine thick as ink. In comparison to bathtub gin this seemed a fairly civilized relief. But even so it was a kind of exile, you might say, at home. Out of some public vestigial memory there was here an ambiguous respect for literature and the other arts.

Nevertheless, most writers felt out of the mainstream of American life. Many went to Europe in true exile. Henry James had already become an English subject; Eliot did later on. Frost was in England for awhile, but he resisted the influence of Pound and returned to the New England country-side. The two westerners, Hemingway and Scott Fitzgerald, were much abroad. John Peale Bishop settled down in a chateau in France and was rescued by Allen Tate who, there on a Guggenheim, persuaded him he was a good poet. He finally came home. Sally Wood also mentions E. E. Cum-mings and Slater Brown; and of course there were Edmund Wilson and Malcolm Cowley, then among the editors of the *New Republic*.

Devotion to literature and its crafts, then, was what all writers of serious intent felt in common. There were certain differences. Easterners and those west of the Mississippi gathered in New York City. They were uprooted and the city was a haven. They did not examine their nativity to see what was wrong and how they could mend it. This would have meant a restora-tion. Instead, they looked to Europe and the economic theories of material-ism. Communism, socialism, and sympathizers with both differed widely from the southern attitude. Southerners not only had a sounder view of history, they had suffered it. Defeat in the 1860s had darkened the South's knowledge of the past but had kept it in a singular way alive as part of the present. There are always a few to defect. These gave to the eastern public a perverted romanticism of a peculiar society of outcasts, which existed only in the minds of the descendants of abolitionist ancestors.

Southerners generally did not feel uprooted. They went to New York because that was the place where writers and publishers were. They gener-ally came home. The southerner's conscious entanglement was the family and its long cords. And the family remained, although its larger meaning as the unit of a community had been stricken. To eat your bread in sorrow and feel an isolation where once you had been among your peers taught you the nature of the world as nothing else could. For example, as writers learned, they were not accepted at home until the eastern establishment gave its praise. This was Allen Tate's complaint. It led him to write to John Peale Bishop that the Republic of Letters was the only republic he believed in. Defeat had destroyed the political republic in the South. Elsewhere the former Union had been replaced by a plutocracy masquerading as a democracy.

It must be said, if briefly, that the Twelve Southerners, the Agrarians, were not taken in by abstract political and economic theories. They by common agreement saw what was needed: to restore what was lost, if possible, and restrain further subversion of not only southern but the general well-being. They reaffirmed the history of their inherited European culture. It had a name, but the name had fallen into disuse. It was, of course, Christendom.

Of peculiar relevance to artists is the fact that the Christian state was based on craftsmanship. It recognized that all the cooperating opposites that we encounter continue in a state of stress; and it is this stress which the crafts, by giving form to nature and human nature, reduced to meaning. The craftsman worked to make a living, but also to the greater glory of God. This glory he felt in himself as a faint but persistent reflection of the source, God as creator. As God's human artifact, he was made and not begotten; and so he could make. But it must be understood that only God creates. Man, the artifact, imitates what the created world holds; but into this imitation he puts his essential self, not the ego. And the craftsman is forever remaking by his talent what he sees, because he is unique; that is, he is a man or woman who is a part of mankind but can never be repeated. To state this another way: the craftsman interprets in a singular way what God the creator has done—not the whole, always only the part that contains the essence of the whole. By the act of making objects for use, as well as to glorify God, he fuses the quick with the everlasting. It is the adversary's role to confuse—that is, to make the divine work meaningless. This sense of the artifact, because it depended upon the Creation, visibly and concretely made of Christian Europe one community. The varieties in customs and mores emphasized the common belief.

As belief in Christianity began to wane, history—or man judging man—gradually took its place. This was better than nothing, but to look to the dead for guidance in crises is to see dust. And that is a poor substitute for prayer. And when prayer becomes uncommon or even forbidden, the Word degenerates into a flux of words that deform the Christian and turn him into the momentary man, stepping St. Vitus's dance as the clock ticks.

By the accident of her birth Caroline Gordon wrote out of this older and richer inheritance. Ford Madox Ford taught her the discipline of craft and what a commitment meant. She responded with quick understanding, because she was brought up and lived under the customs of a hierarchical society. *Penhally*, her first novel, had for its subject the dissolution of this society. If not the general subject of her work, it certainly provided the enveloping action. Victory, after the moment of exultation, becomes dull. Defeat lingers in the psyche. It may be tragic, but it teaches the ways of the world, that the dragon always lies by the side of the road. You learn that you can lose what you cherish, and this lingering sense of loss constantly finds ways to remind you that it may occur again.

Knowledge of this in no way caused Caroline to argue or write polemics. In the seven years when her husband and his companions bestirred themselves over agrarian and related matters, she was sympathetic but left the impression that it was not her proper business. She would say things like "Allen has gone to Nashville to confer with the brothers." At times she would go along, because the meetings were often social occasions.

A woman who writes either fiction or verse, particularly if she is married, has problems a man doesn't have. Keeping a house makes daily demands. If she has a child, her responsibilities obviously increase. Neglect of her work or child can make her wretched, and the demands of each usually conflict. Once in Memphis, when the Tates were living in the Golden Oak Nest, Caroline had worked too late to prepare much of a supper. Her little girl Nancy complained, "Mama, I don't care what those Confederate soldiers ate." Quoting her mother: "It seemed to me so unreasonable when I had just been reading about men picking blackberries as they went into line of battle." So immersed was she in the battle of Chicamauga that, in writing a business letter, she would ask the year. She knew the month, she said.

Caroline Gordon's apprentice years were passed during the Great Depression, and this lasted some eleven years. It was a time of short rations for many, and the artists suffered. At times the Tates were out of food. Making a living was chancy and hard, but they did it. For the short periods when Ford Madox Ford was in this country, Caroline worked as his secretary. Once she typed for the Communist brother. This was always said in half jest and irony. She tried potboilers, but the pot boils best when something is in it. Tate managed to sell essays and reviews to such magazines as the *New Republic* and the *Nation*, and this without joining any clique.

In a 1925 letter to Sally Wood, Caroline wrote, "I'm pretty low just now. Mother took Nancy back to Kentucky with her several weeks ago. I was feeling so feeble I couldn't combat the various forces that were operating against me. . . . You see, I really had her only one day for myself." The two constant conditions of this time were money's uncertainty and the family dramas. They combined at that time in a decisive way. Caroline's mother had arrived without breakfast to find that there was no food in the house. She replenished the larder but took the baby home with her. Being from a large farming connection she could not understand not having food in the house. Money, yes; but food? This situation put her in an invincible position for taking the baby. Caroline: "Of course all this devotion is partly because she never was allowed to have her own babies." This alludes to Miss Carrie, Caroline's grandmother, the matriarch of the family and owner of Merry Mont. When she married a cousin, she required that he leave his farm and move onto hers. From that moment, her sway was never threatened. Her will was absolute, toward nature and human nature. She had no screens in her windows. It didn't suit her to breathe sifted air. Her cows never ate wild onions. Her son-in-law, Brother Gordon, would give loud guffaws at this. This wonderful laugh he passed on to his daughter. When Merry Mont was overcrowded with kin and connection, Miss Carrie fed them by rank. The closest of kin mostly first, but not necessarily; kin or no, it was her favorites who ate first. Those in disfavor got what was left.

Caroline's family was really a close community of three families—the Meriwethers, the silver-tongued Fergusons who married the Meriwether heiresses, and the Barkers. They lived on thirty thousand acres of land, mostly in Kentucky. Before the War of the Northern Invasion, it had been a prosperous community. At Merivale the mistress had her own orchestra that would play for her as she danced from the dining room. Upidon, I believe, was a Ferguson place. With marriages and intermarriages, there was surely some eccentricity, but it never bothered anybody. It gave subjects for conversation and laughter, when the weather allowed. One old cousin of sound mind and good heart asked Caroline, then a young girl, if she would like a watch. Of course she would. He reached into the air and picked her one. "Here, my dear," he said. There is a matter for wonder at another kinswoman who twice flew around the room from the mantel as perch. There was also a cousin, rational in most ways, who thought she was a pea and carefully avoided cracks in the floor. When a daughter came to look after Miss Carrie, then in her eighties, it was plain she wanted no looking after. Her mother told her that if she had no better memory than the daughter, she would offer herself to an institution. The daughter replied that she would but for the fact that she was head of one. Returning to Merry Mont on a visit, Caroline Gordon saw the three women sitting on the porch. This gave her the idea for *The Women on the Porch*.

But it can't be said enough that when the writer uses material close at hand, in fiction this material can never be biographical. The moment the material goes through the crucible of rendition, the meaning surpasses what might be called its source. If the action turns out well, it is archetypal. There is no way to reproduce actual persons in fiction. Certain qualities, yes; but the moment the subject is immersed in the invisible forces in the mind, it gives out an artifact, not a reproduction of human beings. Only God does this. So it was that Henry James, to whom Caroline looked as master, never listened to the end of a story, only enough to release his own story. The workings of this part of the mind we all know in dreams. In dreams and to a heightened degree in visions, those we know in the daylight world present themselves in disorientation—deformed or displaced—and in actions which, implausible to consciousness, seem perfectly natural and acceptable. An art through its craft controls the imagination toward a believable end. The mystery remains. Caroline Gordon rarely failed in understanding or control.

After Morton Street, the Tates spent the winter in Tory Valley, in upper New York State. They rented part of a country house for eight dollars a month. Here they spent the winter near the Cowleys and Browns. Hart Crane lived with them, which proved unfortunate. They reached a pass at which they did not speak but pushed notes under doors. Caroline's references to this are brief. "Hart is a fine poet, but God save me from ever having another romantic in the house with me." What she does mention shows how and what the fictive mind can see. "Our landlady, aged sixty five, fell violently in love with Hart. It was a sort of Eugene O'Neill situation—this pathetic elderly person in love with a young homosexual. . . . Her husband has been in an asylum for the insane for the past five years. He fancies that he is a girl and wears beads around his neck and flirts with a fan!" And again, "We have with us now, to add variety to the scene, a madcap virgin from Greenwich Village. I fear I use the word virgin loosely. . . . Her father, Mr. George Cram ("Jig") Cook, of Davenport, Iowa, fancied he was an ancient Greek, so after founding the Provincetown theater, and whisking about the Village in a leopard's skin he betook himself to Greece where he went about in robes and fillets etc. and finally died with the appropriate publicity. . . . [The virgin] begins to twitch if the conversation strays from sex a moment."

In Tory Valley the pattern of their lives together began to show distinctions that could have been a threat to the common grounds of marriage. But they were young and in love and, more important, they were becoming artists. It was over making a garden. This is the clearest instance. Allen would not hoe, but he didn't mind washing dishes. Caroline says this: "I never want to live in town again, but I think Allen would be reconciled, although he is quite content out here with our friends to afford society. He has the strangest attitude toward the country—the same appreciation you'd have for a good set in the theatre. I think Allen feels toward nature as I do toward mathematics—respectful indifference. He walks about the garden hailing each tomato and melon with amazement—and never sees any connection between planting seeds and eating fruit." My own father once spoke to Tate of Captain Beard as a literary character. Tate blushed and laughed in an embarrassed way, but of understanding, that this was the South's attitude towards its ornaments, to be accepted but not taken too seriously. Tate saw himself suddenly as inheritor to this attitude. Or rather to this role of artist—a part of, but parted from, the basic occupations of society.

This disposition of his never changed. Years later, at Benfolly, Caroline would get excessively vexed when Allen passed drooping tomatoes and never even saw their wilt, much less got water for them. Also, being a landlord with tenants was a game that interested him briefly. He never understood that he did not have enough arable land to interest a serious farmer, nor could he. He was always on the move. His mother lived out of trunks and in hotels, and he the youngest child was with her. This is no explanation for adult behavior entirely, nor is the move to make a living that either; but move they did. The woman is traditionally the muse. When as poet she finds herself in her own court, she is beset by singular difficulties.

By now this should be seen as the burden of this foreword: working against the pressures the writer receives. And this includes the publisher's demands for publication dates that always envision the book as finished, never in the making. I'm not saying that such is unnecessary. Some of it is needed, or the book might never get written.

On Tate's Guggenheim Caroline found ease and a letting-up from imposed diversions. Nancy had a settled widow for nurse who kept her sometimes overnight. They went to many funerals, and Nancy learned to patronize her parents as Americans. In looking at *The Battles and Leaders of the Civil War* she saw a picture of Stonewall Jackson. When she said, "Oh, there is Monsieur Stonewall Jackson," her parents began to think the time had come to take her home. Living in France this first time seemed, on the whole, one of their best moves. Caroline liked the cafés and there seemed not to be so many bouts with flu, which became a frequent problem over the years. Paris winters can be grim, and so she found when her Guggenheim took them back. There was some consolation that Sally Wood went with them, but circumstances even there kept the two friends mostly apart. Even Caroline's Guggenheim did not ease their living, since much of it had to go for debts. And nothing can quite sap the energy as the quiet threats of indebtedness.

A woman of less vitality and devotion could never have written eight novels and several books of stories. There was much visiting back and forth, and there were parties. They would seem childish, I'm afraid, today. We played charades and word games, or who could remember and recite more verse. I seem to remember that Robert Penn Warren won at this. We dressed the parts and had props. I don't remember eating a poor meal at Caroline's house, whether she had a cook or prepared the meal herself. Once we sat down to a magnificent mutton roast, but Ford was in a fret. He took a piece of bread and tore it into bits and threw it about the table. Another time Arkansas poet John Gould Fletcher, with a big head and almost as big a ring on his finger, was dining at Benfolly. He was an habitual talker, and during one long discourse he held a biscuit in his hand. The cook, Beatrice, removed it quietly and put a hot one, buttered, in its place. Fletcher never knew the difference.

It helped that Tate didn't mind helping with the domestic duties. I remember once in preparing for a party, he skillfully ironed Caroline's long evening gown, all the while talking with animation but never missing a lick. It seemed the most natural thing for him to be doing. It was the habit of a craftsman accidentally turned to a lesser thing, but with no less attention to skill. He taught my wife where to begin in ironing a shirt.

How far the burden of running a house interferes with writing may be seen in a letter Caroline wrote from my father's place in Alabama. The Tates

were on their way to a writer's job, when it was canceled. She writes, "We
decided to move on to Cornsilk for our annual visit. . . .

> I never saw such a place for work as Cornsilk. The first morning I
> was there I walked as in a trance into a secluded corner of the dining
> room. I dug myself out a spot by removing several bushels of peanuts,
> a mediaeval cuirass, three or four demijohns of cherry bounce etc., set
> up a card table in the spot thus cleared and almost without thinking
> began to write steadily. . . . And the strange thing was that this spot—
> it's about two by four—this spot which proved such a wonderful
> place, I couldn't even see it at first for the peanuts and things. Well,
> God moves in a mysterious way. . . . Writing there I produced fifteen
> thousand words in one week. . . .
>
> It is too bad you didn't land at Cornsilk during your peregrinations
> with your book. I am convinced that you would not have had to
> expend so much moral energy getting it written. I think it is the
> spectacle of Andrew's father's unbridled energy. As A. says, he begins
> the world new every morning. This sounds annoying in a person but it
> isn't in him. Running half a dozen farms doesn't satisfy him—he
> specializes in making fancy desserts for dinner. Comes in from the field
> around eleven o'clock attended by two field hands, shouts for a quart
> of whipped cream and starts in and makes something marvellous for
> dinner.

In the spring of 1937, at Benfolly after two years' absence, she writes,
"The Fords arrived last Wednesday and we've shaken down into a routine—but not without strife. I took Janice [Ford's wife] by the horns last
night before she'd had time to get really obnoxious and explained to her
that while I seemed very feckless I had in my way a system and that it didn't
include French cooking by a Tennessee negro or by me either. We had for
dinner yesterday spring lamb, home grown strawberries, new potatoes and
cauliflower with Hollandaise sauce. A damn good dinner I call it; I knocked
off work at ten to cook it. Janice said if I'd only told her in time we could
have had the cauliflower Polonaise. 'No, we wouldn't' says I, 'we like it
better Hollandaise.' It's dreadful to feel that way about a guest but I knew
she would run me nuts and ruin my book if I didn't smack her paws off the
bat. When I think of all the people I've had here, feeding them on a shoe
string (financially if not literally)."

This indicates a kind of heroism which only the woman as artist can
accomplish. She did not neglect the common duties and calls on her place
and station in life; but, no matter the circumstances, nothing diverted her

radically from a devotion to and practice of her craft. Contemptuous of the fad to read and judge an author by his political views, she penetrated deeper into Europe's cultural sources, its shaping forms, through the Roman Catholic period, and at last still further back into our classical heritage. She searched the mythological mind of prehistory with all the care of an archaeological dig. The result was her last novel, *The Glory of Hera*. She made human the actors of myth—the gods, the demigods, the heroes, and all the destructive forces personified—which is eternally a part of life. At the same time she kept, through her enveloping action, the aura of actors performing superhuman tasks. The gods and goddesses accountable only to Fate acted also, out of this supernal omniscience, at the same time showing human inclinations. This increased the mystery by allowing mortal beings to suffer the intimacies of immortal wills.

She did not intend to stop here, but to write a contemporary novel, using the lives and families she belonged to as a counterpart to *The Glory of Hera*. Using these, not as a chronicle but as fiction, to render over vast stretches of time what remains contiguous and forever true. She did not finish this project. The dragon that lies by the side of the road moved and blocked her path.

She was buried in San Cristóbal, Mexico, in Chiapas province, where Europe in its dissipating venture met but did not resolve, as she did not, the contradictory meaning within the pagan and Christian mysteries. She received the Roman rites. At the grave site her daughter's housekeeper buried food and drink in the earth to sustain the spirit until its final release. This could only take place when the family, after the proper time, gave a last feast, shared by the quick and the dead, upon the mound used for table.

ANDREW LYTLE

Prologue

These letters were never meant to be published. I found a box of them in the attic when we moved but did not have time to open it for many years. When I did, I found to my surprise that the letters painted a picture of a group of young writers trying to do good work and make money enough to live on—Caroline's husband, Allen Tate, Robert Penn Warren, Andrew Lytle, Katherine Anne Porter; the northerners like Malcolm Cowley, Hart Crane, E. E. Cummings; and then the Englishman Ford Madox Ford, who employed Caroline as his secretary at first and ended up getting her to dictate her manuscript to him.

The letters form almost an autobiography of Caroline Gordon during those years—an unusual picture of a woman who, while turning into a professional writer, was able to live a complete woman's life with her husband, a little daughter, and many friends, in the midst of poverty, uncertainty, family connections, and the traditions of the Old South, which she and Allen never forgot.

In the summer of the year 1924, an historic migration occurred when southern writers began moving north. They wanted to be nearer publishers, magazines, and critics, all in or on the outskirts of New York. I, too, had migrated to New York City, though from only as far away as Rochester and for quite different reasons.

I was alone in our apartment one day when the doorbell rang. There stood a memorable figure, a young girl like and unlike me. We were about the same size, but her coloring was startlingly different. My hair was a nondescript brown, while hers gleamed blacker than a raven's wing, matching her eyes set in a masklike face, magnolia white as—I learned later—only southern faces can be. There must have been a letter or a phone call. She said at once, or at least very soon, that one was never so happy as when asleep, and I must have shown her a couch, because she dropped off in a minute.

Then I remembered that this was the girl my brother had taken out in a canoe on Canandaigua Lake, one of the Finger Lakes near Rochester. Caroline, whose mother was a Meriwether of Kentucky, naturally had visited on her way to New York the only Meriwether in the North, "Little May," who had been a famous belle. It was said in Kentucky that you could always tell the plantation where she was staying by the number of horses tied up in front. Much to the anger of the local young men, Little May had married a New York newspaperman, Sherman Morse, who had soon retired to grow apples on the beautiful hillside of Canandaigua Lake, where my brother was visiting. He had told Caroline that he had a sister living in New York City who was also interested in writing. This small event produced a lifetime friendship between the North and the South.

Caroline had been doing newspaper work in Chattanooga and keeping a thermos of coffee under her bed and an alarm set for 5 A.M. so that she would be able to work a little on a novel before going to the office. No wonder she joined the trek north. There she found newspaper work too, I believe for Berton Braley, who had a syndicated column. Texas Guinan, a nightclub singer whom she had interviewed, took a fancy to Caroline and would call at three or four in the morning.

My shorter migration had taken longer. The family in Rochester had failed to provide me with that *sine qua non* of a writer, an unhappy childhood. Quite the contrary. We were a large family and lived in the country, though my father, a lawyer, went into Rochester daily, as we did too, for school.

The First World War had begun just as I entered Wellesley, where I was considered to be headed for a literary career. I could not forget the war though, and I felt—somewhat uneasily—cut off from the real world. By junior year, our more adventurous men friends were getting restless. They would suddenly disappear from their colleges to join an ambulance corps or the Canadian army. But the *élan* of the beginning soon turned grim, with bayonet drill, with the submarines following troop ships, worst of all, with our men really getting into the trenches. The thin letters arriving at the dorm stamped "officer's mail opened by censor" changed everything. By senior year, there was only one feeling among our classmates: How can we get in too? I was one of the few who managed it.

The army needed nurses and called for young women who were willing to "train" at army camps, supposedly just as nurses then trained in civilian hospitals. Actually, these trainees were put to work on the wards, learning by doing.

In the fall of 1918, a college friend, Ellen Montgomery, and I boarded a bus in Boston full of doughboys going to Camp Devens, to whom we explained that we were bound for the base hospital. At the camp, we were stopped by a sentry surprised to see two young girls. One of the men waved his hand. "Nothing wrong, Corp. There's only us soldiers here."

That was my exit from the ivory tower. It was good preparation for friendship with Caroline Gordon, whose ivory tower had collapsed in the time of her ancestors, with Lee's surrender.

I was at Devens long enough to learn to share my patients' dislike for civilians. They were people you couldn't talk to about the reality of war. And so, once I went home to Rochester, I finished becoming a nurse. Afterward, as a visiting nurse, I lived briefly in a tenement house with another nurse who was also eager to get to know our patients better.

Naturally, a returned soldier, somebody one could talk to, showed up. Stephen Raushenbush had enlisted in an ambulance corps and had been through the worst of it. But now he interested me in the labor movement. Steve had obtained an interesting job. The Fund for the Republic engaged him to live among the coal miners as one of them to see if there was a chance of nationalizing the industry as there had been talk of doing in Britain. A wife was no handicap if she was a nurse, so I went with him. After that, we spent some time in Washington, where Steve told his findings to liberal senators. Then we went to New York.

It soon became obvious that the labor movement did not want intellectuals. My husband's friends had most of them gone into the Brookings Institution. But he had not become reconciled to this. We drifted to the cheapest quarter, Greenwich Village, where Caroline came to visit.

When she woke up, it was as if we had known each other for years. I can't remember anything preliminary. We talked about what interested us most—writing. I was trying to turn back to it, having collected almost too much to say. She had on her shoulders the weight of her ancestors, the whole plight of the South and its lost war.

Our friendship may have seemed odd—our lives had been so far apart. She had gone to a small southern college; I to a northern one. Yet although, as Virginia Woolf said, a woman writer needs a room of her own, she needs something else as well. Men who write often congregate in groups. Women do not, or they did not then. But many women writers have had sisters—Jane Austen had Cassandra; the Brontës were provided for; Emily Dickinson had Lavinia; Virginia Woolf, even though a member of a literary group, depended a great deal on Vanessa. But Caroline, who had no sister, needed a substitute. And though our backgrounds were different, our foregrounds were the same.

She was still working on her Chattanooga novel[1] but spending her evenings with people like Malcolm Cowley, Slater Brown, and his wife, Sue Jenkins, and Allen Tate—all as careless of where they lived or what they lived on as she, devoted only to the way to put words down on paper.

Quite soon after our meeting, Steve and I had an attractive friend over for dinner. I phoned Caroline to ask her too. She said, "No, I can't. I'm going to marry Allen Tate. Ask my roommate to dinner. I don't want her to know."

For more than a year after that, we lived in Greenwich Village, Steve and I in a basement, Caroline and Allen in shabby rooms. There was a lot of cooking in both places, all with the cheapest of materials. When we were seeing each other almost daily, the masklike face disappeared. It was what Caroline showed the world—a defense always ready and often useful against "outrageous fortune." Privately, she looked warmly at one and laughed a great deal.

The Tates' visitors were literary, mostly poets. Poetry was so important nothing else mattered. They most enjoyed days when everyone sat at the table talking from lunch until dinnertime. I was caught up too. Caroline had to cook far more than I, and this was when her southernness became apparent. Never did it occur to either of the Tates that they couldn't invite a guest for a meal. Many were people they didn't even know, young men who came to discuss their work with Allen. To them, Caroline was the mistress of the plantation; Allen, a southern gentleman—despite the fact that these hereditary roles didn't fit the real scene.

Southern girls of my generation reminded me of the women in the Middle Ages whose husbands had gone to the Crusades. Their mothers had had to run the plantations themselves and to cope with the stealing of stock, grain, furniture, and everything else by northern soldiers, not to mention the burning down of their homes. The experience had produced a strong race of women whom I admired as I had their medieval forebears. My college friend, Elizabeth Pickett, was one of them. Robert Penn Warren has said that all of the southerners of that generation, male and female, felt like double persons. Everyone was himself and one of his ancestors.[2]

When Caroline became pregnant, their lives had to change somewhat. As an ex–visiting nurse, I cared passionately for babies, and I stayed around. At the end, I was sitting by her bed at the Sloane Maternity Hospital, timing her labor pains, and Caroline was grimly talking about her novel, her white face flinching now and then. A door opened, and thinking it was a nurse, I turned around. What was my surprise to see Allen, clutching his cane (he never dressed like a Villager), his face more ravaged than Caroline's.

His friends had clustered round him, Caroline said, before she went into the hospital, determined to see *him* through this ordeal, plying him with what passed for liquor in those days.

He had escaped from his friends.

Within a week or so, as I remember it, various crises had got hold of me. My husband had no plans that included me. My brother Remsen, who had been studying painting in Paris, had been very depressed when he had visited us, and I had reason to worry about him.

Now that Caroline was doing so well and was in the now serious care of Allen, I decided on the spur of the moment to take a ship to France.

It was lucky that I did.

My brother had been living in deplorable conditions and taking no care of himself whatever. Within a short time he was seen to have a fever, which rapidly mounted. I called the ambulance for the American Hospital at Neuilly and boarded it with him.[3]

Life was too complicated and uncertain to write to Caroline for a while.

1. This first novel was never published.
2. *Robert Penn Warren Talking: Interviews, 1950–1978* (New York, 1980), 115.
3. We two older ones of the Wood children had spent the summer of 1914 in France with our parents, living with a French family near the Etoile while my father pursued business dealings for a client in Normandy. This gave us some experience in getting to know Paris, though not the Latin Quarter, which my brother had discovered on a later trip.

47 Morton Street, New York City, 1925
To Sally Wood, Traveller's Bank, Place Vendôme, Paris

Friday

Sally, darling:

I've thought of you every day—but I've had nothing to say to anybody. This last week has been such a mad whirl. You left so suddenly I hadn't time to get used to the idea; I haven't realized it yet, in fact. I miss you terribly; that you'd know without my telling you, though.

I'm pretty low just now. Mother took Nancy back to Kentucky with her several weeks ago. I was feeling so feeble I couldn't combat the various forces that were operating against me. It struck everybody as the "sensible" thing to do. I know, and knew at the time, that it was a very mad thing to do, aside from my personal feelings. I think Mother had been planning it ever since before Nancy was born. At the last moment I weakened and was going to refuse to let her go, but I saw Mother would have collapsed. She had borne everything amicably—wild people like Dorothy Day, Peggy Cowley,[1] etc. dropping in—just so she could get Nancy, and I don't know what she'd have done if it had fallen through at the last. I never saw anybody as mad over a child. She could hardly put her down a moment. All our modern ideas of not handling them were swept aside—Mother always had a perfectly good reason for picking her up this particular time.

I feel a little like the Lamb of God taking away the sins of the generations. Of course all this devotion is partly because she never was allowed to have her own babies. Now if I can just keep my hands off of Nancy's we may get back to normalcy in a generation or so! I don't know what having Nancy will do for Mother—it seemed to mean new life. It is doing all sorts of things to me, though. I've felt paralyzed for weeks. You see, I really had her only one day for myself. I wish you could have seen her more. She is the darlingest baby. I could never have let her go but I was afraid Allen would break down trying to work day and night too . . . . . and I was feeling so rotten I couldn't think clearly.

I've started in working. This is really the first day I've been able to do anything, though I've gone through the motions.

I do so want to hear from you and to know how things are going with you. We have dined once at 38 King Street since you left. It was all very nice and things went off rather smoothly, Bethy[2] doing the honors very nicely. I was sad, of course, being there, with you away, and Allen observed after we got home that it had been a pretty tense evening. . . .

. . . .

Mary Maxfield is here, "hooking" again.[3] She is looking fine, with lots of new clothes. I haven't been able to see anybody, though, I've been so much occupied with domestic affairs.

Please write when you can,

With much love,
Carolyn

1. Caroline later modeled the saintly character in *The Malefactors*, Catherine Pollard, after Dorothy Day, the famous Catholic activist. Peggy Cowley was Malcolm's wife.
2. Elizabeth Rauschenbusch, my sister-in-law.
3. Caroline's former roommate, the one from Canandaigua Lake; she was husband hunting.

Remsen spent most of the winter in Leysin, a tuberculosis sanatorium on a Swiss mountain, where his health improved. After Christmas he was allowed to come farther down from the heights to Caux, a village above Montreux, to an apartment we rented in a peasant's house. The peasant family and the cows lived on the first two floors, and we lived above, but it was all on such a steep hillside that we stepped out of our door onto the ground.

Tory Valley, Patterson, New York, February 5, 1926
To S. W. in Switzerland

Dear Sally:

How are you?

I wish you would please write to me. I have thought about you every day almost and wished so much I could see you. You dropped out of our lives so suddenly—I haven't realized it yet. And I still haven't learned to get along without you.

In her last letter May referred to Rem's being sick—had he been sick really?

We are living in the country—out where Bill and Sue's place[1] is, you know. It is lovely. We have half of a big old farmhouse—nothing to do but keep fires going, cook and write. It is so wonderful after New York—our last weeks there were so hectic. I think I was going mad or something—I know I couldn't have stood it much longer.

Nancy is in Kentucky with Mother and Dad. She weighs over twelve pounds, laughs out loud, sings and is getting a tooth. (At least Mother says so, though it seems fearfully early.) Dad writes us a paean in her praise every few days. He maintains that she is the most beautiful baby he has ever seen. I think she is going to be blonde. Her eyes are very dark blue. They send us kodak pictures every now and then—kodak pictures aren't much when you want your baby, but they help some. We hope to have her here in the spring.

We are planning to stay out here indefinitely. Living is so marvelously cheap. In two months we have spent twenty eight dollars for food, and our rent is eight dollars a month. It sounds almost unbelievable, so near New York. The natives are all grand—they think we are mad, but like us anyhow.

We are going to have a garden in the spring. Meantime I am getting in training by sawing wood. I have progressed rather slowly as a sawyer, but today Allen announced that I was actually getting good. Allen, by the way, has developed a whole new set of talents—he makes a wonderful countryman. I was afraid to urge him to come out here as he'd never lived in the country before, but I'm very glad we came now—he likes it as well as I do.

Bill and Sue, of course, are a great joy. About the only urbanity we have left is gathering for tea each afternoon at one house or another—and when the moon is full we have a cider party.

Rura cano as Catullus observed. Really, it's great . . . . .

I am writing another novel [*Penhally*] . . . . . I can't tell you exactly what it's about yet, though. It's just in the last two weeks, that I've been able to write anything. But now at least I'm able to put words together.

Allen is doing a lot of reviewing for the Nation and the New Republic—enough, in fact, to live on.

Just now we are snowed in. The mail is brought to the foot of "the mountain" and we flounder over for it. We snowshoed there today—some of the drifts were at least seven feet deep, and we went skipping right over. . . . . I don't know when the roads will be clear again.

Please, Sally, write to me. You don't know how much I miss you. If you come back to New York in the spring you must come out and make us a visit. Allen sends his love—much love from

Carolyn

. . . .

1. Sue Jenkins and Slater Brown, known to his friends as Bill.

Tory Valley, May 15, 1926
To S. W. in Switzerland

My dearest Sally:

I was sitting in my study writing on my novel—some ten thousand words are already written on it—when Allen came bringing your letter. It is so good to hear from you, Sally. I was just on the point of writing again when your letter came.

I do wish you'd write oftener: you don't know how I miss you. My last letter was such a stupid, confused thing I don't blame you for not answering, however.

I was in town in April—the first time since we came out here. I'd been in Washington visiting my brother; Allen came in and met me. We felt quite luxurious staying at the Albert and taking hot baths! Of course we drank a little and saw a few people, but the hot baths were the brightest lights.

I saw Keg[1] for a brief space. I had such a time seeing him at all. My time was limited and one night I'd counted on seeing him after nine I was detained by a stupid drinking party. I wanted a little advice from him—on "pulling my novel together." After making and breaking several engagements I finally found him sitting in his office behind a door which said "Giant Power or something", and we had a nice chat until Allen came and interrupted us. He gave me some news of you, said he was worried about you. He'd done some more work on his novel. I wondered if his éducation sentimentale hadn't advanced a little. My suspicion is based on some-

thing very vague. In my novel a young gentleman is in love with somebody else's wife. The mood of the book is a slowly increasing madness;
I explained to Keg that I wanted to introduce reality into this unreal
scene and chose a love affair of this kind as the most poignant example.
Keg observed quickly that there [were] other things that had more reality
than illicit love affairs. . . . . I feel rather silly, retailing conversations in
this way.

I don't know about whether there's any advantage in having a large
number of experiences. Shall I tell you what Allen thinks about you?
(He'd scalp me if he knew I was quoting him!) That you'd be much
happier if you didn't theorize about life—simply went ahead and did what
you wanted to do whenever you could! But then Allen hasn't any New
Englander in him!

Just after I sent you Allen's poem he up and wrote another one
you'll like better. It's the only thing of the kind he's ever done. The
Nation's publishing it some time. Allen had a very fecund period a few
weeks ago: in fact it became almost indecent the way he produced poems.
Any moment he was likely to be seized with labor pains.

We are leading a very pleasant life now. The country has just become green—it is very lovely. I have been wading in the brook every day,
picking cowslip greens. Some days I sprawl on the grass and pick dan-
delion and dock, then we cook them and eat them with much relish. We
are gardening very vigorously now. I go into a perfect frenzy over the
clods. I shall spare you the enumeration of what I have planted, but it is a
hell of a lot. And in the cold frame I have some of the most admirable
lettuce imaginable. Allen, I fear, will never make a gardener. I get a few
rows a day out of him, though. I have the most beautiful black cat. He
has lovely green eyes and when we garden he walks around us, licking
our legs.

The valley is quite populous now. The Bovings, our Danish neighbors are just a little way off. Bina Flynn and her Italian husband come up
to their place every weekend. Romolo is a giant—from some moun-
tainous section of Italy—he used to be a radical leader, but now he's in
the real estate business and quite American. He makes the most marvellous Italian dishes.

Hart Crane went off to the Isle of Pines a few weeks ago, accompanied by Waldo Frank. Hart is a fine poet, but God save me from ever

having another romantic in the house with me! We had material for a Eugene O'Neill play in this house this winter. Our landlady,[2] a worthy soul of sixty four, fell violently in love with Hart. With his departure we fell heir to much space. I am writing now in my "study", a darling little white room upstairs. It adjoins a grand big bedroom, wherein sits Mrs. T's pride, "the old, antique" bed. It is made like a sleigh, and is a devil to sleep in. I am quite overcome with all this space, after that terrible little cooped up apartment we had on Morton Street. We don't ever want to go back to town to live—but we do hope to have a month there next winter—during that dreary after Christmas stretch. But I'm not bored or side tracked in the country—less so than in New York. I'm not at all an urban person, you see. I love to have space around me, and I love to dig in the dirt and walk in the woods. Allen is quite contented out here. In fact he says he is happier than he's ever been in his life. We lead lives of strict sobriety. When visitors bring liquor out we complain a little before drinking it!

I find that having a room to work in of my own enables me to write—I couldn't write a word all winter.[3] I hope to have my novel ready to offer by fall. McBride's[4] by the way, have suggested that Allen write a novel, and say they might publish his poems if he'd furnish a novel to take care of the expense. I wish I could offer mine in lieu of his! Don't mention the novel project by the way. It's all in the air as yet, and nothing may come of it.

I enclose pictures of Nancy. You needn't return these as I have now a regular gallery of her pictures. You will see beside her one half a negro baby. The negro baby hight Vergil Lois, is just Nancy's age, and breast fed. Mother says she is not as heavy as Nancy. Nancy weighs seventeen and a half pounds and gains steadily each week. She seems to be a model baby. Mother and Dad are crazy about her. Mother is going to bring her up for a visit this summer. Dad wrote yesterday, however, that I must realize that it is only for a visit, that we are not prepared to take care of her and that they do not propose to jeopardize the progress she has made. This is the most explicit statement I've had yet of an attitude I've been aware of all along. I can't blame them. I want to have a talk with Dad somehow before I do anything decisive. I'm really afraid Mother will go all to pieces if Nancy is taken away from her. We think we may work out some system of dividing the year between the two households. Nancy, in that case, would have a more varied experience than most children. Whether it would be bad for her I can't say.

Allen is moaning for food downstairs. He is able, however, to send his love.

Allen was quite annoyed when Keg told him he was to have a section of the New Republic on giant power or coal or something like that. He thought it was quite disgraceful that they could spare all that space to economics when literature went begging.

I must go and throw together some food.

Thanks so much for your letter, dear Sally, and please write again. I worry about [you] when I don't hear for so long. I want to see you; I wonder if you'll be back this fall? We'll look for you out here.

Much love,
from Carolyn

1. My husband's college nickname, useful in the coal mines.
2. Mrs. Addie Turner.
3. Hart Crane had constantly interrupted everyone.
4. Robert M. McBride and Company, New York book publishers.

I wrote Caroline that, having lived with French people for some time, I was beginning to adopt their point of view. I had found that they lived in the present, not the future as the Americans often did. This was preferable—restful and enjoyable. (See Faulkner's letters from Paris about the same time.)

Tory Valley, spring, 1926
To S. W. in Switzerland in a villa in Caux above Montreux

I was a-writing in my study on a pot boiler wherewith I hope to redeem the family larder when your letter came. I am glad that you are writing me something about yourself, at last, for it's been awful not to know just what was happening to you. Of course I realize, though, that it's very hard to write anything about yourself to anybody when as you say you're in the process of being made over.

. . . .

I am at this point writing a series of pot boilers in an effort to accumulate enough money for Nancy's railroad fare up here—Mother's rather. Mother, who is as wily and designing [a] female as ever lived, has us. She has spent so much on us that I can't urge her to make the trip up here unless I can furnish the money, and it's so damned hard to get hold of. She writes now urbanely that she will have to defer her visit until August, because my aunt Margaret who has been planning to go to see the baby can't leave home until the middle of July. Of course it will be too hot to travel in August. All I can do is to point out that it is a little more important for us to see Nancy than for her to be inspected by her aunt, and to observe also that I know exactly what she is up to.

Of course this is a minor irritation when I think of how wonderfully Mother has cared for Nancy. She really seems to be the model baby. She wrings the necks off of toy ducks and geese with one twist of her wrist to the admiration of her grandparents, yells lustily when she doesn't get what she wants and shows many other signs of being very vigorous and alert.

I amazed myself by making forty dollars the other day, my first contribution to the family finances for some time, so now I'm trying to do it again.

McBride's have told Allen that they will publish his poems if he'll write them a novel within the year—so he's trying to outline one. I haven't the least idea whether he *can* write a novel—it seems that if he could his thoughts would have turned that way long ago—and neither is he, but he's anxious to get his poems published and this seems the only way to do it. So soon there'll be two of us writing novels in this house.

Tory Valley is a lovely place now. We lie around in the grass a great deal, garden a little, and get little else done. The winter was a million times better than it would have been in New York, but it was a horror in some ways. Hart Crane was with us. Our landlady, aged sixty five, fell violently in love with Hart. It was a sort of Eugene O'Neill situation—this pathetic elderly person in love with a young homosexual. The situation gets more poignant as we have seen her past life gradually revealed. Her husband has been in an asylum for the insane for the past five years. He fancies that he is a girl and wears beads around his neck and flirts with a fan! "It wouldn't have been so bad when he was here," she told me, "if he hadn't been so set on hiring help. He'd drive into Pawling and sit on the street corner in his wagon and hire any young man he saw to come and help him on the farm. Then I'd have to go and borrow the money to pay them from the neighbors." And now he, her husband, or "Blind Jim" as the neighbors call him, is out of the asylum, and we are instructed not to let him in if he comes tapping, like Pew on the window pane!

This New England country life is so different from country life in the south. I am quite fascinated by it.

To cap the climax of our winter's drama, a young sailor arrived in Patterson with his ditty box, prepared to *stay* indefinitely, just a week after Hart had sailed for the Isle of Pines!!!!

We have with us now, to add variety to the scene, a madcap virgin from Greenwich Village. I fear I use the word virgin loosely but it seems to have departed from its original meaning. Her father . . . fancied he was an ancient Greek, so after founding the Provincetown theater, and whisking about the village in a leopard's skin he betook himself to Greece where he went about in robes and fillets etc. and finally died with the appropriate publicity. This child is an unedifying spectacle of what may happen to young people these days! She begins to twitch if the conversation strays from sex a moment, and suddenly began to boast in the midst of dinner last night of her prowess in birth control by muscle contraction—a method she says she learned from some Hindu. I found myself observing tartly that it seemed to me a matter of where the sphincter muscles were placed in the body. But I suppose if one has a father who celebrates Dionysiac rites at the age of fifty one comes easily to believe in that sort of thing. I begin to think that I must be Puritanical; I can't be comfortable around exhibitionists.

We are eating our own lettuce! You can't imagine how we thrill over it. I am still quite crazy over my garden. Allen and I quarreled violently over the garden the first few weeks, but now we understand each other's limitations better. He realizes that I must finger the soil and I see that he will never really enjoy hoeing. So I don't try to drive him to the garden and he doesn't try to drive me out of it.

I wonder when you'll come back to America? I can't urge you to; though I want to see you so much. It must be a relief to be over there in many ways. *If* we should both sell a novel Allen and I may go over—but that of course is all prospect.

. . . .

Next Day: Since writing the paragraph above I have gone in swimming, idled away an evening in talk, slept eleven hours, and now I'm upstairs resolved to get 2500 words done on this damn story before going forth at three this afternoon to the Cowleys' house warming.

Sally, darling, I do miss you! I feel a little stir of admiration when I think of you. . . .

I must to work.

Love,
Carolyn

Remsen had moved still farther down the hill to Lausanne. His lungs seemed to be clear, but there was a question of bone involvement. There was no question of a return to Paris. He was told to row on Lac Leman every day to recover his strength. I made a trip to Paris to place two of Remsen's paintings in the Salon des Indépendents and store the others.

We had been advised to spend the winter in the south of France. This, of course, was during the French depression, and it was much cheaper to live in France than in America. In Vence, Remsen reorganized his life and began to paint. I decided to spend the mornings writing in English and the afternoons speaking French. As we were getting settled in, this letter arrived from Caroline.

Tory Valley, September 9, 1926
To S. W. in Vence, Alpes-Maritimes, France

Dear Sally:

It has been over a month since your letter came. I found it very interesting. Your situation interests me, aside from the interest I feel in anything that happens to you—but you'll be sniffing at the novelist in me if I develop that point. But I have thought of you a lot this month, wondering what happened, and how you settled matters.

I am very glad you write to me without as you say rounding off the corners. You can do it safely. I understand that you yourself have changed a lot since last fall. . . . Please write and tell me what's happened since Keg went over. I was simply dumbfounded when he told me he was going . . . . . and have been ever since.

Downstairs in the "settin room" Allen is making a version of his poems to assault a publisher with. McBride's seemed on the verge of taking them, then at the last moment weakened. Damn all publishers. An outline of my second novel is now in the hands of John Farrar, curses on him. But I won't be able to think of novels till fall.

For in the middle bedroom Nancy is taking a nap. She takes two a day, thank God! She went to sleep this time with tears in her eyes, clutching my finger with both hands and one foot. She is horribly afraid she'll miss something. She and Mother have been with us two weeks now. I am sure you would feel that all your efforts in her behalf were worth while if you could see her. She is extremely vigorous and healthy—and the merriest baby I ever saw. She snickers to herself almost all day, occasionally breaking into a loud guffaw. Allen has never known a baby intimately, so he is [in] constant amazement at the uncanny things all of them do. She looks rather like Allen, has golden hair and lovely blue eyes, and a lovely Cupid's bow mouth.

However we have our troubles in spite of all her loveliness. I think it would kill Mother if we took her away from her, yet I can't let Nancy be brought up the way she will be brought up if she remains with Mother. It is no worse than I foresaw when I let Nancy go—in fact I painted the picture for Allen at the time. He says that he thought I was exaggerating, and that my fears were all due to my nervous condition— but admits now that it is all exactly as I prophesied. Mother is—indescribable. She is mediaeval in spirit. Her ratiocinative processes are those of the schoolmen of the middle ages. Imagine such methods applied to every day life in this century! The result is appalling. She has no mental life outside this system, which her whole being is constantly defending. Fortunately or unfortunately, she still has her natural affections—this is what complicates relations with her so much. And of course she is simply mad about Nancy. In the rearing of Nancy she hopes to correct all the errors she made with me! Poor Allen is frequently embarrassed when she says to him quite naively, "and you see how Carolyn turned out." He realizes that he is the bad end to which I have come, in Mother's opinion, but he doesn't think he should be called upon to cry out on my ruin. We have decided to leave Nancy with Mother another winter, then snatch her away at any cost. When it comes to a choice between Mother and Nancy I am quite capable of being ruthless. But just now I honestly don't know whether it's best for Nancy to risk our uncertain fortunes. It is fiendishly cold here in the winter. Then too, there are times when we simply don't eat.

We hope to go to town for a month or so. We have raised almost enough food for next winter! I feel quite proud of my carrots, beets, salsify etc. We expect to store the pantry shelves, then go to town, stay as long as our money holds out, and take refuge here again when broke.

I am still quite infatuated with life here in spite of all its difficulties. Nancy is yelling, so I must go. Please write. Lots of love.

Carolyn

Tory Valley, fall, 1926
To S. W. in Vence

My dearest Sally:

Your letter's just come. I am so glad to hear from you and to know something more of your affairs which seem to grow more complicated each time you write. I didn't imagine, though, that you and Keg would find it possible to take up things again, although I rather hoped you could. . . . Being involved in such a situation as you're now in—where there's a compulsion strong enough to direct your life—is the most satis-factory experience one can have, I believe. Having had such an experience and complicating my life immeasurably by it, I still hold this opinion. But oh, Sally, I'd like to see you happier in an easier fashion! I do look forward to our being together again—when you're tired of Europe. I can't help being rather anxious about your health. If you *should* have a year of inactivity after an operation I'd like to have the chance of waiting on you—really if you ever should want a quiet time in the country this would be a fine place to come. And you know how delighted we'd be to have you. I fear Tory Valley would seem rather tame after Paris and Lausanne though—we play croquet! Yes, we have come to that!!

. . . I had a passion this spring for feeding everybody who came out strawberry shortcake—marvelous wild strawberries were everywhere then. As a matter of fact, I do very little housework, though. Just now I'm working pretty steadily on my novel—twenty thousand words done. I write all morning and then cook a little while Allen washes stacks of dishes. Allen is an angel about dishes and things like that but he *won't* work the garden. But as I prefer the dirt to dishes our arrangement works well.

Just now I'm all by myself. Have been for three days. It's long enough, too, to live in a house in the country by yourself. Allen's been in

town, seeing editors and publishers etc. He returns this evening, and in a
little while I must go down and round up some food for him and for Bill
and Sue who are coming down to eat dinner and hear what news there is
from the city.

I suppose Nancy and Mother were here six weeks. They were harried, hectic
weeks. We couldn't enjoy Nancy much because Mother wouldn't let us.
Nancy is a darling, though. I am crazy about her, and Allen is too. She
suddenly began to talk while she was here. Her vocabulary included
"Allen," "Tat Tat" and "Boone" (our hound dog.) She was somewhat
confused as to her paternity, addressing Allen and Boone interchangeably
as "Daddy," but that was not surprising under the circumstances.

I suppose I try to put the situation as regards Nancy rationally
because it seems so hopelessly involved emotionally. I don't know what to
do. Mother is the sort of person with whom no one can have a satisfactory relationship. She uses theology—the theology of the first century
church—as her weapon of offense and defense—in the affairs of every day
life. She is enormously learned in this lore—before Nancy came she gave
all her time to it for five years. Unless you have seen it in operation you
cannot imagine what an effective weapon it is. After a week of Mother's
society I begin to think the fathers of the church were men of superhuman intelligence. The system really takes care of every human foible, if as
Mother piously avers, you can just "lay down your mind and take up the
mind of God." I, who want to keep what little mind I have can't agree
with her there, so nothing I say has any weight with her, coming as it
does from "the carnal mind." She has a great scorn for the modern, who
confuses Christianity with humanitarianism. She sees that "the mind of
God" is capable of cruelty, and she uses cruelty to gain her own ends,
always of course within the strict letter of the system. As she is very
careful to make her actions consonant with the system she remains always
virtuous. I think she came heartily to hate Allen for he made her uncom-
fortable—she has always disliked me. Nancy is to become all the things I
have failed to be!!!! You can imagine how that prospect pleases us. I can
of course take Nancy away from her—Allen was on the verge of doing it
half a dozen times while Mother was here, but that is a very hard thing to
do. Mother, in spite of having taken up the mind of Christ, still retains
her natural affections. She is a person of strong passions, and she has set
her heart on Nancy. I really think she would collapse if we took her away.
Then I feel some responsibility towards my father. She always makes him

suffer for any disappointment that comes to her. He and I have had a sort of gentlemen's agreement ever since I was fifteen or sixteen, to help each other out when we can.

My disapproval of Mother, my indignation against her—and Allen's—is all on moral grounds. And she feels great disapproval of us too, so we're completely antagonistic. At the same time she insists on stressing family affection. We're going to let her have Nancy another year anyhow. After that I don't know what we'll do. Nancy will probably decide the matter for herself eventually, though; so there's no use in bothering. Meanwhile I'm trying to finish this novel before I do anything else.

* * * * * * * *

It is a wonderful golden morning. Yesterday I gathered a lot of elderberries, and I'm going to start some wine today. There are dozens of things like that to be done this time of year. I enjoy them very much. We hope to go to town for January and February, although I'd just as soon stay up here. I don't know whether we'll be here next year. I'm making some money writing pot boilers, and Allen makes a little more all the time. We now have one regular hack job which gives us a regular income of thirty three dollars a month! This seems a great deal of money after starving all winter. As we make a little more money I see us going back to town. I never want to live in town again, but I think Allen would be reconciled, although he is quite content out here with our friends to afford society. He has the strangest attitude toward the country—the same appreciation you'd have for a good set in the theatre. I think Allen feels toward Nature as I do toward mathematics—respectful indifference. He walks about the garden hailing each tomato and melon with amazement—and never sees any connection between planting seeds and eating fruit. Allen, by the way, has changed a lot in the last year. He's certainly a more integrated person.

Please write to me oftener. What you tell me about your health in this letter makes me want to keep in closer touch with you. . . .

I failed to mention last time I wrote how pleased I was to hear about Rem's pictures. I wish I could see some more of his work.

Love,
from
Carolyn

The Tates had decided against another winter in Tory Valley. I had been ill in
Lausanne before the move to Vence but recovered in the warmth and sunshine.

27 Bank Street, New York, fall, 1927
To S. W. in Vence

Dearest Sally:

I've been wanting so much to hear from you—now that I know
you've been sick I realize you haven't felt like writing. I had lunch with Keg
yesterday and he told me he was thinking of going over, and that your
mother would be in town this week. You must have had a hellish time. I
wish I could see you and get some news of you first hand; it's maddening
to hear only through other people.

I haven't written because—well, a dozen or so things, two attacks
of grippe a couple of jobs and the usual struggle for existence.

. . . Allen's poems are with the same people now, but they are
rather snooty about them. I took them with the recommendation of Ford
Madox Ford for whom I've been working as secretary, and now he's
trying to get them published in England. He thinks an English publisher
will be more likely to take them, that they're more like English poems
than American. Sometimes I think no American publisher will ever take
them.

Have I written you since we became janitors? We have an apartment, half of which we rent, for our services. It's rather hectic at times but
better than having a steady job. I've been doing odd jobs, proof reading
for a month or so, then working for Ford—and now he's passing me on
to Elinor Wylie when he leaves in February. He's awfully nice, and I love
to see him take his sentences by the tail and uncurl them—in a perfectly
elegant manner. I don't believe there's anybody writing now who can do
it so elegantly. At times he almost weeps over my lapses into American-
isms. "My deah child, *do* you spell 'honour' without a u?"

I'm still trying to write a novel but don't get much done. . . .

Nancy is thriving in Kentucky. She has jaw teeth now. We got
proofs of some photographs the other day. She is a massive child with a
wide grin. I think she's probably taking after either her Uncle Bill or her
Uncle Ben,[1] both of whom are six footers. It's been so long since I've seen
her now that her picture is rather dim in my memory.

I hope to see your mother while she's in town. I hope she'll send me a note after she gets over there and lets me know how you are. I worry about you a good deal.

Love from both of us,
Carolyn

1. Bill Gordon, Caroline's brother, and Ben Tate, Allen's brother.

When Remsen had fully recovered, he married Anna Van Houten, a painter who had been a friend of his first wife. I had then changed my address to live with the de Ladébat family, who had two daughters about my age. One of them, Monique, had already published a short novel.

27 Bank Street, New York City, November 20, 1927
To S. W. in Vence

Dearest Sally:

What a life this is! I have been trying for months to write you a letter and here I sit on Sunday morning hell-bent on correspondence though there doesn't seem to be any more time Sunday morning than any other. I am so glad you urged Anna and Rem to look us up. We did enjoy them so! I wish we could have seen more of them. But it was good to get some news of you and to find out that I might write to you. I got my last letter back some months ago, and that dampened my ardor considerably. Your life there sounds awfully nice. And what an address you have! Surely at such a place a person could get a few minutes to herself each day! When, if ever are you coming back?

This is the weekend of the Yale Harvard game. I rather expected to hear from the Morses but so far no call—it may be that they didn't come to town. I have not heard from May in months.

By the way, there is a chance—a small chance—that we may be coming to France some time this year. I don't think things will really turn out that way so I'll not explain the various factors of the situation—it's supposed to be a great secret anyhow—but wouldn't that be grand? I get quite up in the air when I even think of it.

. . . I managed to write two [stories] this summer—in the midst of the most frightful uproar. One is coming out soon I think in one of these "younger writers" magazines, edited or rather collected by a mad Irishman named McSorley.[1] He says he'll pay with the second issue but I doubt it. Our dear friend Red Warren descended on us this summer with his fiancee and here they stayed for six weeks. I, of course, got nothing done. The fiancee—her right name is Emma Cinina Elena Anna Clotilda Maria Borgia Venia Gasparini Brescia—felt that she must live up to her descent from the Borgias and raised as much hell as she possibly could all the time. It wasn't so much because she is really rather a stolid soul but it was enough to keep either of us from doing a bit of work—except that once I just elbowed them all out of the way and wrote a story in two sittings. I would have thrown her out of the window the first week but for my deep affection for Red. . . .

Allen is writing a biography of Stonewall Jackson. We took a trip in a Ford this summer over the battlefields in Virginia—it was simply grand. We took a camping outfit along and slept out, mostly in tourist camps because we were too lazy to hunt for water at night. Next summer we plan to drive to Kentucky to see Nancy. Mother was going to bring her to New York in October, but she (Mother) has been quite ill, and we thought the trip would be too hard on her. So we haven't seen Nancy since she was eight months old! She is a very buxom young woman, five pounds overweight for a boy. Dad wrote me the other day that it was certainly strange "that two such ordinary people as you and Allen could produce such a remarkable child and when I look at Nancy I think so too. Of course a large part of her robustness is due to you. I can never forget how you looked after me before she was born. It seems years and years, Sally, since I've seen you.

I must do a little work, housework. I am at present acting as secretary for Ford Madox Ford, running this house and my own apartment. Ford will be going back to France soon, though, and I won't have so much to do. My job with him is really ideal; he comes over about three times a year and stays a month or so. I have long periods in between for my own work with certainty of employment when he comes back.

Do write, Sally. I have gone quite long enough without news of you. . . . Allen sends his love too.

                                        Carolyn

1. Possibly Edward McSorley (1902–1966), one-time journalist, publicist, later novelist, short story writer, who also wrote articles and reviews.

Obviously, letters were lost at this point. Caroline must have written that Allen had had Mr. Pope and Other Poems *published after* Stonewall Jackson, *both in 1928, and that he had received a Guggenheim.*

My brother had been feeling quite well in Vence and had become home-sick for America. He went home in the summer, and I was about to follow even though, by that time, I had become devoted to France. I had to have surgery and had seen too much of foreign medicine to stay away.

Caroline sent this letter from a tenement house inhabited by other writers and called the Cabinet of Dr. Caligari after the celebrated movie in which everyone was crazy although one did not realize it at first.

561 Hudson Street, New York City, late winter, 1928
To S. W. in Vence

My darling Sally:

How grand to hear from you! I am overcome. I have felt like breaking your neck on occasions the last few months, but now that your letter comes I am touched. Isn't it hell that I go across just as you come back? Don't come. Stay. We have counted so on seeing you. Please don't come over—do you have to?

About the apartment: I am tempted to take it, but darling, we don't even know what country we're going to be in. We may go first to England. We haven't made any plans yet really. Both of us have been in a sort of fog about personal affairs. Allen has to whirl in and write a biography of Jefferson Davis before we leave and I have been trying desperately to finish a mystery story (a sort of shot in the dark that I have been working on this past year) before I even think about going. I finished it yesterday and had just sat down to revise the ms when your letter came. Things then being as they are I guess we'd better not take the apartment. I am anxious to spend as much time as we can in the country. We've been pent in the city two years now and we both feel the need of a little rural air frightfully. And the bars of Paris don't tempt me much: I know too well the kind of people who'll be sitting around them.

. . . .

Yes, Nancy is with us—at my elbow, in fact, at this minute: let that account for any incoherencies. She is a perfect dumpling—I wish you could see her. She talks incessantly and says some very good things. I must say that Keg is the first young man who has walked into this house (and God knows that far too many young men walk into this house) who hasn't been bowled over by her charms. His verdict on her was that she certainly talked fast! Her courtesy uncles prize most the remark made to Donald Clark.[1] She showed him a hideous headless doll and said "This is my big baby, Donald." "Oh," says he, "Parthenogenetic, I suppose?" "Naw," says Nancy, with equal aplomb, "Santa Claus done it." She urges us constantly to efforts in her behalf with: "Go on, Daddy and make me a living." "A living" is any piece of typewritten paper. She picked several up from Allen's desk one day and said "Is this my living, Daddy?" and when he said it was she observed "It's mighty thin, Daddy." But she really is a darling, and doesn't wise crack any more than the average baby. We had a hell of a time with her for several months after I brought her back from Kentucky. My father met me at the station and told me that she was "the worst spoiled child in the United States" (privately of course,) and that he didn't know how I would ever manage her. We did manage however to establish a routine for her in the course of several weeks, but it was certainly hell while it lasted. She was used to being rocked to sleep and all that sort of thing.

We are living now in a fine pre-Revolutionary tenement house, known as The Cabinet of Dr. Caligari. I am quite devoted to the place in spite of its many drawbacks—no hot water etc. 561 Hudson Street, Telephone Chelsea 6744. If we should be out of town when you come which God forbid I'd love to have you stay here, if it isn't too rough for you. On the chance I am going to include directions for establishing yourself here. Get hold of Katherine Anne Porter, either by telephoning or standing in the hall and shouting her name. She will have our key and she will introduce you to the ways of Caligari. I will tell her that you may appear and she will be on the lookout for you. I know that it is hard to pin yourself down, but would that you had given some date for your arrival so that I might arrange my affairs accordingly! I shall never get over it if I miss you.

Oh, Allen's book is going swell. It actually looks as though he would make something out of it. It has sold three thousand in three weeks. I haven't as yet taken in the fact that by fall we will have enough money on hand for at least two years living. It doesn't seem possible. We have literally not known where the next package of cigarettes was coming from these last two years. However I have pretty well gotten used to it now, and I don't worry about it.

. . . .

I have little to show for two—or is it three years—work. This book I have just finished, and three fourths of another novel, and two stories. That is all I have been able to accomplish. It is these young poets from the South—they call us up as soon as they hit the Pennsylvania Station and they stay anywhere from a week to a month. I have gotten a bit bitter about it.

. . . .

It is now time that I jerk this place into some semblance of order and get some groceries in for the weekend.

Please try to arrange to be here the latter part of June if you can. I just must see you.

Allen sends his love. I wonder if you are aware of the great admiration that young man has for you? We are both agog at the prospect of seeing you—so is Nancy.

Love,
C.

[added as a postscript]

. . . .

I am wondering whether I ought not to cable you about the apartment—but alas I am broke at present.

1. Perhaps Donald Clark (1888–1966), then associate professor of English at Columbia and shortly to take over as editor of the annual volume of *Columbia Poetry*. He would have been introduced by his colleague, the Tates' friend Mark Van Doren.

561 Hudson Street, New York City, August 17, 1928
To S. W. in Rochester, New York

_____

Dearest Sally:

I have just gotten back to New York after coursing madly over the country in a Ford for over two months. Della Day[1] has just told me about the telegram you sent me on your arrival. I cannot tell you how sorry I am not to have been able to meet you. I saw Keg the other day and he told me that you were going to have an operation. You may by this time have had it. I do so hope everything goes well, and that you will be recovered soon. It was certainly rotten luck to miss you. I have been so anxious to see you.

. . . .

It is perhaps well that you did not stop in our apartment. It seems a terrible spot after all the green open spaces we've seen recently. I have been stupefied and appalled by the city ever since I got back—and I was perfectly adjusted to urban life when we left. We will be sailing in about six months—if we sail at all. My mother is very ill—that is, several doctors have said that she cannot live long, and I cannot bear to go abroad under the circumstances.

If you can, write me, Sally. I am anxious about you.

Much love,
Carolyn

1. Dorothy's younger sister, who, with Forster Batterham and Dorothy, lived across the street from the Tates.

I did not go to the Cabinet of Dr. Caligari because my family met me in New York, and I returned with them to Rochester. I was put out of commission for a long while. The operation was followed by rheumatic fever, for which there were at the time no such remedies as there are today.

561 Hudson Street, New York City, late August, 1928
To S. W. in Rochester

Dear Sally:

I have begun to feel these last few months, years, in fact, that you are a sort of wraith out of my past, any sort of communication with you seems so impossible. . . . I am glad to learn that you are at last on the same continent, though it is fiendish to think that I probably won't see you. I wrote you about a week ago, but . . . [we were told] you didn't get the letter. A friend came in while we were away and in straightening up our papers buried your mother's Rochester address and I've never been able to find it, so I just addressed you in her care, Rochester. We have been home about three weeks now, after over two months of coursing

over the country in our Ford. I didn't know about your telegram from the
boat until I arrived. I am so sorry I wasn't able to meet you. It looks as
though we're fated to miss each other. I answered your Dijon letter but as
I addressed you here at Caligari you doubtless never got that either.

I am glad to hear you're going to have your operation and get it
over with. I do wish you were able to travel here or that I could get down
there to see you, but I don't suppose it can be managed. My own affairs
are in great confusion just now. I think I'll be going south for a visit of a
week or ten days very soon, probably next Monday. We sail the twenty
eighth of September. How I wish you were going to be in France this
year! By the way, if you have any addresses to give me, please do. We shall
feel rather lost, I'm sure. We know very few people abroad, though you
do run into people all the time, I suppose.

. . . .

It looked for awhile as though we might not go abroad this year
after all, but it's finally been decided that we will. My mother is quite ill,
at least the doctors have said that she can hardly live more than a year. It
is cancer of the breast. It seems almost impossible to leave under the circumstances, yet she will not hear to anything else, so we're going on.
We may come back, however, before the year is over, to be with my
father. . . .

Do write me, Sally. Address me here and Allen will forward if
I've left town. I really don't know just when I'll be going. I wish I could
see you!

Much love,
Carolyn

561 Hudson Street, New York City, fall, 1928
To S. W. in Rochester

_____

Dearest Sally:

You must have been impressed by my complaints of your insub-
stantiality to send me such a lovely and tangible proof of your existence!
The ring just came a minute ago and I am quite overwhelmed by it. It is
just the sort of thing that I adore—and I must admit that it is extremely
becoming to my large, dark brown hand. I shall wear it whenever I am

not washing dishes and think of you. No, I shall wear it only on dress up occasions. Anyhow I think is is lovely and it was sweet of you to send it— but how I do wish I could see you! It does seem too fiendish to go abroad without seeing you. Our tickets came today, by the way, tickets and labels for baggage etc. For the first time I realized that I am really going. Nancy never loses sight of her projected journey. "That," she says kindly to visitors "is my Yurrup hat." She even has some geographical information: "There is a lot of sand at France," she says, "and I am going to play in it."

I wonder if you got Allen's book of poems [*Mr. Pope and Other Poems*], and how you liked it? He was quite annoyed because last Sunday the Tribune announced his book as "by the author of Stonewall Jackson." I am waiting for the Times to come out with "The author of Stonewall Jackson tries his hand at verse." That will quite finish Allen. The idea, somehow, amuses me a great deal.

. . . .

I got in three days work the other day, then took cold and have been sitting round doing nothing but read Virginia Woolf three more days. Oh, I think she's marvelous!

I am ashamed of myself for letting Little May think I was coming all summer, but I have come very near losing my mind this summer, what with family troubles and all, and other people's annoyances seemed very vague to me.

Your advice about the clothes I hug to my bosom. I think I will just get myself one or two things that suit me. I haven't had clothes I liked for four years now and I am pretty sick of it. I have just made myself the love-liest gown I've had in many a year, though, and I'm still absorbed in wonder over it. I fell heir to an evening cape of gold cloth, and I made a dress out of it—a very dark brown velvet basque on a long scalloped skirt. It is marvelous. I don't yet see how I did it. I have been sewing madly on this garment for two days, crouched in a welter of young men from Vanderbilt. This is the time for the annual irruption. I have never seen anything like the way they come—some I never even heard of before appeared yesterday. There will be about two more weeks before they flutter south. Poor Nancy is more confused by them than I. She has about six adopted uncles now. Yesterday she looked in and saw another one and said: "Now what Bill is that, Mama?"

I have a story I'll send you.

I am afraid we can't come to Rochester, though I simply hate to leave without seeing you. We are, as usual, somewhat short of money. We tried to be prudent and divided the Guggenheim installments so we get the largest ones after we get over there. We have just enough money to get there and last three months.

Allen sends his love. Don't bother to write him unless you feel up to it. I know that the feeling of letters owed can be very depressing. He knows that you got the poems, and he knows that you like them. I'll have some kodak pictures of Nancy soon. Much love, Sally.

561 Hudson Street, New York City, September, 1928
To S. W. in Rochester

Dearest Sally:

I was immensely relieved to get your letter. It was mighty good of you to write—I know it must have taken an effort. But I had gotten awfully anxious to hear from you. I was about to write [a friend] for some proof of your continued existence.

. . . .

Don't bother about the list of addresses unless you feel quite up to it. I'd be interested of course in your recommendations, more than in anybody else's, but we have collected lots of addresses. A young man from Nashville blew in yesterday and gave us detailed instructions, where to spend our first night in Paris, our second night, our third night in London etc. etc. We are to go into hotels and say: "A bed for the baby at once!" If there is delay we are to snort: "What no bed for the baby? What sort of place is this?" and turn on our heel, our family heel, as it were and only be lured back by reductions in prices, protestation and so on. I can see how Europe would be a perfect rest cure if one followed his advice—one could take out all sorts of irritations on the hapless restaurateurs and hotel keepers. I can't see myself getting away with it, though.

No, I didn't know that the ring was for the forefinger—such an idea never entered my head, but it is grand on any finger.

. . . .

I don't imagine we'll stay our full year in Europe—Mother's condition makes it improbable. It is really too much to leave everything on Dad.

I am sort of suspended, waiting to know whether I'll go home or not. I think now I mayn't go. I imagine Dad's decided that it's best after all for me not [to] come, but I can't take up anything else or finish anything till I know, for after all, one going into my home needs all her resources, mental and moral.

We sail the twenty eighth.

We think that Allen will make three to five thousand dollars out of Jackson. We are both quite stunned over it. We are going to slap the money quickly into a place in Pennsylvania. We already know the place. You drive along through the woods by a brook, and suddenly there is an old stone bridge and you look across this vista at a beautiful old stone house. It is one of the most beautiful places I've ever seen. A little above the house is a gorgeous rock lined pool, so baths will never be any problem. We hope to get back towards the end of next summer and get the place. I hope you . . . can visit us there then. We have to get the place very quickly or we won't be able to hold on to the money.

. . . .

> *Love,*
> *C.*
> *Tuesday, Wednesday or Thursday*

Written upon arriving in London, October 8, 1928
To S. W. in Rochester

My dearest Sally—We got your letter with the notes before we left. It was awfully good of you to write all those letters, and I'm sure the time will come soon when we'll be glad to meet people. Just now, however, I am too fresh from Caligari and the crowds that swell and turn south to be at all lonely. I'm rather pleased to reflect that unless we look up your Hamish Patterson[1] (who sounds charming) there is nobody I know in London except Paul Robeson, the negro actor, and an offensive Jewish poetess.

Allen has gone out to Bayswater to find lodgings. Nancy and I repose at this hotel. We landed Sunday after a fearful voyage. A storm, two points below a hurricane, the captain said, raged for four days and nights. None of us were sea sick, but we got quite morbid. Allen refused to take off his clothes at night, and vowed that he would never cross the Atlantic again under any circumstances. Just before we landed I was requested to sign a letter of eulogy of the captain who stayed on the bridge three days & nights and like Allen, never changed his clothes. I was surprised to find that this eulogy was the work of Allen—surely the most florid piece of writing he's every done!

There were forty Rhodes scholars on our boat—really quite terrible creatures, most of them. The honour of Tennessee is in the hands of a young man named Dogberry, who had the effrontery to refer to me as "the wife."

We expect to stay in London about a week, then hunt up some place in the country and live there until January. Allen wants to stay in England till then for the libraries. I am disappointed: I could afford a nurse for Nancy in France, but not in England. Six weeks, with no interruption, would enable me to finish this novel I've been working on now for three years—but I see little chance of getting the six weeks. I am getting a bit bitter about it.

This is the eighth of October—I am wondering if you've had your operation yet and how you are. I do so hope you'll be entirely recovered soon, dear Sally. Let me hear from you when you can.

I shall be anxious for news of you.

Love,

C.

[added as a postscript]

We think now we'll go to Vence this winter, in which case your letters will certainly be presented. It's nice to have the prospect of seeing your friends.

1. A Scottish painter who had both wrists shot at Gallipoli.

Paris, France, December 2 and 3, 1928
To S. W. in Rochester

Dearest Sally:

Your letter came just as we were leaving Oxford. I have been trying for days to get a moment to write to you, but getting settled always seems to take so much time. I was surprised to hear that you had put off your operation till November. I had been hoping to hear that it was over. I am, of course, awfully anxious to hear from you. Let me have some news as soon as you can. In the meantime, much love. I think of you very often. I am so sorry you are not in Paris now. We miss you. We keep saying, "How nice it would be if Sally were here!"

We are settled—thanks to you—in the Hotel de Fleurus. We are very comfortable. It was a great comfort to have a place to come to, without parley. We seem to waste a great deal of time in parley.

Ford has about persuaded us to stay in Paris for the next few months. The railroad fare to Vence, Montpellier or any other place we had thought of, is quite an item. And it seems that living expenses will be higher there now than at any other time. I haven't as yet seen any of your friends, except Anna, whom we saw night before last. We are going with her tonight to some negro place whose name I cannot remember. . . . We missed seeing Cecil Wright[1] and his wife, and Hamish Patterson. They were in London—he had a show there—while we were in Oxford. As for Harold Stearns[2] I cannot feel any desire to know him (with your description in mind). People who make a cult of drink bore me terribly, even friends of yours, dear Sally. I know that they are amusing at times, as people are always saying of them, but my experience has been that you have to wade through such dreary wastes for those few moments, that it's hardly worth while. [E. E] Cummings, for instance, I regard as one of the greatest bores that ever lived. He will sit for hours gearing himself up to make some brilliant stroke—when it comes out it is usually something like "Fuckaduck." Perhaps I wrong Mr. Stearns—he is probably a charming person—but I can't help fearing he's like that.

I have to dress for lunch. I'll finish this later.

[Written on top of address—probably added because of lack of space]

No, Nancy is not shy. She particularly likes strange gentlemen, and will deliver greetings gladly. I hope we will yet see Cecil and Margaret Wright. They sound awfully nice.

December 3. I understand now why you wrote so seldom when you were here—there seems to be no time, though where it goes I don't know. We had tea yesterday with Anna at her hotel—the only place in Paris, she says, which would take her dog in. I was anxious to see some of her work, but she had only two pictures there, and some sketches. I liked them very much. Why doesn't she go on painting, instead of fooling around at the Sorbonne?

It looks now as though we would not get to Vence. Anna tells me that living is just as expensive there as in Paris, and there is the long rail-road journey too, to consider.

. . . .

I worked like hell when we were in Oxford. I have my novel—the one I've been on three years—about half rewritten. It will be a relief if ever I get it off. Oxford was a grand place to work.

I can't thank you enough for all your recommendations, particularly for sending us to this hotel. It suits us perfectly, and the location, I think, is ideal. Ford, by the way, lives just around the corner.

The Dome and Rotonde are really quite terrible, don't you think? A sort of super-Greenwich village. They actually appall. Allen says the Select is better. I haven't been there yet.

I have just gotten out your long letter of advices, written before we left, and going over it, find many, many things I wanted to know. It was awfully good of you to take so much trouble for us. This is a poor, dis-jointed letter, I know. The truth is, all my energy as a correspondent just now goes into letters to my mother, who will hardly live through the winter, I think. I try to write every day, and recount most of Nancy's bright remarks, and when that is done I am pretty well exhausted.

My love to your mother. Do get her, or Alice,[3] or Rem (to whom also we send greetings,) to drop us a note and let us know how you are. We are so anxious to hear.

Much love, Carolyn

1. A British painter whom we knew in Vence. He had been a king's courier during World War I and had arrived in Russia in the middle of the revolution, getting out with his life but not his health.
2. Editor of *Civilization in the United States* (1922). He didn't believe there was any and so fled to Europe.
3. My sister.

There was a gap here due to my prolonged illness. I had gone to Chapel Hill, North Carolina, in the fall for the benefit of a warmer climate and then to Florida where I must have contracted the typhoid fever that declared itself on

*my return to Chapel Hill. This time I was unconscious for six weeks, but oddly
enough, I recovered. There were more letters from Caroline than from me.*

Paris, July 9, 1929
To S. W. in Rochester

Dear Sally:

I wonder if I will ever have another letter from you?

All the news I've had of you this winter was a note just after your
operation, relayed by Anna. I would like so much to know how you are,
what your plans are and so on. It is about time for your semi-annual
letter, don't you think? Anna said there was a rumor that you were coming over this summer. We got rather worked up over that, but as no word
has come from you I have decided there was nothing in it.

We are staying in Paris about a week longer—until Ford returns
from New York and we can deliver him the keys of his apartment. We
have had it five months now and it has been a great joy. It is just opposite
the Senate. Our windows look out on Saint Sulpice. This has been a marvelous location to which you directed us. I don't think I'd ever want to
live anywhere else in Paris. Nancy plays in the [Luxembourg] gardens
every day with the same group of French children. Her French is much
better than her parents', and quite fluent. I notice that she even talks to
herself and her imaginary family, the Keder-Jenkinses, in French now. We
have decided, though, that it is about time to bring her home. Her favorite book is still "Battles and Leaders of the Civil War", but the other day
when she was looking it over she observed "There's Monsieur Stonewall
Jackson." We really can't have that!

We plan to go south in a few days. I have no idea just where. Antibes probably, may be Cagnes, because it is cheaper. I am very anxious
for Allen and Nancy to lie around in the sun and get the grippe germs
completely out of their system. One reason I have [not] written you oftener—did you ever get any letters from me? this winter is because we
have been having steadily one hell of a time. First we had grippe, then
grippe again, and then more grippe: three main bouts, with slight attacks
sprinkled in between. I never saw anything like it. It was a terrible winter
here. Everybody had this peculiar grippe with complications, abscesses in

ears, weakened livers etc. As soon as the grippe was over, two of our friends began having hysterics. They had them so hard and fast that we had to drop everything and look after them for weeks and weeks. Then we had the grippe again. Then Allen's publisher wrote and said there was another biography of Jefferson Davis coming out this fall and Allen had better make publication on September 20 if he didn't want to lose money. Allen leaped out of his sick bed and began typing madly. I also began typing madly. We continued to type madly day and night until the fourth of July when that damn book was dispatched to the publisher. We then went out and celebrated our freedom by getting drunk with Hart Crane who is over here spending his grandmother's legacy. And now here we are, a little dazed but quite ready for the summer. At least I am here; Allen is in England seeing people.

I got up this morning, determined to work—I had to drop my work for a whole month to help Allen—and I am anxious to make time before things being to thicken up for the summer. Friends came in and asked me to go shopping, but I said no, I would work. I discovered however that I simply couldn't work, so I got on a bus and went over to the Guaranty Trust which now ornaments 4 Place de la Concorde. After getting me some money I stopped and had coffee at a cafe on the rue Royale, then I thought I would walk around the Madeleine and after that I would have the beginning of my chapter in my head. The first thing I knew I was in Trois Quartiers buying a beautiful pink wool sweater and a new hat, to say nothing of some underwear.

When I got home a few minutes ago, it was four o'clock, and I haven't the least idea where the day went to.

It is so nice here now, though still a little cold. I cannot get used to its being so cold in July: Allen is positively bitter about it. He makes patriotic speeches about the climate; he even put a dig at it in his book. "Young men," says he, "who found it inconvenient to go to war, suddenly developed bad health and had to go abroad to recuperate in the fogs and drizzles of northern Europe."

Did I tell you Allen got his Guggenheim Fellowship renewed, which means perhaps another six months abroad? If it's all right with the foundation we want to come home this fall, though. At least Allen does. I don't. I have a grand little maid for five hundred francs a month who takes complete charge of the house and keeps Nancy out in the gardens at least five hours a day. If it hadn't been for the grippe and the hysterical friends and Jefferson Davis I would have gotten a lot of work done. As it is I have had several weeks completely uninterrupted.

Anna came through the other day, on her way to Juan-les-Pins for the summer with the children. I wouldn't have known Freda, she has grown so much. We had them all together one day—and what a day!—in the gardens, and Freda spent the night with us. Anna has enlivened us with several visits this winter. The time before she let Orgal¹ spend the night with us. We enjoyed her too very much. Anna almost persuaded me to go to Juan-les-Pins this summer. We may land there yet. In any case we will see her if we go to Antibes or Cagnes. I suppose you have heard what a time Anna had in Holland this winter. She seemed overjoyed to be back in France. She arrived here on one of the worst days of the winter, in the midst of a stretch of weather that was almost driving us mad, and she kept looking about and sniffing this horrible gray air, and saying it was so springlike and bright! May I never see Holland!

Stella,² Ford's former wife, has just finished painting a portrait of the Tates *en famille*—Allen and I, held together in space, by Nancy, as it were. It sounds as if the composition were pretty funny, but it really isn't. Pavlich Tchelitchew³—I wonder if you've ever seen any of his work— observed that Nancy's head was quite *moyen age*, whatever he meant by that. He didn't say what her parents were like. I'll send you a photograph if Stella gets back from England before we leave.

transition⁴ in its last issue announces a revolution of the word. They are through, they aver, with "monotonous syntax, the banal word etc." I wish I had that proclamation here—it was really very funny. Every one of their banal and ungrammatical statements was reenforced by a quotation from Blake: "The tigers of wrath are stronger than the horses of instruction." I begin to think that they aren't, reading transition. A new magazine has sprung up, called Tambour.⁵ It is edited by a Jewish lad of eighteen who ought to be in school learning the parts of speech. Although he actually cannot write a grammatical sentence he is taken quite seriously and lectures his elders sternly at times in the pages of the Mercure de France, his own publication and elsewhere. The first issue of his magazine contained an attack on "the old men of '99" (elderly creatures like Malcolm Cowley, Hart, Allen) who, doddering on the verge of the grave put out their palsied hands to strangle young talent. God, how fast we get on!

I have a story—the best I have ever written—coming out this fall in a "little" magazine published by Yvor Winters, called The Gyroscope. The story is called "Summer Dust," and has been turned down by practically every living publisher. I am glad to see it published at last, as it is the best piece of writing I have ever done.

E. W. Titus—do you know that slightly sinister figger?—has bought This Quarter, why nobody knows, and is getting out his first number quite soon.[6] 4 rue Delambre, if you want to send anything. That horrible Pierre Loving[7] told me they needed fiction. Titus turned that story of mine down on the ground that it was not complete in itself. It has four episodes, rather loosely hung together.

Oh, damn it, how nice it would have been if you could have been here this winter! And how hellish it will be if you get here just after we leave! . . . Nancy still speaks of [a mutual friend] enthusiastically—he brought her the first box of candy she ever received from a young man. I regret to say that she took it to bed with her, leaving a dozen people sitting around candyless. I believe we did steal from the child while she was asleep. . . .

. . . .

I wish I did have some French—but I just can't bother with it now. It upsets me to even think about it when I'm trying to write. Of course I pick up necessary phrases from the concierge, waiters, our femme de menage etc. It's all the conversational French I'll ever have, probably.

What is Rem doing? And how is he? Give him my regards.

Please write me and tell me how you are, and what your plans are. I do want to see you. My love to your mother,

Much love,
Carolyn

1. My brother's dog.
2. Stella Bowen was Ford's Australian wife, a painter.
3. Pavel Tchelitchew (1898–1957), Russian-born "neoromantic" painter and stage designer.
4. A monthly magazine, later a quarterly, edited in Paris by Eugene Jolas and Elliot Paul, April, 1927, to spring, 1938. One of the most influential of the little magazines, its aims were to publish a "re-evaluation of Romanticism," a "campaign for the 'Revolution of the Word,'" and a "new philosophy from sub-liminal and preconscious materials" based on the writings of Carl Jung. Besides Tate himself, other notable contributors included Hart Crane, Joyce, Hemingway, Kafka, Gertrude Stein, William Carlos Williams, and Malcolm Cowley.
5. Published by Harold J. Salemson, February, 1929, to June, 1930, it printed both English and French writing. Salemson criticized other such magazines for being esoterically exclusive and writers of the twenties for being too preoccupied with "form" at the expense of "matter."
6. A "little magazine" begun in 1925 under the editorship of Ernest Walsh but suspended

after three issues when he died. It resumed under Edward W. Titus (1929–1932) with contributors such as Robert Penn Warren, William Carlos Williams, Cummings, Winters, Louis Mac-Neice, Paul Valery, Ernest Hemingway, and Sherwood Anderson.

7. Loving wrote on drama, publishing a number of critical essays in various literary magazines. His recent book was *Revolt in German Drama* (1925).

Unites States Lines, January 5, 1930
To S. W. in Rochester

We dock tomorrow morning, they say, after a ghastly trip. We are going, I think, to the Cavendish Arms, 23rd St. & 7th Ave. while we hunt an apartment. My address is: Care Frank Lappin, 81 Jane St. New York. Please write if you can. *Can't* you come to New York before we leave? We expect to stay there three months, then go south to hunt up a farm—provided Allen's publisher isn't enough affected by the Stock Market crash to forget his magnificent promises. In Virginia, the farm will be, I think.

I *hated* leaving Paris. God, how I hated leaving Paris. I didn't do much to amuse myself there—just sat around in cafes, but it was all so nice & easy. I gained 15 pounds, in spite of working like a dog! You won't know me.

I left half of a novel in the hands of Ford Madox Ford who's going to try to get me a contract from Harper's or some of the other publishers who appear so thickly in the spring. God knows when I'll finish the novel if Ford can't land me an advance.

If you have any short stuff on hand send it to Yvor Winters, Box 286, Palo Alto, California for his "little" magazine The Gyroscope. The Gyroscope is suspended now. However, Winters intends to publish next year two issues (large.) He can't pay anything.

I am writing this in the Social hall while six children of as many as four nationalities are "swimming" from rug to rug. *Please* write.

Love,
Caroline

[added as a postscript]
I have four short stories to show you, all written in the last six months. I never could write short stories until I went to Brittany and then I burst out with 'em like a rash.

Caroline must have realized that, since we still couldn't see each other because of
my prolonged illnesses, she would have to catch me up on events by letter.

364 East Twenty Sixth St., New York City, January 21, 1930
To S. W. in Chapel Hill, North Carolina

My poor dear Sally: What a frightful time you have had. I am so
very sorry about it all. I knew that things could not be going well with
you, but I didn't know exactly how they were. I have been so anxious for
news of you, and now comes this disheartening letter. . . .

Your letter came back to me from Paris. Oh God, how I want to be
back in Paris! I complained all the way home. I think it was grief at leaving Paris made me so sea sick. We had a hellish crossing.

We lived this winter in the little hotel by the Odeon, Hotel de la
Place de l'Odeon. I got to love that *place* very much. I really miss the gray
streets more than anything. I would like to be walking home from the
Closerie des Lilas now along the rue d'Assas. But this is no sort of line to
hand you, in North Carolina. I don't know a single soul in North Carolina who could lighten a day for one. Chapel Hill must be terrible. Well,
New York is terrible. I thought I would go mad the first few days, what
with the rocking of the boat that still went on in my head and the uproar
of Twenty Third Street. We are settled on Twenty Sixth street now, just
off Ninth avenue, in a two by four furnished apartment. We plan to stay
here till the first of June anyhow. We have so many plans that I hardly
know which one to hand out. The last plan is to get my grandmother,
now nearly eighty, to give me my slice of Merimont[1] now and settle down
there instead of buying a place in Virginia or Pennsylvania. There is a
little piece of land, cut off from the rest of the farm by the big road that I
covet. It is on a beautiful little stream, "Hatcher's Branch" (we call them
branches, you know; brook is literary,) with an enormous spring that
already supplies water power to one house. I have been going over the
farm in my mind all day, rounding up cabins. I think we might put a
couple of cabins together (I know people who have had cabins moved)
and make us some sort of house. Any place where there was room enough
to turn round in twice would seem pretty swell to me, after living in this
two room apartment. I have written asking my grandmother about giving
me the land. I can't see why she should object. I know she would be an-

xious for me to settle down there. She regards living anywhere else in the world as pure madness, and I am her favorite, or was, until I married. She really likes only very thin virgins, born on her own land. She can't bear any of the grandchildren who were born off her land.

I enclose a drawing of Nancy's. The title, "Man with Hair" is her own. She draws a great deal these days. The poor child is having a hard time, shifting her base so often. She had a nice old Frenchwoman for a nurse this winter and got terribly French. Towards the last, for a month, that is, I left her with the old woman all the time, even at night—I was working awfully hard on my novel and Nancy had [a] habit of rising at five o'clock and singing little French songs in a piercingly sweet voice. She acquired a great scorn for her parents because they were Americans. The remark she made to me most frequently was "You don't know, Mama, you don't know." Her English is very poor now, about where it was a year ago. She cannot handle the verb at all. She has been thinking in French, you see, for about a year. She still talks to herself in French, but I suppose she will lose it very rapidly.

Our last days in Paris were very hectic. Christmas came on, with lots of gayeties and I was carousing of nights and working all day on my novel for the last three or four weeks. . . . Ford took me by the scruff of the neck about three weeks before I left, set me down in his apartment every morning at eleven o'clock and forced me to dictate at least five thousand words, not all in one morning, of my novel to him. If I complained that it was hard to work with everything so hurried and Christmas presents to buy he observed "You have no passion for your art. It is unfortunate" in such a sinister way that I would reel forth sentences in a sort of panic. Never did I see such a passion for the novel as that man has. I have known him for several years, and he has been hounding me to show him my novel all that time. But you know I never have anything in a state to show anybody. And besides I never thought he would like it. I did show him some short things which I myself rather fancied, some of them a damn sight better done than the novel, and he would mumble in his moustache "Beautiful writing, but I don't know what it is all about."[2] Then finally I drags this novel, only half finished over, and he flies into a great rage and accuses me of concealing it from him until there is no time to do anything and so on and so on. I left the manuscript, half finished, with him, and he is going to try to get me a contract and an advance on

it. I have no great hopes, however. It is hard to do anything with a half
finished manuscript. Anyhow I am settling down in this very apartment to
try to finish it before we go to the country. I have taken the plunge and
engaged a maid to come every morning, from nine to one, so I can work.
I enclose, by the way, a short story.[3] Don't lose it, but you needn't bother
to send it back right off. It is coming out in the Gyroscope, ought to be
out now. You might send Winters something for next year. He is suspend-
ing the Gyroscope but plans to get out two issues during the year. He
can't pay anything. I've told you this before?

. . . .

Anna was off for Vence for the winter last time I saw her.[4] Anna
really does what Henry James said once he did love France better than any
man. She is a queer gal. I never saw any of the literary productions. When
she mentioned them I always said "For God's sake why, when you can
paint?" (No, it's the Latin Quarter Anna loves.)

There is a new magazine, "The Miscellany,"[5] at 26 West Ninth
Street. They have asked me to contribute. A group of Yale lads, I think
they are. If you have any short stuff on hand send it there.

There will certainly be room for you on any place we get in the
country. We will just drag up an extra cabin while we're about it, so you
can feel independent. No, really, I think we could make you comfortable
enough, and there would be no stairs. So you must come, as soon as we
get settled. Couldn't you come to New York this spring, though. The
Carteret, on Twenty Third street, is a good place to stay, quite cheap, and
very comfortable, much more comfortable, say, than the Albert. Unfortunately we haven't room for another object in the apartment. I debate
about buying a tea strainer because I don't know where I'd put it. We
have a fair sized living room, though, in which Allen and I sleep, eat and
work. We cook in Nancy's bedroom and wash dishes in the bathroom. It
isn't so bad, though, as long as I have a woman to keep it clean.

I say let all of us that can turn Catholic at once. Yes, you must have
plenty of servants to abandon yourself to your emotions, even to what
mind you have. I can't write when I'm doing scullery work because even
when I get the time my mind won't take hold of any problem.

But I must go to bed. I am so glad to have heard from you. Please
write again. I have been so out of touch with you and have hated it so.

You must come to New York this spring. Much love from both of us,
Carolyn

1. Caroline's mother was a Meriwether, the name of a Virginia family whose best known member was Meriwether Lewis. Their family place near Trenton, Kentucky, was sometimes spelled this way and sometimes spelled *Merry Mont*.

2. The War Between the States had not been in Ford's experience, but he was destined to learn about it, as well as much else in the life of the South.

3. "The Long Day."

4. Anna had been to America with her two Dutch children to visit. She found no cafés or Latin Quarter environment and so returned to France. My brother had been too ill in France to wish to go back, however. These feelings persisted and ended in divorce.

5. A bimonthly that lasted one year (1930–1931), notable for critical articles of high quality and poetry by men such as Winters, Williams, and Conrad Aiken. Among its four editors were Frederick Dupee and Dwight MacDonald.

By this time, Allen had published Stonewall Jackson: The Good Soldier *(1928),* Mr. Pope and Other Poems *(1928), and* Jefferson Davis: His Rise and Fall *(1929). He had become very well known and had a great deal of influence with other writers.*

His brother Ben, who was very well off, knowing of the Tates' plan to live in the country, helped them buy a house. It was on the Cumberland River near Clarksville, Tennessee. Caroline always called it Benfolly. It was in what she spoke of as "the old neighborhood" next to Kentucky where her ancestors the Meriwethers had settled when they came westward from Virginia. The Tates often went to "spend the day" with Caroline's grandmother, Miss Carrie, at Merimont, a short distance away. Caroline was her favorite grandchild. Caroline's father, whose character later inspired several short stories and the book Aleck Maury, Sportsman, *had left those parts before the Tates came, but several Meriwether aunts and uncles and numberless cousins lived nearby.*

Once, when I was visiting, one of the relatives was looking at a collection of family photographs that Allen had over his desk. Pointing to one of them, he asked, "Who's that?"

It was Baudelaire, but Allen replied, "That's Cousin Charles."

"Oh yes," said the young man.

Benfolly was not far from Nashville, the headquarters of the Fugitives. It naturally became a gathering place for southern writers.

The following spring, though I was still rather feeble, I decided that I had been spared especially to see certain people and that Clarksville was on the way from Wrightsville Beach, North Carolina, where I had been recovering, to Rochester, New York.

Clarksville, Tennessee, July 31, 1930
To S. W. in Wrightsville Beach, North Carolina

Your letter has just come. I was wondering if you really had gotten my letter, and thinking pettishly that *your* telegram was probably merely the preliminary to one of your lapses into silence. We are so thrilled that you think now you can come. I hope to God the altitude and temperature are right! As for hay fever—I personally don't know any sufferers from it in Clarksville—that may be just my ignorance. I know, intimately, though—that is I am acquainted with the ailments that afflict the three or four thousand members of the Meriwether and Barker connection and I cannot recall one that has hay fever. But then they are probably not very sensitive. Stop, Howard Patterson spent two or three years here recovering from asthma, and got quite recovered in our salubrious climate. Is that fact of any significance? It's no good my calling up the local doctors. They do not recognize any ailment except malaria. I was in bed with a temperature of 103 the other day and the doctor came and said "I don't know what's the matter with you, but I'll give you this hypodermic of quinine and if you feel better you have malaria." As time dragged on I did feel better, so the ailment goes down as malaria.

Our hill—probably the most beautiful hill in the world—will not bother you. It is shaped just like a crouching lion. The lion's head and shoulders front the river and the house sits on, say, his forehead. One drives up his spinal column, right to the front door; the ascent is gradual and you do not realize till you get out on the big porch how high up you are. It is swell, at night, when the lights in the town come out.

. . . .

As I told you, I believe, there is a bedroom on the ground floor, so you need never climb stairs. I thought you were going to stay the whole month? Your being here won't interfere with our work. We go straight to our typewriters in the morning, but in the afternoon we are always free. Do stay as long as you can. It has been such a long time since we have seen each other, and God knows when you'll be down this way again.

It will be a godsend to have somebody to talk to besides the kin. I am getting pretty tired of them. There is no amusement here except driving around to various creeks to go swimming. Still, there is always talk. And we are making some beer today.

Now, please don't let anything interfere with your coming, and come before the middle of August if you can—and arrange to stay as long as you can. I wish you could be here in the fall. It is gorgeous then. Lovely, warm weather usually up to Christmas and a heavenly blue haze over everything.

Love. I am so excited at the prospect of seeing you, and so is Allen,

C.

[added as a postscript]

Nancy regards the French period in her life as something that had better be forgotten. She is a little ashamed, I think, of having been so won over to the French. She came to me one day not long ago and said: "I am a little Homerican girl now." She is learning now the vernacular of the country people. She saw one of the negroes going by the other day and observed "He ain't never been no good since he fell off that wagon." She thinks that I am abysmally ignorant. She asked me the other day if a cow that we passed in a field had milk in her and I answered absently that no doubt she had. Nancy eyed her critically and said "Naw. You don't know. Heifers don't have no milk in 'em."

Clarksville, August 12, 1930
To S. W. in Wrightsville Beach

We are so thrilled at the thought that you may come after all. Don't weaken for God's sake. It has been hellish here all summer. The drought, though, has been frightful everywhere. It seems to be breaking now. We have had a good rain and the weather, for the last seventy two hours, has been delightful. We will probably have grand cool days from now. We have them coming to us.

There is a letter here for you, from your mother, I ween. Haven't sent it on because I thought you might appear any minute.

I can't believe the mosquitoes are much of a menace. This, as anybody will tell you, is a high, healthful plateau—not swampy and peculiar like Arkansas and Mississippi. Of course I was sick and John Ross [the doctor] said it might be malaria, but he has lived years in the tropics and is malaria-mad. I still maintain that it was the result of the contemplation of the objects amassed by Allen's mother in one lifetime that threw me into a fever. It would have thrown anybody into a fever.[1]

I told Nancy that you were coming and prevaricated to the extent that you didn't speak much English. "I can't fool with that lady much," Nancy said, "I have forgotten most of my French." You might address her in French right off the bat and see what her reaction will be. Her flirtations with language have been interesting. When we brought her back she was translating each remark she made in English from the French. Now she translates, if at all, from the African.

I hope we'll get a wire now any day saying you're coming. I shall be terribly disappointed if you don't make it.

love,
Caroline

[added as a postscript]
I am writing in the half dark, on Allen's typewriter. I trust you can read this.

1. Allen's mother had died the previous July (1929) while he and Caroline were still in France.

At this point, I made a long visit to Benfolly on my way back to Rochester, staying in a room next to the kitchen on the lowest floor of the house. This floor was almost a basement in the upper, or front, side of the hill and simply a ground floor room at the back of the house, where the hill sloped down to the Cumberland.

Besides my room and the kitchen, this floor contained a long dining room that reached from the front to the back of the house with a large fireplace in the center. This was the gathering place of the household not only for meals but between them. Caroline's desk was at the Cumberland side. In the center the long table made a convenient place for manuscripts to be laid down—temporarily, of course. The fireplace heat reached far enough for quite a few people to gather around. Later, it was agreed that the room resembed a Paris café.

Clarksville, September 10, 1930
To S. W. in Rochester

Sally, darling:

Don't answer this letter. Yes, I know that's a bit domineering, but never mind.

It is really quite desolate here without you. Beatrice[1] feels it keenly. She said "Miss Sally wasn't company, but she was a lot of company." I feel a little conscience stricken when I reflect that I went back to smoking the day after you left and the day after that I took Hind Tit and Oedipous[2] to Cousin Lucy's! Allen went to Nashville[3] the day after you left and I was here all alone for several days, so naturally I got to smoking again. It was really grand here one night—the night I wrote three thousand words, knocking off at half past eleven. The miasmal mist rose from the river in great clouds. It actually curled up over the back porch. It was almost like being on a boat in a storm. Quite a spectacle.

It took to raining constantly, too, of course, immediately after your departure. I doubt if there is any pollen left in the whole country. I have been to the woods and got creeper and ferns and so on and we are doing lots of planting. There is so much activity outside this morning that it is hard for me to work. Mr. Perry's two mules dash over the lawn dragging wagon loads of dirt. They are followed by Jim Hughes, our able colored henchman, Doug, Mr. Perry's white vassal, Mr. Perry himself, Allen, Nancy, Freda,[4] and all the chickens. There is a great deal of shrieking, shouting, clucking and so on. Violet Emma[5] and I alone remain aloof. You won't know the old homestead when you see it again. They have dug out and gravelled a circular drive. They are taking all the dirt they've dug up and have filled in that horrible, yawning hole and all the bare places around the house with it. They are also putting turf around in great slabs. It is going to look pretty swell.

That fierce Highland shentleman, McGillicuddy, was here yesterday to re-apologize for his conduct on the night of Willie Lee's orgy.[6] He is travelling these days by bus—the Ford, which his father had bought, especially for his leave, having been irreparably injured. He is anxious to marry Marion[7] and take her to China, though he reminds her often, she says, that the Henrys are dastardly lowlanders and that it will be quite a come down for him.

Allen and I went day before yesterday to the cemetery to attend the funeral of Uncle Will Douglas Meriwether. Nancy was much cut up because I wouldn't let her go. She said "I went to a funeral every day in Paris with Madame Gau," and doubtless she did. Uncle Will (Nancy's great-great-great uncle) was ninety four and going strong. Everybody was convinced he would never depart this life, so it was quite an event. Among the kin present was Margaret Meriwether who said that Little May was coming down in October. Can't you join forces, or at least arrive here somewhere near the same time? I think it would be fun.

You cannot imagine what it was like here when Freda was in heat! I chained her under the lattice, but some of the suitors dug her out. The fiercest Romeo was Mr. Perry's white dog, Billy, who seems to be a cross between a dachshund and a bull dog. I finally had to keep her up on the big porch and he stood under it yelping all night. It is over now, though, and what a relief! Stoner[8] complained that he almost had a wreck getting out by the porch, the dogs nearly upset his truck.

Katie Dos Passos[9] says that Humanism is like M. Valdemar, the corpse who was always being resuscitated in Poe's story.[10] Each time he is brought to life he is a little more putrescent but manages to breathe and speak a few words. Did you see Rebecca West and Collins at it in the last Bookman or was that before you left?[11]

I do hope you're keeping on getting stronger. I assure you that you will find this quite a little health resort in October. The season has already turned towards fall and the air has that exciting feeling. The Cowleys say they will get here about October seventh. I wish you could get back by then. They are very amusing and good company.

Love from all of us. My warm greetings to all the members of your family, including Michael,[12] who probably has you all wrapped around his finger by this time.

C

[added as a postscript]
Frederick O'Brien writes asking that I send a photograph for reproduction with his article on "The Best Short Stories of 1930" which comes out "shortly" in the Boston Transcript. So I have to dash to Nashville tomorrow and get a picture taken—and here I haven't even decided what I'll do with my hair this fall! Darling, would you, if you can without exerting yourself, yank on to this copy of the Transcript? Anybody named

Calkins ought,[13] at least, to have kinfolks who read the Transcript—or at any rate there are news stalls in your city. We are so remote here there is no chance of my getting hold of any paper except The Leaf, and I want to send O'Brien's article to Perkins at Scribner's.

1. Caroline's maid and cook.
2. Cats.
3. The collection of essays *I'll Take My Stand* was being issued by the Nashville Agrarians.
4. A dog.
5. A cat.
6. McGillicuddy was some kin of the Meriwethers. Willie Lee, a young, blond cousin or friend of Caroline's, could not hold her liquor.
7. Caroline's cousin, Marion Henry.
8. A taxi driver and handyman, easily available because of his interest in Beatrice. Allen told me he considered him a member of the staff.
9. Wife of John Dos Passos.
10. Edgar Allan Poe, "The Facts in the Case of M. Valdemar."
11. Seward Collins (1899?–1952) was an independently wealthy Princeton graduate who bought the *Bookman*, which became a forum for humanist debate. Collins became editor of the magazine (1928–1933) and then changed its name to the *American Review* (1933–37). He was interested in the Agrarians and printed many of their essays. Rebecca West resigned as English correspondent for the *Bookman* because she was so angry at their treatment of Allen. (See also Caroline's letter dated January 7, 1932.)
12. A brand new nephew.
13. My cousin Mary Whiton Calkins was professor of philosophy at Wellesley.

The Fugitives by this time had turned to prose also. They expressed their fondness for the Old South in a new title, calling themselves Agrarians. They were against northern industry's migration south, and since the North was involved in the Great Depression, any sort of change was looked upon with great interest. I'll Take My Stand was published as their joint statement—a symposium.

Few of the Agrarians had farms as their ancestors had. Caroline was the nearest to the old ways, surrounded by the Meriwethers still living on the same land. And Andrew Lytle, a new recruit, possessed a father with a plantation farther south.

Clarksville, October [3?], 1930, but mailed with the following letter
To S. W. in Rochester

This letter is stale now.
Dear Sally:
When we got up this morning the miasmal mist was dashing over the prow of the hammock enough to make you sea-sick. I take a walk

around the house before breakfast and get all the sensations and highly virtuous feelings of one who takes a cold bath every morning, but by eight or nine o'clock the sun is shining like blazes. Really, this weather is too grand! You must come back soon while it's at its best. The grand weather, of course, prevails everywhere, but the mist is our own special feature. It's very exciting. When you look out of the dining room door at breakfast time you can't see anything, and then the whole valley slowly emerges.

In spite of all the good weather I hauled off last week and wrote a short story—the life and some of the works of Mr. Suiter. (I hope he doesn't sue me for libel or take after me with an axe.)[1] I enclose it on the chance that it may amuse you. Don't bother to return the copy but park it in a safe place. I sent the other two copies I made off, one to Scribner's, one to Eliot,[2] thinking that he *might* think the English would recognize murder even among Americans. He always writes back that the English couldn't understand a word I write.

We sit around waiting for the Cowleys to heave up over the bridge—they're due here now, but we've had no word from them since they made their plans, Sept. 18. Ford is also vaguely supposed to roll this way.

We have a new maltese cat, shaped like a Boston bull terrier. His name is Uncle Penn. (Fear not; he is cold and haughty, by nature.) We had to name him Uncle Penn after we re-christened Violet Emma Emma Cinina Elena Anna Roma Clotilda Borgia etc. . . . . but we have had no word from Uncle Penn himself since he left these parts and fear that something has happened to the nuptials. We all wonder but are afraid to ask.

The Symposiers are having a great time. An Ivanhoe suddenly appeared in the list, Stringfellow Barr, editor of the Virginia Quarterly Review, who writes an article in said review to the effect that industrialism is a swell thing, let's whoop it up in the south etc. This gives the Nashville brethren a chance to accuse him of selling out. They then proceed to recriminate each other in the pages of the Tennessean, New York Times etc. even brawling a bit on the A.P. wires.

"It is time," thunders Mr. Ransom[4] "for the leadership of the South to pass out of the hands of the Old Dominion," and so it was, in 1859. The Virginians were always indecently commercial minded.

The pea hay in the bottom has been cut and is being raked up now in stacks. Mr. Perry says we ought to have five ton for our share and thinks he can sell it for forty dollars a ton. We think that is pretty swell. We also have a fine turnip sallet patch on the side of the hill.

I must go back to that damn novel. I thought it would kill me to write that short story, but writing short stories has one advantage—it makes writing a novel seem such easy, pleasant work that you wonder why you ever took it so hard.

I do hope you're free of the curse of hay fever by this time. Your seasons get along so fast up there you ought to be.

> *Love,*
> *C.*

[added as a postscript, dated October 4]
Nancy had a grand birthday party and behaved angelically. Beatrice made a beautiful cake and I made a dog sandwich apiece for each of the little critters. I am proud to say they noticed that it was a dog before devouring it.

The electric light poles have been cut, we hope to have light in a few weeks.

1. In the story, "Mr. Powers," the character did use an axe.
2. T. S. Eliot, whom they had met in England.
3. John Crowe Ransom.

Clarksville, October 20, 1930
To S. W. in Rochester

I wrote you a letter the other day but it doesn't seem to have gotten mailed. We were overcome by the grapes—which by the way arrived in perfect condition—and stunned by the grand basket of apples that arrived yesterday, also in fine condition.[1] I had forgotten how good the apples are up that way. These are marvelous.

We were highly entertained by your letter—the description of Monsieur Babbitt as well as the wedding party. I trust the roast beef banquet came off all right. But I am past the point of worrying about whether parties turn out well. This last week has been hectic. First the Cowleys came on their way to Mexico, then Ford drove down with Harold Loeb,[2] Sue Jenkins, and Loeb's girl, Marjorie. We had a grand time, going in swimming—we had several balmy days when it was enjoy-able—drinking corn liquor and talking. Only Ford made me go over every inch of my manuscript with him which kept me pretty tired all the time. He lectured in Nashville and we all went up to support him during the terrible tea at the woman's club and an even more terrible dinner at the Hermitage which should have been nice as the guests were hand picked. I was certainly glad to get back to Benfolly after it was all over. Red Warren and his Italian bride hove in, and Bill Bandy[3] and his bride and one or two others. "Miss Sally's room", as Beatrice faithfully calls it, let come who will, hardly got its sheets cold before another pair of guests crawled in. They are all gone now and Allen and I are all alone, except for several new cats that have come to live with us. (Some fiend drops these cats at the gates, I am convinced. Every other day one suddenly appears on the front porch.) Freda, I fear, is dead. She disappeared while we were away in Nashville, though we had left the house open and Beatrice here for the express purpose of feeding her. I am feeling pretty sad over it. She was such a darling dog.[4]

I sold my story about Mr. Suiter to Scribner's for two hundred dol-lars—did I tell you that I was writing a story about him? Ford is going to try to persuade them to let me make a trilogy of my Penhally novel but I don't think there is any chance. It would be swell if they did. I could fin-ish the first part at my leisure, knock off a few short stories which they seem anxious for and get through the winter in fine shape. By the way, young woman, they write me rather pathetically that "it is so hard to get any stories with real emotion in them" and ask me not to neglect to send them anything that I come across. They take of my stories only those dealing with murder, sudden death and the like, which is not as inconve-nient as it sounds, my mind running as it does—but you could doubtless work up a "real emotion" in some more subtle way. Do do something about that story when you come back.

We are awfully thrilled at the thought of you and Little May com-ing down. Please don't give up the idea and the sooner you start the bet-ter. October is the best month here, though it looks like we'd have a No-vember Indian summer this year. Anyhow, do come as soon as you can. We are digging in for a long stretch of staying at home, with practically no company.

. . . .

Harold Loeb, the villain of The Sun Also Rises turns out to be a very nice person, as indeed I thought he appeared to be in that book.

Ford showed me pictures of his young Russian Jewish painter wife[5] and I liked her face and thought she looked like a gal who could do without fine clothes if it should be necessary, which ought to mean something in a man's life even if it rarely does. He brought us a portrait of Julie[6] that she'd done. It had captured a quality of Julie's which is the thing I always remember her by, so I liked it. (Julie is his little daughter, Nancy's "chere amie.")

This is all the news from us. You are an angel for arranging for me to get that Transcript article. I suppose you just bodaciously wrote and asked them to send it. I never thought of so bold a measure, partly because I never worked on a paper where such a request would have received the least attention. Thanks a thousand times for the grapes. They are gorgeous. We had them in the big silver epergne thing for breakfast while all the guests were here and they looked grand besides being so good. We still have a round left.

Please come as soon as you can. Love from all of us,

C.

1. I had sent the Tates grapes and apples from Canandaigua Lake.

2. Harold A. Loeb (1892?–1974), prototype of Robert Cohn in Hemingway's *The Sun Also Rises*. With various associate editors, like the Tates' friends Slater Brown and Malcolm Cowley, he published the avant garde magazine *Broom* (1921–1924) featuring early work of writers like Hemingway and Crane.

3. William T. Bandy (1903–), contemporary of Tate at Vanderbilt. He also spent time in France in the 1920s preparing to become a professor of French. He is now professor emeritus at Vanderbilt.

4. Freda wasn't dead after all—just lost. See Caroline's letter dated early January, 1931.

5. Janice Biala.

6. Julie was the daughter of Ford's Australian painter wife, Stella Bowen. She lived with her mother in Paris, where the Tates had met her.

Clarksville, November 3, 1930
To S. W. in Rochester

Dearest Sally:

Nancy's box just arrived and she is in transports. I was just thinking that I must get her a sweater to wear under her coat which is a trifle light and rather dreading the ordeal (Clarksville having practically nothing to offer infants) when lo, these grand affairs arrive. They look adorable on her! And you are an angel to remember us. But—WHEN are you coming? It enrages me to see all the pretty weather slip past and you not here. You cannot imagine how gorgeous it is now. The hill opposite the filling station is especially beautiful. The reds and yellows are set off by the very dark green cedars. I hadn't realized before how lovely those cedars are.

We have no company now except Andrew Lytle who has settled down here for a long stretch—until he finishes his biography of Forrest. I am struggling with Shiloh and Missionary Ridge and Allen is on the verge of starting Lee. Our conversations are all highly military, and are no doubt highly amusing if anybody were to overhear us.

The Southern Symposium "I'll Take My Stand" is out. It has worked up into quite a book. I want you to read it. You can read it while you're here. . . . The boys are all going over to Richmond November 14 for the debate between "Agrarian Ransom and Industrialist Barr" as the Papers have it. I'd like to go, but don't see how I can make it. If you and Little May are heading this way please let me know. And please let me know your plans anyway. I haven't written Little May, chiefly because I've been so occupied with nagging details as well as trying to get on with my work, but I have thought about her every day and I shall be so disappointed if you all don't come. Please don't change your minds!

We are planning quite a party for Thanksgiving. You must be here then. Red and Cinina and of course Andrew and perhaps another two or three from Nashville. Andrew is furnishing the turkey, his own turkey!

We have to go out to Merry Mont in a few minutes to eat dinner, middle of the day dinner. Nothing will satisfy Miss Carrie but an oldfashioned spend the day party.

Must collect the buttermilk jugs etc.

Love,

It was after Thanksgiving when I visited Benfolly on my way to Florida. The doctor had told me to avoid a Rochester winter.

Caroline and Allen were hard at work. Andrew Lytle was there writing Bedford Forrest and His Critter Company *(1931). One met him pacing about the house with blank eyes, giving military orders. "Then General Forrest said, '. . .'" Only occasionally did he become himself. Most of the time he actually* was *General Forrest.*

Since everybody in the house but me was immersed in the War between

the States, I found it quite restful. It was all in the past. It had been World
War I, in which none of the others had been involved, that had changed my life.

All of my men friends had been overseas—not only all the men I knew in
college, but those I'd met with my brother in France and Switzerland. The lost
generation did not consist solely of Americans; it included the British and, to
some extent, the French. Of course, the Frenchmen were used to fighting for
their own country. All of the very few men our age who were left alive had been
wounded in some way, at least psychologically.

Life had proved different from what we'd been brought up to believe. But
I was slowly getting mended. Those people who were all living before 1914 happened took my mind off it. And Caroline, so resolute, so constant and unde-
terred by any difficulty, was the perfect companion.

One of her habits was never to let anyone get into serious conversation at
breakfast. It was certainly true that being distracted then often spoiled a morning's work. At Benfolly everyone was free to go directly to his or her own typewriter. This was extremely good for me and good for the others. Of course, it was
more useful for prose than for poetry. Allen wrote quite a lot of prose—reviews
and biographies—but he was not as attached to a schedule as other people. I
asked him when he wrote poetry, and he said, "Oh, when it rises up in me."

Hart Crane would not have fitted in well at Benfolly, but later, it was
just what Robert Lowell needed.

Clarksville, January 8, 1931
To S. W. in Delray Beach Florida

Dearest Sally:

Your Christmas, with the bottle of whiskey and the nudes and I
suppose time to contemplate them sounds enchanting. There was one
night here when I wished for you—we danced in the parlor and had quite
a good time—but all the other times I was damned glad you weren't here.
This is the first morning I've been able to sit down to the typewriter in
two weeks.

But business first. Marion Henry may come to Delray to tutor the
children of Juanita Carsey. . . . The Carsey family is all up in the air. The
old lady finally died—and left all her property to Willie Lee's Mother. She
left the imbecile son, Overton, to her too, and his care may well offset the

material benefits. Anyway the Jim-Juanita Carseys are suing and for weeks
they were all there together, not speaking. Willie Lee ups and gets married during it all—to Fred, not Magus! Magus appeared just in time for
Christmas, but he had neglected to write Willie Lee just when he was
coming, so Fred took advantage of it to sweep Willie Lee into matrimony.
I enclose, if I can find it, Willie Lee's picture from the Leaf. Isn't it marvelous. That starry sorrowful look, I fear, is directed to poor Magus who
never even saw his love alone after two years of separation. Willie Lee
brought them both out here one night, Magus sticking along on Fred's
date. As they were leaving she drew me aside and said (rocking a little in
her cups,) "Carrie, whish would you take?" "My God," I said, "have you
got to decide tonight?" "I shink I have," says Willie Lee and reels off into
the dark—and out of our lives. I think the whole thing was really brought
about by the Clarksville Girls' Cotillion Club. It is comprised now of girls
under nineteen and when Willie wasn't in on the Christmas dance she just
had to do something.

The oranges were grand. There's nothing I'd rather have had. They
helped me to bear up under Christmas as nothing else could have.

I do hope you've gotten over the moving into the apartment. I'm
rather worried about you. . . .

We have got on to a good liquor supply, seven dollars a gallon and
just about twice as good as Between the Rivers. You can actually drink it
with pleasure!

Allen's father, his brothers Ben and Varnell, Ben's twelve year old
son and Varnell's wife all had a sort of business conference and family reunion here last week. It was very strenuous, but came off very well. Mr. T.
and his eldest son, Varnell, had last met in a sleeping car fifteen years ago
when Mr. T. was attempting to kidnap Varnell's little boy to save him
from the awful fate of having a stepmother, so there was some constraint
at first. However they all got pretty chummy before they left. I could not
but admire Ben's generalship. We had to have a fire going in every room
in the house so they could plot and counter-plot. They almost froze to
death while Beatrice and I rushed around making up the fires, sweat dripping from us. Varnell has Allen's features with looking out of them the
most childlike nature you can imagine—it is really amusing to see them
together. The sister-in-law, usually characterized by Mrs. Tate as "that
frivolous, floozy flapper" turns out to be an earnest Christian scientist
which is almost as bad. She was pretty bitter.

While they were here the one social event of the year, for me, at least, came off and we had to miss it. Mister Rob's[1] neighbors had an old-fashioned hoe down at his house. Everybody in the community, of every class was there. They had to go out and bring in the leader of the chain gang to call the figures. Tragic that Andrew couldn't be there, wasn't it?

Nancy is learning to read, figuring it out for herself. E she says is for "E, like eva one you want, k for decayed teeth and R like Ah, Ah!" Ma[2] undertook to give her a little religious instruction, but Nancy tripped her up the first round on the virgin birth and Ma gave up. "I never understood it very well myself," she said.

Your criticism of The Ice House[3] sounds neatly its death knell. I told Allen as much when I finished the story, but he insisted that it wasn't so, that the whole story could be transposed into any other frame, and so it could, but what casual reader would stop to do it? The partizanship is accidental, but still it is there.

Red Warren has written—for the American Caravan—a thirty thousand word story that interests me very much and reminds me in one way of your work.[4] It is a fine thing, all atmosphere, though the action comes off. The curious thing about it, though, is the contrast between the handling of the action and the atmosphere. Paragraph after paragraph of such beautiful writing, the view from a window, the way the house sits among the trees—one passage where a woman comes into a dark room bringing a lamp, one of those old fashioned glazed lamps is one of the finest things I ever read. The frosted globe and the little wreath of flowers that is painted on it are perfectly realized. But the action throughout is rough and barely adequate. His descriptive paragraphs are very much like yours. I think you'd like the story. It will be in this year's *Caravan*.

I have got to get lunch, Beatrice being prostrated after the company.

Let me know how you are and how you are getting along. I told Marion to write you.

                              Love,

[added as a postscript]
Nancy adores her stockings.

1. Caroline's uncle.
2. Caroline's grandmother, Miss Carrie.

3. A short story collected in the *Forest of the South* (New York, 1945). See Caroline's letter dated February 21, 1931.

4. The story was "Prime Leaf," which appeared in *American Caravan IV* (1931), 3–61. *American Caravan* was a yearbook that appeared under various similar titles and with interruptions from 1927 to 1936.

Clarksville, early January, 1931
To S. W. in Delray Beach

Dearest Sally:

It is terrible that I am only this minute answering a telegram that said "Wire answer."

. . . .

Also, I have had off and on and was having when I should have wired you a frightful toothache. Largest tooth I own, takes me by the seat of the pants and lets me see exactly how a turkey looks over a log. Isn't out yet. I dose it with Guiacol and intend to keep on dosing it till I have finished this damn novel [*Penhally*]. I am really scared to death. I have figured out that I have as much to write as I've already written, and have to get it to Perkins by summer, anyhow, and I can see now that things will be thickening up by that time on this hill.

I know that I have lured you here several times with false promises of delights, but really now you must come by in the spring, just this one time. I will be through writing then—you won't know the old place. And is Little May coming up? *Please* persuade her to if you see her.

Little by little we improve too. Your room this time will have a typewriter table, the kind one has always yearned for. I found it out at Merry Mont beside the stove. Really, a darling, once I got it sandpapered and waxed. Also we are going to build a guest cabin—you don't have to stay in it—round there among those locusts, by Violet Emma's grave. Yes, she died very gently in the night. We kept the news from Nancy who was at Merry Mont at the time, uselessly it turned out. Her eyes shone with pleasure when she finally was told. "I believe I'll dig her up," says she.

We now have a tenant. Jesse Rye and his bride, both aged eighteen. They arrived with a hound dog and a kitchen stove and we have spent most of our time since getting them a mule—it turned out to be a horse—beds, wagons etc. Allen is developing the true landlord spirit. He told me that when they went to the second hand furniture store, Jesse kept demanding all sorts of fancy things. "Like what?" I asked, thinking perhaps a radio. "Like chairs," says Allen sternly. "I told him there was nothing doing. Why, Jesse, I said, you can sit on a box." Jesse brought into our lives the other day the one true agrarian. His little brother, aged ten. He stood on the brow of the hill and gazed at Clarksville as if it were a dream city. "He's jist crazy to git to that town," says Jesse, "I told him hit was mighty common oncet you see it, but he ain't never been to a town." "Never seen a town?" I asked. "He's been to Lone Oak," Jesse said.

Allen is in Nashville, ostensibly to work in the library. He has finally decided that he'd better do something about Lee.

Freda is in heat—if you want all the news. She is "engaged" as Nancy says to Mister Bodo Cross, Pat Henry's dog. We now have a fox hound pup. Some fiends threw him into the river from the bridge and he swam out and staggered up the hill.

My novel is turning out a mess. And this is no mock modesty. Too much stuff and not organized. I am sick over it. Nothing to do but stagger on with it.

Edmund Wilson has written a book that you will want to read.[1] I will send it [to] you when Allen gets back and finishes it. Essays on Proust, Yeats, Valery, Stein, Rimbaud. I want to hear what you think of his Proust effort. He published a shorter version in the NR.[2] The essay will interest you, I think.

Jesse is going to try to make a living raising a market garden. I am hoping that we will get enough vegetables for the table out of it, but I can't see how he can make a living. We have built him a log cabin in the hollow by the spring. The loveliest spot and the cabin is beautiful, built of hewn logs, chinked with clay and lime in the old fashioned way. They even got the shingles from an oak tree here on the place.

I have written eighteen hundred words and am somewhat depleted so forgive this incoherent letter. I must now go and feed the hound pup. Do let us hear how you are getting on. Florida must be grand. It is very mild here, but unnaturally dry. Dust rises when you work the ground—in January! We have been out of water for over a month.

Love,

C.

[added as a postscript]

I trust Anne[3] turned out to be a comfort.

I have been complimented frequently on my red hat.

K. A.[4] is getting restless, insists that she will arrive here in August with a rosewood grand piano, silver mirror, Mexican chairs, rugs, pottery and so on. "I will just bundle them up and bring them along," she says! I have no idea that she could stand this climate, but I think she will get a Guggenheim and so will go abroad, but a winter in Paris would be her finish, I am afraid. I am really awfully apprehensive about that.

This typewriter, which Mr. Dickson lends me while my Royal is being repaired is incorrigible. I cannot go on. I am sure you will not be able to stand it.

I do hope you're comfortably situated. Dad writes almost lyrically from his Leesburg boarding house.

I got a hundred and fifty dollar advance on my novel out of Perkins. He persists in regarding it as almost finished, which is disconcerting. I am going to dive into the muggy depths of that Civil War story and end the agony this week if possible. If it goes on any longer I'll lose my reason.

We all send love and miss you so much,

As ever, c.

[added as a second postscript]

Please preserve this copy of "The Ice House." I have no other. Darling, *could* you send it back? That is, if it's not too hard to mail things there.

Allen has burst out with three poems—one a day, I believe. I enclose Allen's poems.[5] He, by the way, is distressed because he didn't get to read the outline of N.C.[6] He says his head was in such a fuzzy condition that night that he forgot it completely till the next day.

1. *Axel's Castle* (1931).
2. *New Republic.*
3. My sister Alice had friends in Rochester whose child had been advised to spend the winter in a warm climate. My sister telegraphed me in Florida to ask if I would take her, and I, always the R.N., wired back yes. Anne Carver, age six or seven, was my Christmas present.
4. Katherine Anne Porter.
5. One of the poems she sent was "The Cross."
6. The book I was working on.

Caroline sent me Edmund Wilson's Axel's Castle, *as she had promised. I also received a letter from Allen later that year.*

Clarksville, August 21, 1931
From Allen Tate
To S. W. Delray Beach

My dear Sally:
    The passages from Proust are very interesting, and I am thinking of
using one of them as the motto or text of the book. It was mighty sweet
of you to take all that trouble. Much obliged, as the agrarians say, till
you're better paid. These copies of some new poems may amuse you, and
if you're feeling critical tell me what's wrong with them. You promised
before you left to show me a piece of your work which would interest me
because it deals with *ideas*. It has never arrived. Caroline says to write and
to come on down. The weather here is fine—cool, but just warm enough
to make swimming necessary.
                        Love from us all,
                        Allen

    P.S. You must read Andrew's *Bedford Forrest*. It's very fine.

*Beatrice was Caroline's favorite maid. Bringing the morning coffee to the table,
she would ask softly, "How the story going, Miz Tate?"*
    When John Gould Fletcher[1] *was at Benfolly to dinner, he would become
so interested in talking that his gesturing hand, holding a biscuit, would be
forgotten and the biscuit would get cold. Beatrice, seeing the misfortune, would
butter a hot one, gently remove the cold, and replace it. In the kitchen she would
shake her head. "He forget everything, old Uncle John Jule."*
    *I thought Caroline had treated the Yankees exceptionally badly—even
for her—in "The Ice House," and for once, I objected. At first she listened, but
not for long.*

Clarksville, February 21, 1931
To S. W. in Delray Beach

Dearest Sally:
    Do go and hold your head under a pump. You are quite off about
The Ice House. When I say "If that ain't a Yankee fer ye!" I am not ex-
pressing a judgment on Yankees. I am merely recording the attitude,

deplorable as it is, of two Virginia urchins in 1866 or whenever it was. I
know, from observation, from history, from family tradition and so on that
such would have been the attitude of these urchins. The phrase, however,
is a sort of makeshift. I wanted to end the story on "Thar ain't a whole
man in ary one of them boxes," but neither Allen or Andrew would admit
that what had happened was clear with no more than that said, so I had to
go a little further than I wanted to go. But enough of The Ice House. It
has had a little private circulation and is now laid away in the old desk
that I got in from Merry Mont the other day.

     I am glad that Anne is proving a comfort and evidently not as
much trouble as children ordinarily are. Having spent the winter in good
works why could you not come up here this spring? If you did want to
come you could fix up a story that would wring your mother's heart of
how you had to take Nancy off my hands while I finished up my book.
You really owe it to us to be here some time during the really good
weather. We are going to try awfully hard to get that cabin built. It will
be just around the smoke house slope among those locusts—I think they
will give enough shade—near enough to take baths here, if there's any
water and near enough to be safe from marauders, but far enough for you
to feel independent, in case you were in that mood. As for trusting Nancy
with you for a longish spell—just try me some time!

     About Katherine Anne. She seems to be set on coming here, and I
should certainly be pleased to see you two hooked up, as it were. I really
think you'd enjoy her, and of course it would mean a great deal to her. I
believe that she will get a Guggenheim fellowship, though, which will
mean that she will go abroad. She could stay in Mexico, but I detect signs
in our friend of being tired of Mexico, so I fear she will make tracks for
France. Of course a winter in Paris would finish her. I am right worried
about that. The Guggenheim awards will be made in March, in about
three weeks, Allen says. In the meantime I am writing to K. A. about my
friend, but she already feels that she knows you she has heard us talk
about you so much.

     Edmund Wilson, Raymond Holden and Louise [Bogan][2] all
drifted in here the other day. Raymond had had several of his secretaries
on the New Yorker dictate letters to us but none of them arrived, so we
knew nothing of their plans until they phoned from Nashville. We were
out at Summertrees[3] when the call came and rushed home to find Beatrice
hopelessly drunk. Yes. It was a blow to me too. I couldn't have been more

shocked if I had found your mother sprawling in a gutter. She was maudlin. It was my own fault, though. I told her I thought a good strong toddy would help her cold. She wouldn't even let me in the cabin, just snickered and said "Unh-unhh" as I pounded on the door. The next morning a contrite face appeared at my bedside. "It was that hot water, Mrs. Tate" she said.

The Holden-Wilson visit was quite funny. Louise H. had told Leonie Adams[4] everything we ever said about her just before they started down and Leonie had written wanting to know if it was all true. We had spent hours at it and had gotten a great deal said. Poor Allen was very apprehensive when Louise hove in. He feared we would smite hip and thigh, but I was so upset over Beatrice that I really couldn't pay much attention to it. There is nothing to do about Louise anyway. She is absolutely irresponsible and a born alcoholic.

You should have seen Edmund inspecting the tobacco being stripped in Mister Rob's barn. It was mean, I know, but I let him nibble the tiniest tip of a leaf. Not a chew, you understand, just a nibble. He went into a slight convulsion.

We drove the Holdens and Edmund up to Nashville day before yesterday. They stayed at the Andrew Jackson that night and we had a sort of party. Did you every play "Murder"? It is a grand parlor game.

Andrew is here at this minute finishing up Forrest. He wants us to go to a dance at Monteagle[5] tonight. It seems a wild idea to me. I am trying to stand firm, but will probably weaken.

Ben's fiancee is very ill. We have taken her dog to keep for awhile. The chauffeur came solemnly driving him down from Cincinnati the other day. He is quite sweet, very spoiled, of course. He makes passes at Freda, though I have explained that she is old enough to be his mother and affianced besides to Mister Bodo Cross. He is very Cymric, Alfreda's dog. They call him Whiskers, but I am going to re-name him some noble name like Cadwallader or something.

You are quire right about Edmund's Proust essay, Eliot too. It is just exposition, but so beautifully written.

I will let you know as soon as I can about K. A.'s plans, or rather you ought to get into communication. She won't have the least idea what she will do, though, till the awards are made. She will tell you, of course, that she is coming here in August.

The jonquils are blooming. The willow leaves are just out, and

things are getting quite spring like. We have peas and cabbages and lettuce and squash planted. And I have tomato slips growing in the house.

The Carseys are suing Willie Lee's mother.

Do arrange to come to us for a while this spring. If you and K. A.
are really coming we will put a dog run between the rooms of the cabin.
Really we could get the cabin up inside of a week. Andrew is going to fell
some of the trees next week.

I have to decide whether we are going to Monteagle and pick some
turnip greens. Write when you can.

Love,

· ·

1. An American poet (1886–1950), associated with the imagist movement and later
with the Agrarians. He received the Pulitzer Prize for his *Selected Poems* (1938).

2. Raymond Holden (1894–1972) was an American poet and novelist who wrote
mysteries under the pseudonym Richard Peckham. He and Louise Bogan were married.

3. The plantation of Cousin John Ferguson. Caroline's letter of August 20, 1931,
recounts the dismay caused by the article Wilson wrote for the *New Republic* based on this
visit.

4. An American poet (1899–   ) who had stayed with the Tates in London and
France. Her published volumes to date had been *Those Not Elect* (1925) and *High Falcon* (1929).
Whatever his opinion of her as a person, Allen had generous praise for her work. (See his
Sixty American Poets, 1896–1944 [Washington, D.C., 1945], 1.)

5. A Chautauqua-like community five miles from Sewanee.

Clarksville, May 4, 1931
To S. W. at Wrightsville Beach, North Carolina

Dearest Sally:

What has become of you and can you find it in your heart to pass
us up this time? I do wish you could be here these next few months. They
are really the best of all. I agonize over our writings a bit and then rush
out and lie flat in the sun and then rush in and agonize a bit more and the
days go by, rather pleasantly on the whole. . . .

What *are* your plans for the summer? Can't you come here and stay
at least until the hay fever season opens? I'm looking for Little May and
Margaret next week. I had hoped you would come along with them.

I have not sent you Axel's Castle as I promised nor have I sent my
sister in law the trunk containing the effects of her husband's first wife. I
am in short a worm. But I can't do anything about it. Allen and I have

made simultaneously, though, a sort of discovery—regarding the works of Ernest Hemingway and the middle west which we will din into your ears when you arrive.

We have not had any visitors since the Holdens and Edmund Wilson, except the Nashvillians who came down the other day for a picnic. It being so early in the season the picnic was a very sketchy affair—we got about three feet from the house with the food.

Is Anne [Carver] still with you? And how did she work out?

K. A. Porter got a Guggenheim, but says she is going to stay in Mexico till she finishes her novel.

We have a Jersey cow named Daisy Miller and an electric refrigerator. The cow is very erratic but gives marvellous milk. Did I tell you we also have two tenants—Jesse and Florence Rye. They speak beautiful archaic English and steal everything they can lay their hands on. They call Beatrice "Ma'am" and Stoner "Mister!" They do not seem to be composed of flesh and blood. I had some folks from Nashville here not long ago. I had intended to give them for a country treat turnip greens and poached eggs. Beatrice kept evading me about the eggs and finally she broke down and said "Aw, Mrs. Tate we can't have no eggs. Jesse went through the kitchen just before supper." Two dozen eggs he picked up as he went through! The way he happened to get the eggs was that I had called him into the house to give him half a cake. It is an infringement of the system to ever give them anything, but they really don't have enough to eat, so I said to myself Be damned with the system! Allen, in his innocence, engaged Jesse to do a day's work on the yard one day just as we set out for Nashville. As soon as the car disappeared Jesse hitched up his horse, went to town and charged a lot of things on our grocery bill. We discovered it of course and gave him hell. I, knowing well how the sytem worked, foolishly thought that Jesse being only eighteen, might not know, so thinking to discipline him a little, I said, "If you are going to do things like that you'll have to hunt another home." Whereupon Jesse, who consulted his lawyer immediately after charging the things replied, "It don't make no difference what I do. I can come up here and have a fuss with you all every morning and you can't put me off this place."

And this is true. The contract between the landlord and tenant— purely verbal—must be fulfilled but it is practically impossible to prove that the tenant has violated his contract. It is a very good law and yet it works out very strangely. If the landlord gets a man who is a thief and an incompetent he simply has to stand him till the year is up and then he can't even put him off his place if he doesn't give him written notice on the very day that the contract is up. If he waits a day later the tenant has a right to live on that farm another year!

I feel like one of these women who knows she is going to have another baby before the one in her arms is weaned. I have the subject for my next book.[1] Two families, white and poor white, living on the same farm. The situation seen through first the eyes of one and then of the other. Each regards the other as his natural enemy. I am sure that Jesse thinks it perfectly proper to steal from me. I *should* regard him as so much vermin. Little May's uncle, Morris Barker, was killed by one of his tenants. You can just see how the situation piles up through the years. It is complicated, of course, by money, when the tenant comes out owing two or three hundred dollars each year the landlord will keep him on, hoping to get his money back . . . . . But you cannot have any very lively interest in all this!

Do write and let us know your plans. And please do come by here, if you can. I'm quite hungry to see you. We say each day we wish Sally was here. It is really lovely now. The woods are perfectly white with dogwood. The turnip sallet patch that extends along the whole side of the hill is in bloom—one long stretch of yellow. It is a marvellous sight.

Love, and please write,
C.

1. *The Garden of Adonis* (1937).

Clarksville, Tenn., May 1931
To S. W. in Wrightsville Beach

Does this sending of books mean that you aren't coming this way—and why ain't you? Do write and tell us your plans and don't pass us up this summer. I have been in a state of complete moral deterioration for over a month, absolutely washed out, but am now recovered, praise God. I am within three chapters of finishing this horrible book. I'd hoped you'd be here to celebrate with me.

Little May is here, but I've seen her only twice, as they have brought her mother to Guthrie and she has to spend most of her time with her. She looks well and very brown and healthy.

Dad came by the other day on his way to Normandy on Duck river. He couldn't stay but a day, having fished all winter he had no time to lose. I never saw anybody as brown, he looks almost like a negro.

Do write and tell us where you're going to be and that it's going to be here.

Love from all of us, including the new dog, Whiskers.

c.t.

[added as a postscript]
Poor K. A. She is still in Mexico trying to finish her novel. I got a letter from her the other day. Hart Crane has moved in on her and she wanted to know what she should do! He came one night, very drunk and admired extravagantly an empty room. The next morning he arrived cold sober and moved into said room, and there he stays, getting up very early in the morning to turn on his victrola, caroling and drinking beer and so on.

Clarksville, May 30, 1931
To S. W. in Wrightsville Beach

Dearest Sally:
This idea of Rochester annoys me extremely. Oh, I do wish you could come here this summer. I have an idea that we could make you more comfortable than we did last summer. Our electric refrigerator, for instance—to think you won't get any of those little cubes! . . . . And I will be through my book, Deo volente, before the week is up and Allen will have Lee off his hands by the middle of July.[1] And Anne, of course, would be a godsend. I went out and borrowed Lucy May and Eleanor the other day in desperation.

. . . .

Little May is here. The neighborhood is agog with parties for her. I haven't been to many of them, though. I have been working all day and until ten or eleven at night, a heavy bromide, some troubled sleep and back at it. But I really see the light. Two more chapters to rewrite, a little going over the whole thing and I am through. It's rotten, of course, but still I will have it off my hands for weal or woe. It is a little like coming out of the penitentiary. Even the glimpse of freedom excites me. I went to pieces pretty badly the other night. I got frightened when Allen told me plainly that the last chapter, the climax that I had built up to so fondly simply would not do. My hands got to shaking so I couldn't even hit the keys. Finally I told Allen he had to write it then if it didn't suit him. He wrote a few pages and I got interested trying to fix up what he had written—it seemed to me so impossible—that I worked out of the fit.

The little dress came. It is darling. Nancy will adore it.

Yes, K. A. got a Guggenheim. I have not even written to congratulate her. . . . . or condole. Hart Crane moved in on her the other day, portable victrola, African chief's costume and all! He came one night, very tight, admired an empty room in her house and arrived next morning to occupy it. Yvor Winters wrote me, though, that he had moved out. She talks of going to Europe, I know, from a letter she wrote to Elizabeth Roberts.[2] I'll write K. A. next week.

As for us God knows what we will do this winter. We haven't even tried to think past this summer. But we will feel so exuberant with these books off that we may do anything. Lord, I wish we could be there together!

. . . I will send you shortly a photograph of me which isn't as bad as they usually are. Publicity harried me to the studio. The German photographer called one pose "Deeply thinking." It looks a little sick.

Howard Baker[3] and his wife came by here en route from Paris to California. They tell us that Ford's new wife is desperately in love with him . . . . . such grand news. And Ford and Janice who seems to be an awfully good sort are at Toulon. If you do go over let them take care of you a bit. It would give Ford such pleasure and he really doesn't worry you.

Andrew is through his book and deep in thirty three acres of strawberries. They ought to be finished now, though. He won quite a victory over the publisher who wanted to cut it. We saw him at Columbia the other night where Don Davidson made mincemeat of William S. Knickerbocker,[4] in the interest of agrarianism. I was pretty harried and I told Allen that if Andrew said anything soothing to me I was going to slap him in

the face. Andrew came up, redder in the face than one of his own strawberries—he had been straw bossing three hundred recalcitrant niggers for
a week or two. His first remark was "I think I am going crazy."

I do so hope you will feel all right from now on. It is a damn shame
that you have had another bad winter. I thought Florida was doing all
sorts of things for you. Maybe you need the waters of the Cumberland.
We have the new raft built now, as large as a room, it rides high on the
water, mounted on five enormous steel drums. It is really palatial. I am
dying to start swimming.

But I must get back to that wearisome young man. I killed two
men yesterday, one a suicide, one just shot down in hot blood I
can't help it though, it works out that way.

Let us know, anyhow, what your plans are. Much love,

[added as a postscript]
Freda is on the verge of puppies.

I *know* I could make you more comfortable than last summer because I am not going to even try to do any writing for a month or two
anyhow, & I will be bursting with energy.

1. He did not have Lee off his hands then—or ever.
2. Elizabeth Madox Roberts (1886–1941), an American novelist, poet, and short story
writer known for her treatment of the pioneers of Kentucky and Virginia.
3. A California poet and writer of fiction (1905–   ), member of Yvor Winters' coterie,
associate editor (with Winters) of the short-lived *Gyroscope*. He may have met the Tates in
Paris, where he lived for a year. (Allen included him in *Sixty American Poets*). He later published Sally Wood's story "Breakfast in the Country" in his *Magazine*.
4. Knickerbocker (1892–1972) was a professor and the editor of *Sewanee Review* from
1926–1942. Allen's brief tenure in that post immediately followed Knickerbocker's.

*Anne Carver was still staying with me in Florida, and even though Caroline
had invited her, it would have been too complicated to take her to Clarksville
with me. So I did not visit the Tates on my way north that summer.*

Clarksville, probably early summer, 1931
To S. W. in Wrightsville Beach

Well, go on to Rochester then, and come here in the fall. I forbore
to mention it when I wrote before, but I swear to God I believe we're

going to have another drought exactly like last summer. As Mr. Perry says the way hits a-doing hits a whuppin up to it. We have not a drop of water at this moment. We bathe in the river and bring drinking water from town. Really don't miss water much except that I hate to see the vines I was cherishing around the house all drying up.

This house from which a great many people have just gone out is now empty except for me and Beatrice and Uncle Doc. Andrew is being exhibited in a book store in Nashville today and Allen and Red and Cinina went along to do him honor. I remained to go over my novel one more time—and now I am writing to you. The novel, I suppose, is finished, but the first chapter in the third section is so bad that it may ruin the book which otherwise I believe would come off very well. The knowledge depresses me but I am so weary I can't think of anything to do about it. All the young men and the young woman read and read and wrinkle their brows and suggest things to do, ranging from two thousand to five thousand words and I keep wondering if I could squeeze out one more sentence.

. . . .

When Nancy took the little white box that contained the dress you sent in her hands she said "It's not silk, is it?" sort of hoping against hope. She was truly thrilled to discover that it *was* silk! She wore it on Confederate Memorial Day, belt and all—she dotes on the belt. Andrew made an impassioned speech, following on the heels of the mayor who had just remarked that we were all one country now and so on. "Gentlemen," says Andrew bowing to three palsied veterans who sat with mouths agape and hands cupped to ears "You have not fought in vain". "The world war . . . . . Hanh!" says Andrew, "why should I fight to collect Mr. Morgan's loans . . . . ." and a shocked silence falls on the whole graveyard. Andrew was suffering the after effects of cholera morbus at the time he made the speech which made it all much fiercer. A greenish light which I mistook for zeal for the Lost Cause would play over his countenance . . . . . it was really fine.

I must get back to that damned novel. Let us know how you get on. . . .

Love.

Clarksville, August 20, 1931
To S. W. in Wrightsville Beach

Dearest Sally:

I have been wondering how you've spent the summer and how you are and what your plans are for the winter, though I suppose it's rather early to be talking of that.

We are in a sort of in between time here, Allen still struggling with Lee but seeing a little light and I, trying to pull myself together to start another novel, for which I've already signed the contract. I'll be sending you a copy of "Penhally" in a day or two. Later I'll want you to tell me what's wrong with it, besides the things I already know. Just now I'm so depressed over certain aspects of it that I can't bear even to think of the damn thing.

I do wish you could come by here this fall. We won't be as harried as usual, for one thing, and it would be a joy to have you here one time when I wasn't worrying over a book. The weather has already turned a little towards fall, very bright blue days, but no leaves turning yet—it's just in the air. The river shows it mostly. I always enjoy swimming more when the days begin to be numbered.

I am sorry to tell you that we have another Hind Tit—Second we call her, but she *never* claws the screens. We found her sitting in the middle of the road one night, cars running right over her and she purring peacefully, exactly in the spot where we found Hind Tit I. The cats, in fact, multiply amazingly this time of year. One dropped on me out of the top boughs of the cedar tree the other day and three others just strolled up. Only about seven, so far, not counting Nancy's Primrose Ann who lives in the woods. Freda's puppy is adorable. Nancy named her Wigwam—Wig, she says because she wiggles and warm because she's warm! Nancy starts school the first week in September!

. . . .

We have really suffered for society this summer. There isn't one soul in Clarksville with whom one can spend a social hour. And all the agrarian brethren have been away. Red and Cinina will be in Nashville this winter, thank God. I can't hand Cinina much but I adore Red, and he is a sweet creature to have around if you have any time at all to play. We are plan-

ning a houseparty sometime after the middle of September. Can't you
come along before then?

    We have also formed a sort of poker club which meets of Saturday
evenings at the Laniers,[1] which ought to be a godsend this winter and put
off the evil day when we have to learn Contract. We want to go to New
York if we get hold of any money, but I don't imagine much will be coming in. I have to sell three thousand copies of my book before Scribner's
advance is paid back even. And everybody says it is a frightful season.

    Stark Young[2] came by a few weeks ago on his way to Texas to visit
his aged aunts. He was just back from Italy where he had been decorated
by the king and had his little ribbons and things in a satin lined box to
show his aunts. We made him wear them one afternoon calling on Cousins May and Mag. He is a very entertaining person, the most fluent talker
I have ever heard. It just flows on and on, very good stuff too, with a little
bit of acting thrown in every now and then to heighten things. He did
one thing that Allen said he wouldn't have done for anything in the
world. He patted my fierce grandmother on the hand and said "You're
such a dear old thing!" She liked it too. "Such a pleasant gentleman," she
said the next day.

    Phelps Putnam[3] also came by not long ago, with his Guggenheim
fellowship stuck up his sleeve. He acquired a Southern accent while he
was here and refers to himself now as Old Marse Phelps. Edmund Wilson
who has been out in Sante Fe reports that Phelps' main parlor trick now is
reciting his poems with a Southern accent, Hasbrouck and the Rose, especially. I always said it was particularly fitted for that. It is really killing to
hear him: "I mean the flowah toahds which mad haouah by houah, ah
travel brokenly . . . ."

    Did you see the New Republic article that Edmund Wilson wrote
about Cousin John Ferguson?[4] The symposium boys are all as mad as
hops, of course. He did a very nice impressionistic study of Cousin John
and Summertrees, then threw the agrarian symposium in along with the
lavendar and old lace, giving the impression that they were all sitting
around under the trees, reading Greek and brooding on their ancestors. It
really was a dirty trick, I thought, though of course Edmund didn't mean
it that way. It's simply that people can't see anything that isn't already in
their heads. We took him out to see Mister Rob who, though he isn't as
easily classified, is much more interesting than Cousin John, simply as a

case. If he had been a starving miner Edmund would have understood his case, but as he wasn't he didn't see anything there at all—but Summer-trees is more the sort of thing he expects to find in the south, so of course he leaped on it.

Do you realize that Ivanhoe is one of the most magnificent perfor-mances in the way of a novel that's ever been written? I'm reading it for the first time since I was a child. It's a shame to let children read it in high school the way they do. It's the most gorgeous thing—the whole feudal pageant passing before you and all very cleverly put together. The whole thing is grand.

Little May and Phelps hit here together as she may have told you. We didn't see much of her as she had to stay pretty close with her mother and aunt, but we had one picnic down on the raft (the New raft, a very swell affair that rides high on the river) and she spent a day and night with us.

There isn't any other news of us that I can think of. We have learned how to make some pretty good beer and are making enough to lay in for the winter.

Do try and come in time for the house party!

love from all of us,

c.

1. Chink and Lyle Lanier. Lyle, an Agrarian, wrote "A Critique of the Philosophy of Progress" for *I'll Take My Stand.*
2. Young had recently been awarded the order of the Crown of Italy while he was in that country to lecture for the Westinghouse Foundation.
3. A Yale poet who lived in New York, he was associated with a group of writers that included Edmund Wilson, Waldo Frank, and Quincy Howe. Malcolm Cowley talks of Put-nam's interest in the labor movement in *The Dream of the Golden Mountains* (1980), 74. In *Sixty American Poets*, 125, Allen said that his two slender volumes contained some of the best poetry of our time.
4. "Tennessee Agrarians," *New Republic*, LXII (1931), 279–81.

Something that Caroline does not mention in this letter is her correspondence with Katherine Anne Porter after Katherine Anne sailed from Vera Cruz. To quote Robert Penn Warren, "In August of 1931 she [Katherine Anne] found herself on a German boat, bound for Bremerhaven, observing the fellow pas-sengers, and keeping a journal-letter for the novelist Caroline Gordon, which was to be the germ of Ship of Fools, *published more than thirty years later."*[1]

Clarksville, August 21, 1931
To S. W. in Wrightsville Beach

Dearest Sally:

I have just moved into my bedroom—to work, you know, among
the old tennis shoes and hair brushes. I have decided that I have a bad
case of agoraphobia which only severe claustration will cure. That parlor,
with its space and the voices from the porch—I can at least lock the door
in here. Having got in here all set to work I will now write to you as a
way of working up to it.

I am glad you're in North Carolina. At least I am if being there will
bring you this way in the fall, and now why shouldn't it if you are going
to spend the winter in Rochester?

Marion Sadler, the son of Dickson-Sadler the druggist (a lovely boy
with beautiful eyes who wants to be a professor of history and falls into a
trance when "Mister Tate" speaks) is upstairs copying excerpts from the
letters of Robert E. Lee, Allen in the next room is writing to T. S. Eliot,
Nancy and little Paul Campbell (185 pounds) are wrestling in the hall, Beatrice is making beer in the kitchen and I really don't see how a person can
work with the summer in such full swing. Besides that I was up till twelve
o'clock last night—Manny[2] is spending her vacation at the Red Gate
cabin and we had a creek party yesterday afternoon. And the night before
Cousin Robin's folks were here and we all got very tight on beer—August
is perfectly bewildering here. I am going away next year if I have the
money. It always thickens up this way. Doug (Brother's son) has just
brought his bride (Hildred Neuernschwander) home—another picnic is
indicated. I suppose I will have made a thousand sandwiches before the
week is over.

This afternoon Nancy is to be vaccinated, preparatory to starting
school the tenth. I can't realize yet that she's old enough to go to school.
She asked me a minute ago "Mama, what does a person do when they go
wild?"
. . . .
Katherine Anne, durn her, seems to have sailed from Vera Cruz
without a by your leave to us. The news comes from Malcolm Cowley,
who K. A. said is now separating from Peggy. Anyway Peggy is in
Mexico.

You are probably right about Marion Henry. If you don't *have* to earn your living people aren't going to do much about it. Allen took her up to see a friend of his, librarian at Nashville—her attitude and address weren't right, but that is mostly just being brought up in this out of the way part of the world where you have to keep saying something pleasant whether you feel like talking or not. She read the proof on my novel in a most business like way and caught all sorts of tricky little errors. She is probably more capable and intelligent than most people making a living.

Willie Lee has been quite ill, pus on the kidney, I think. "Her pancreas," Coach Thumma says solemnly, "Willie Lee was always fond of her corn." She was in the hospital and emerged quite frail and wan looking.[3]

We had the strangest visitor this week—a professor of philosophy at Ohio State named Van Atta. He wrote Allen a year ago about something of his he'd read. Allen answered and they had a little correspondence. Some months later he wrote saying that his wife had just died giving Allen a full account of her funeral, copies of the written tributes and so on and saying he'd like to come to see us some time. We said come, of course and thought no more about it. Night before last he telephoned from the hotel in town. Allen brought him out here and he spent the night. He is rather awkward socially—I thought for the first fifteen minutes of his stay (he arrived in the midst of Cousin Robin, Polly and Jenny Lester) that he was just one of those people who think that all writers are "interesting." But he is really very remarkable, extremely intelligent and awfully nice in a strained, queer way. He is a follower of Spinoza and interested mostly in philosophy, of course, but he seems to understand modern literature and what he has to say about it is intelligent and very much unlike the usual academic reactions. His wife, a German girl evidently very accomplished, died in childbirth a year after their marriage. He had a great deal of feeling about Hemingway's "A Farewell to Arms"; he said that she had been reading it a few months before her death and had found it one of the few American novels she was able to read all the way through. "Now who is that woman," he said, "who writes rather like Hemingway?" He meant Gertrude Stein!

A young sculptor whom John Ransom and those people are very enthusiastic about is coming here tomorrow to make a bronze plaque, profile, of Allen. He's done one of John that Allen likes very much. I expect he's going to be pretty trying. I hope he won't take long.

Dickson-Sadler's, the drug store, is going to have a window display of my book with the author autographing—if the kin don't come and at least stand around in the attitude of people about to buy books I shall be peeved. I'm nervous about it, fearing it may be like getting ready to be married and no groom turning up. I'm also going up to Nashville to autograph at one of the stores. I'll be sending you a copy before long. The books aren't made yet, though.

Your personal affairs hang so delicately in the balance, I suppose, that you aren't giving out any news. Don't go and do anything important without at least informing me.[4]

We have the most remarkable milker, a negro school teacher. He and Allen have long talks. He seems to have thought on all the problems of the day and has a long, considered answer. The problem of race equality he dismisses by saying he has no use for any animal that isn't thoroughbred. He is rather moony and finally confessed that he sometimes wrote poems. He brought Allen one called "Sorrow" that wasn't bad, sort of Biblical in phrasing. Beatrice told me yesterday that she hoped we could get another negro to milk when he goes off to teach school. "You see if it's a colored person I can manage 'em," says she, "but I can't do nothing if it's a white person."

She, by the way, continues faithful to Miss Sally of all our visitors.

Well, I have got to go through the motions of some work. The water is marvelous now. I try to swim everyday.

Much love,

c.

1. Robert Penn Warren, Introduction, in Warren (ed.), *Katherine Anne Porter: A Collection of Critical Essays* (Englewood Cliffs, N.J., 1979), 5.
2. Caroline's cousin, Marion Meriwether.
3. I remember once putting Willie Lee in the shower to revive her.
4. I had been divorced for quite a while and was considering—only considering—a second marriage.

Clarksville, early fall, 1931
To S. W. in Rochester

Dearest Sally:

You seem to be getting the wish so many people cherish—of doing things over after you have enough sense to know what to do. All those beaux sound very alluring to me, the having them, not the particular beaux as I don't know very much about any of them. By all means marry a Southerner if you must marry is my advice. Georgia, you say? I'd prefer a Tennessean, of course, still Georgia is easy driving distance from Benfolly . . . . .

I wish to God I could make you a visit this winter. It all sounds very tempting. I'll do it if it can be worked. It all still hangs on Lee, of course. The book is delayed publication this fall after Balch[1] had persecuted us for weeks with long distance telephone calls. "It's just Mister Balch, I reckon," Beatrice would say easily as she moved to the telephone. God knows when Allen will finish that damn book.[2] We could do almost anything this winter if he only would—he could get a sizable advance on another book he has in mind the minute he finishes Lee.

We are going to Charlottesville in October, last of [the] month, to a conference of Southern writers. Cabell, Glasgow et al and all the Dubose Heywards and so on.[3] I'm going as a stowaway, not being invited. Andrew says he may go along to keep me company and we will be the spectres at the feast. I'll write you a report of the affair. It ought to be very amusing.

The reason I type so badly is because my hands are so cold they won't hit the keys. It's turned very cold after a most hellish hot spell. We've been spending half of every night at the hospital with Red Warren. His mother is very ill, dying, I think, has been since last Saturday. They keep her going with saline solutions and water injected in the veins and all that but I don't think she can possibly get well. We've gone through two nights when we expected her to die any minute, then she would rally before day and sink the next afternoon—it's been a terrible ordeal. Poor Mr. Warren though has had no hope from the first. She was operated on for gall stones a week ago and they found an abscess in the bowels.

My book came out with great eclat in these parts.[4] An autographing party in Nashville and a really much nicer one here at the Dickson-Sadler Drug company. At the Nashville book store we were confined in a small balcony at one end of the shop. A woman came and stood downstairs for a long time staring up at the balcony, from whence, they said, a steady stream of smoke ascended. "Is that the lady that wrote the book?" she asked. "She must be mighty smart, but Lord, don't she smoke a lot!"

I've had some very nice letters—the very nicest (at least it was the subtlest praise) from Lincoln Kirstein, editor of the Hound and Horn.[5] Yvor Winters wrote me that Penhally was one of the five or six best novels of the past two decades. The only thing wrong with it he said is the method. It should have been written in an entirely different way—he has outlined for me the way I must write my second novel! The best review, so far that I've seen is by a Jew we knew in Paris, Cecil Goldbeck in the NY Eve. Post, who actually observed that the book attempted to show the disintegration of the Southern ideal of life. I was quite touched.

I have considered carefully your question about Nancy's present. I believe that the handiest addition to her wardrobe would be a dress, jersey, wash silk—anything that I could set apart as a sort of party dress. She still has the two sweaters you gave her last year and a very sweet little blue sweater and a winter coat. And I have just got her school dresses up to what I consider a fine state—I made her four myself and they are really masterpieces. I have shown them to all her great aunts who have a very poor opinion of me as a seamstress and they all admired them greatly. We have such a time every morning deciding which dress she shall wear to school that I've decided to put all her school dresses in one drawer and let her choose the one that suits her own mood. Then I'll keep one dress on hand for parties and the like which is not to be worn to school. She is still wearing wash dresses—I just couldn't keep woolen dresses unspotted for every day at her age. I have kept her in long stockings every winter up to now but I am thinking of making it three quarter socks this year. Marion Henry says her whole life is marred by the fact that she had to wear long stockings when everybody else wore socks, and a young tobacconist (who wants to be a musician) has just had a nervous break down here. I am sure it was brought on by his first day at school—I well remember it. He came in a white linen suit that had an embroidered collar, but that wasn't the worst. The speller they used in the Gordon School was bright red and during the day he had a slight accident and those white linen pants were pale pink all that day. Nancy has a silver medal (the size of a pea) for her progress in busy work. She says they were given only to the girls. "Uncle Penn got a medal when he was in school," she says, "I reckon they gave them to boys in that school." (The Vanderbilt Founder's Medal, Red says, has fifty dollars worth of gold wasted in it!)

Nancy is very enthusiastic about her school and very ambitious.

The first day she was so excited that she couldn't leave off making letters
till ten o'clock at night and she got up early the next morning and began
making them. She was also quite carried away by the church services but
she is more *blasé* now, says the "Father's prayers are too long." I surely did
tell you her memorable remark about my book? Well, it will bear repeating. Beatrice said "When you get grown you're going to write a book like
Mama." "Don't mention no books to me," Nancy said, "Mama has nearly
drove me crazy, locking herself up every morning." John Ransom's children, by the way, seem to have taken the other attitude. Helen writes
plays about Greek heroes which are produced in school and Reavell(?) [6]
addressed a High school class in Colorado this summer on the wanderings
of Ulysses, stopping every now and then to take a drink, they said, in
quite the popular lecturer's manner. I suppose they have to take things
violently either way. Sometimes I think Allen is distressed by Nancy's
double negatives—but as I tell him they are quite in the best agrarian
tradition.

We have had one violent visitation this summer—a young sculptor
whom Sidney Hirsch[7] discovered. He has made bas reliefs in bronze of
Allen and John Ransom which are really marvelous. They are very different, the two reliefs, very interesting, seen together. Likenesses, both of
them, and something else—something that you would say it was impossible for that boy to do. Allen's is full of movement, "Confederate" most
people say at once when they look at it; John's is all repose. You know
what a complex mind he has and that saintly sort of face—it's all there in
one line, the downward slant of the lip. He has caught the balance of the
man's whole nature in that one line. Sidney says sculptors are always like
this boy—no mind, or rather the mind of a child, the manner, really the
instincts, of a bum. He almost drove us crazy, of course, while he was
doing Allen's head. "Beatrice," he would say at the table, "you certainly
look marvelous in black. Now turn your head just a little to the right."
Allen is going to send him on to Cincinnati. Ben is going to try to get
him some orders and no doubt he can. Nashville is a very poor place for
him, of course. The women there who might give him commissions just
can't get over the fact that he hasn't the manners of a gentleman—but in a
more sophisticated community those very manners might be an asset.

If I can get some photographs of Allen's and John's reliefs I'll send
you some. I think you'd like them. I never have gotten any of my photo-

graphs back from Scribner's. I sent a whole bunch and they promised to send me the ones they didn't use so I haven't had any more made.

Did you ever get a copy of "Penhally?" I ordered it sent some weeks ago?

I must get to work. Love and let us hear from you when you feel like writing,

C.

1. Earle Henry Balch, of Minton, Balch, and Company, publishers of Allen's early books.
2. He never did.
3. James Branch Cabell (1879–1958), American novelist; Ellen Glasgow (1874–1945), a southern novelist popular all over America; Dubose Heyward (1885–1940), a Charleston novelist, dramatist, and poet, best known for his *Porgy*, which George Gershwin dramatized as *Porgy and Bess*.
4. *Penhally*.
5. *Hound and Horn*, originally *Harvard Magazine*, was published from September, 1927, to July, 1934. Its two editors were Bernard Bandler, who became a Boston psychiatrist, and Lincoln Kirstein, who established the School of American Ballet in New York City in 1933 and later directed the New York Ballet Company. The magazine's most notable contributors were T. S. Eliot, R. P. Blackmur, Allen Tate, Malcolm Cowley, Wallace Stevens, William Carlos Williams, Katherine Anne Porter, Kay Boyle, John Dos Passos, and E. E. Cummings.
6. Robb Reavill, his mother, was a classmate of mine at Wellesley.
7. Dr. Sidney Mttron Hirsch, one of the original Fugitives in Nashville, something of a mystagogue and self-taught universal genius.

Clarksville, November 2, 1931
To S. W. in Rochester

Dear Sally:

I am a little tight on home made beer, but I promised myself I'd start work in the morning so my only chance for letters is tonight.

. . . .

I am touched at the idea of your mother giving a talk on Penhally. She flatters me at one point, though. I am thirty seven years old, not a young girl, alas. And as for the war, in a sense I was there. Really, I've been through it so many times in "Battles and Leaders" I have to stop and remind myself that I was neither at Shiloh, Antietam, Malvern Hill nor Bull Run—nor sang within the bloody wood.[1]

Allen and I got back yesterday from the Southern Writers' conference at Charlottesville. Quite an affair. Would you had been there. So Southern—all the writers very anxious not to be thought Southern, everybody so anxious not to let anybody else know that they thought Ellen Glasgow was lacking in intellectual subtlety—everybody, that is, except Paul Green[2] who got up and announced that we were all going to God in a machine. It was such a funny affair—so as I was saying Southern. The atmosphere, I suppose. Virginia is terrible. The buzzards hang all day over the fields—scenting the odor of decay Andrew says. Old ladies of the Green Springs neighborhood hide away in boarding houses. You can pay fifty cents and walk around the grounds of your great great great grandfather's estate—the box is worth two hundred thousand dollars—everything nowadays is valued in Virginia. A professor told me that life had been much pleasanter since the crash, poor devils, the professors, I mean.

The conference was nice. Only one son of a bitch—Paul Green. I got very fond of Ulrich Phillips, Jim Boyd, and one or two others.[3] And Ellen Glasgow is a grand old girl.

Miss Carrie is a cagy old bird. Her apparent reaction to Penhally is conventional pride in having a granddaughter who has written a book. We were both mistaken about Dad. I never dreamed he would take the trouble to read the book, but he has. He is now reading it for the second time! "I read a little in it every day," he says and explains that it amuses him because he knows all those people so well. He too was dying to know what Miss Carrie thought of it. "My cows won't touch onions," he says and roars with laughter.[4]

One more thing about Penhally. The process is reversed. The people first took hold of me and then they produced an intellectual impression. I didn't know what they were about at first. I doubt if it's the right way to write a novel, but that's the way it was.

I must reel off to bed. I really am quite tight, but maybe this is legible. Much love. Do write, caroline

1. A line from Tate's "Ode to the Confederate Dead," followed by one from Eliot's "Sweeney Among the Nightingales."
2. An American playwright (1894–1981), who taught at Chapel Hill. His play *In Abraham's Bosom* won the Pulitzer Prize.
3. Ulrich Bonell Phillips (1877–1934), a Georgia historian; James Boyd (1888–1944), lieutenant in the U.S. Army Ambulance Service and novelist, who wrote *Drums, Marching On*, and others about World War I.

4. A frequent remark of Miss Carrie's, used in *Penhally*. Wild onions eaten by cows can be tasted in the milk.

Clarksville, November 18, 1931
To S. W. in Rochester

Dearest Sally:

What a darling dress, so truly chic and yet such a tender affair! You must have hunted days for it. Nancy is at school but she will be thrilled when she sees it. Her vanity is something amazing. That belt will hit her eye. She does yearn so for a waist line—and she is so fat! Fatter this fall than ever, it seems to me. At least her great aunt, Loulie, says that something ought to be done about her legs.

Do you remember the warm weather we had when Allen and Andrew went to Richmond debating? It is just like that now, warmer perhaps, and God knows it is drier. I am in something of a daze this morning. We had a weekend party, the last festive gathering before we dig in for the winter, and there were dozens of people. We drank beer steadily for two days, but it must have been pretty good because nobody has a hangover. Everybody has gone home except one or two people and I have been wandering around picking up beer bottles and thinking how hard it is going to be to get back to work which I will have to do tomorrow, certainly.

(I am sorry this typewriter skips so, but there is nothing to do about it.)

I have just finished applying for a Guggenheim again. Allen thinks I have a chance, but I rather have an idea that I have been weighed in the balance—against Emjo Basshe [1] and his like—and found wanting. Because, really, when people like Phelps Putnam get Guggenheims . . . . . still Phelps does speak of himself in a very reverential way and that does wonders. Some demon prompted me to write "Oh, Jesus, Hasbrouck" [2] when I was autographing Katherine Shove's copy of Penhally and in the next mail came a long letter from Katherine, all about her and Phelps.

Cousin Carrie Ferguson was at Merry Mont the other day. Says she "What kind of party was it that Carrie and Allen went to in Nashville—a bridge party or a dancing party?" "It warn't either," says Nancy, "It was a drinking party."

A note from my father today says that he has just flown South—he was in a sweat fearing he might delay here too long and miss a day's fishing—I am wondering if you are going to Florida or stick it out in Rochester. Now will you really come here in the spring? I am going to do two long stories this winter and really expect not to be rushed this spring—it would be heavenly if you would come during the pretty weather. It seems so long since you were here.

Loulie (Manny's mother) has gone to Merry Mont to spend the winter under the impression that Miss Carrie was too feeble to stay alone. Miss Carrie is showing more than one flash of her old time form in consequence. She complains of being crowded. Then, too, Loulie started in and washed everything in the house which rather upset the old lady. The kitchen for instance—she had Stella scrub the walls and it appears that they were originally painted gray—I had always thought that it was a dark brown paint on those walls. Ma says that if Loulie doesn't quit carrying on so she is going to tie her legs together and throw her in a haystack as somebody did to old Mr. Unseld the miser not long ago.

Did I tell you Andrew was in love—with one of my Virginia cousins—Sarah Lindsay Patton, only they call her Patty. He stayed at their house all the time we were at Charlottesville. Patty works the garden bare footed—the negro house boy said "I can always tell when Miss Patty's beaus is getting serious. They takes off their shoes." Andrew was bare footed thirty minutes after we arrived. He went over the mountains using his mountain accent and came back with broad A's. I really think he is as hard hit as he will ever be. Patty's father is some sort of official in the administration of the Episcopal church. He was sent to Liberia last year to investigate the condition of the colored Christians and found them selling each other into slavery and carrying on scandalous. He stayed there so long that white people got to looking strange to him—he was telling us about his adventures in Africa while Andrew and Patty courted in a corner. "They gave me two women," says Cousin Bob (he is a little like Dad, only more urbane and *much* more innocent.) "I would have liked to bring them to Jane but I thought people might gossip." Cousin Jane got me off in a corner and said that if Andrew told the story about his little brother

Micajah who come into the world a-bouncing and warn't weaned till he was old enough to go hunting—she said that if Andrew told about Micajah a-bouncin in from hunting and saying "Well, Mammy, let me have it" that the match was all off, that Cousin Bob's adventures in Africa hadn't really broadened him that much.

Those people are coming downstairs. I've got to see about some food.

> *Love. Do write,*
>
> c

[written as a postscript]
Just got Nancy's first report. She got 98 for politeness; 91 for reading; 93 spelling; 85 busy work!

1. Russian-American dramatist (1900–1939), associated with the Provincetown Theatre. He directed several of Paul Green's plays.
2. A line addressed to the title character in Phelps Putnam's "Hasbrouck and the Rose."

I must have visited the Tates this fall because I remember us all sitting around the café dining room table teasing Andrew about some girl related to somebody. Various members of the group were giving him advice on how to conduct a love affair. He finally said, "I don't want to do any of those things. I was just courting her out of respect for brother Tate."

One time, as we were sitting around that table quoting Shakespeare's sonnets, first one and then another, so far as we could remember, little Nancy kept wandering in and out, too polite to interrupt, but wishing to take part. She finally stood by her father holding a book, and at the first pause, read a poem. It was "Matilda: Who Told Lies and Was Burned to Death," by Hilaire Belloc in Cautionary Verses. *It was a great success.*

Clarksville, January 7, 1932
To S. W. in Rochester

Dearest Sally:
I've been wanting to write you all Christmas week but things have

kept getting thicker. That yellow sweater is lovely—I am crazy about it. I wore it all through Christmas and thought fondly of you. Nancy was quite thrilled over hers, too.

. . . .

I sent four copies of "Penhally" to Rochester. Larry,[1] by the way, will probably be thinking you think more of him than you do. I found myself writing that I hoped he'd come to Benfolly some day—and so I do. I hope he'll drive you down some time. Won't he? And when are you coming?

We have just gotten back from Murfreesboro where we went to attend the funeral of Andrew's mother. She fell ill Christmas day—peritonitis, like Mrs. Warren and like Mrs. Warren she was kept alive for ten days or so with saline solutions and blood transfusions. She was such a pretty, frivolous woman—it is hard to think of her dead. She fought very gamely, joking with the family to the end. Poor Andrew is pretty broken up. He is in love—if Andrew can be in love—with one of my Virginia cousins, by the way.

We had a fairly quiet Christmas. Ben, Allen's rich brother, came down for his annual visit of two days and brought his little son. He is really quite a sweet thing. Such a life he leads! You can't help feeling sorry for him.

. . . .

Bernard Bandler who edits The Hound and Horn came down Christmas Day—to investigate agrarianism, he said. He said on leaving that he found it very satisfactory. We enjoyed him quite a lot. He's awfully nice and very intelligent.

I have spent almost all of this day chasing two ponies which escaped from us last night and made off five or six miles through the bottom. I went farther over on the bluff that runs along parallel with the river than I'd ever been before and I found some of the most heavenly vines and things. One beautiful bush that at this season of the year has lovely, blood red blossoms or something that are so fragile they look like they are made out of paper. I brought a lot home with me and put it in the dining room in glass pitchers. Those bluffs are marvelous. Bernard and I did a good deal of walking while he was here—we couldn't get Allen to stir— he never walks unless he has what he calls an objective. One day we went up on that hill across the road. It was mid day and the sun so warm it was like summer and Clarksville looked like a very soft coloured picture post card down below us. I found great tangles of those bamboo berries up there—they have a wonderful grayish sheen which they lose when you bring them into the house.

I am writing this letter in a perfect bedlam—Nancy and one of her little friends who is spending the night are both getting their Christmas baby dolls to sleep. If I am more than usually incoherent that is one of the reasons.

You'd heard about Margaret Meriwether's marriage—to Ross Mc[Gilli]Cuddy who is already in the family and therefore a suitable mate and as Miss Carrie says "Such a fine young man and has such a nice old brick house." I met him once at the family bridge club. Very good looking I thought him, a handsome portly creature of fifty something with gray hair, good, heavy features and a passion for hunting and fishing. They ought to be happy together.

Ford hauled off and wrote a swell piece on "Penhally" (December Bookman) and the Bookman actually ran two terrible pictures of me— much to my surprise. Seward Collins has got to the point now where he refers to Allen as "Even Allen Tate."

Have you been doing any writing? That Rochester life sounds far too partyish to me. You'd better come down here as soon as it's a little warmer and do a little work. It is so warm now, by the way, that the forsythia is blooming and a few jonquils and narcissi—I suppose we'll have a cold spell later.

I trust this letter is decipherable. The children yell louder than ever. I think I'll go take a hot bath to soothe my frayed nerves.

Much love,

[added as a postscript]
One of Nancy's recent remarks I'll risk repeating. I told her she'd better eat her vegetables or she wouldn't be pretty like Cath Wilds when she grew up. She returned composedly "Cath had better try to get pretty like me. I heard her say yesterday she wished she was as pretty as I was."

1. Dr. Lawrence Kohn, the man I eventually married, was too busy to drive anywhere

except to see patients. Our lives were far apart at this time, but as Caroline realized, we were aware of each other.

Clarksville, March 12, 1932
To S. W. in Rochester

I have not heard from you for so long—I do hope you are not having flu or doing anything desperate. Do write and reassure me.

We have just come out of a month's spell of illness that has left us both prostrated. Financial reverses had come so hard and fast that we had gotten to thinking that we couldn't be worse off.

. . . .

. . . Allen meanwhile had a relapse after flu, running 96 [*sic*] the night my fever was so high. He has been in bed for three weeks and dressed for the first time today. I think, though, that he is quite recovered; he stayed in bed long enough to get his strength back this time. Beatrice, by the way, walked off last Friday, leaving us both in bed. I was never so shocked in my life. I am still puzzling over her sudden defection. Niggers are un-fathomable, but I wouldn't have thought Beatrice would do that. I was going to let her go, anyway, once I got up—not being able to pay her any longer—but I intended to keep her till I was out of bed. I had to get out of bed a day or two before the doctor said I could but it didn't seem to hurt me. I have got my strength back and am really feeling fine, though somewhat weighed down by housework. Lord, I hate it. Andrew arrived yesterday, thank God, and is grand, goes to town and gets provisions for us and even helps me wash the dishes like a lamb.

I tell all my bad news first. There is one piece of good news—but Allen says, tell you I am writing with my fingers crossed, or it may bring bad luck. I seem to have some chance for the Guggenheim fellowship. At least they have written me wanting to know this and that, though warn-ing me that it is by no means certain that I'll get one. But *if* I do can't you go over with us? It would be heavenly to all get over together and this—if it comes off—will probably be our only chance. I have a feeling that you will be writing back that you would love to but you have just decided to get married or something like that. That is one reason I am writing pre-

maturely—for fear you'll go and make other arrangements. If we go we'll
have to go this spring, around May, anyhow. We are thinking of taking
the car. Would you advise it?

Do write and let me know how you are and what you are doing.
Love,

caroline

[added as a postscript]
This letter was written a week ago but not mailed in rush of dish
washing. I did get the Guggenheim after all!

Clarksville, March 23, 1932
To S. W. in Rochester

Dear Sally:
The magnificent house arrived duly and has been set up, most ex-
pertly by Allen who had a great deal of fun doing it. Nancy adores it, and
re-decorates the interior a dozen times a day.

I have been a little disturbed by not hearing from you. I'm afraid
you're sick again. If you are, don't bother to write. I remember how letters weighed on me when I was sick. If you aren't sick let us hear from
you—and know if there's any chance of your going abroad with us.

We've rented this house, hurrah—to a German tobacconist and his
bride. He has a boat and loves the river and dogs. Has a fine dog who
though he speaks only German will doubtless prove pleasant company for
Freda—police dog. He takes it over in June. We camp on Miss Carrie till
the middle of July then start out, in the Ford, no doubt, lecture a bit—
(yea, even I will address some remarks on Southern novelists to the as-
sembled old ladies of Monteagle) wend our way to Baltimore whence
we'll sail (most cheaply) on a mail boat line. We plan to make Toulon our
headquarters. I had a cable the other day from Katherine Anne and Ford's
wife, from Paris, but they said they were leaving shortly for Toulon. We
shall be quite a party when we all get there. Now are you coming???

I want to ask a favor, always supposing you're not sick. I enclose a
letter to Nancy's old nurse, Mme Gau. I could never get it written so the

old lady'd understand it. If you're in the mood would you translate it? *Don't* bother a minute if you aren't.

I am trying to write a fairy story in hope of making some money. It is hell. I now return to it. Love, C.

[added as a postscript]

I am quite over my ailment. It's only in the last few days, though. I went finally and had a curetage, Amytal and morphine I believe I took. Not very bad—I'm not stoical like you. I fuss dreadfully when I'm sick, never having been sick much.

I don't think my new novel is going to be as painful a process as "Penhally," being all in the present. I feel it winding up inside me slowly and am counting on France to act as mid-wife. Such a relief to have only two characters. Here's a little song we've been singing much of late (fiddle accompaniment):

What you going to do when the meat gives out?
Stand in the corner with your lip poked out.

What you going to do when the meat comes in?
Stand in the corner with a greasy chin.

The chins are immaculate as yet but we are hoping.

Clarksville, early spring, 1932
To S. W. in Rochester

Your letter has just come. I am relieved to hear from you. I was rather worried. Glad it's no worse than colds, though they are bad enough. Yes, you must come with us. As for getting unsettled again . . . the disasters, you know, are never the ones you expect. Now, you're not likely to fall in love with Ford and I for one will be rather pleased if he falls in love with you. You've already stood exposure to Allen very well . . . . .

Our program? As I say this mail boat line (I can't remember the name; I'm downstairs)[1] is the cheapest passage we've found and we've been deluged with lists and letters. One hundred and eighty dollars round trip per person on a one class boat. Can you beat that? A tobacconist here sailed on one and says it was fine. Certainly the accommodations will beat those I have at Benfolly. Your hundred a month sounds princely. Those damn Guggenheims only gave me two thousand and we have millions of bills to settle before we go. I have no idea how we'll make it. We can't move around at all. Be lucky if we make it sitting still but of course you don't have to stick with us. I decided on Toulon, first, because Ford was established there and second because of Allen's susceptibility to flu. We could spend some weeks in Paris on our way down. I'd like to.

God knows about Janice.[2] I *hope* she hasn't worn off.

I'm glad to know you're working. That's grand. I, too, am going to work—like hell. If the circle at Toulon proves so distracting that Allen doesn't work I'm going to move off and leave you all. I'm fed up on starving.

Can't you come on down as soon as the weather warms up which should be any day and then journey through the country with us? It ought to be rather fun working our way to Baltimore.

I'm expecting any day a letter from Ford telling me exactly and authoritatively what to do. His advice will probably be good. He is so broke he'll see things from our viewpoint. I really like being in his vicinity. To have even one person sort of planning things so you can get your work done helps a lot. And his mild tyrannies will be exerted over Janice this time, let us hope. Really, he never did anything worse than demand that we spend all our evenings with him at a period when he was undergoing all sorts of terrific troubles (a fool doctor had told him he was likely to kick off any minute.)

I wish we could come by New York but we simply can't. We have never been as broke in our lives for we never had as many debts before. I don't see how we'll make it at all, but we will, somehow, for we can't turn down the two thousand.

Allen is sending you a copy of his new book of poems[3]—unless you're coming down here right away.

I hate to leave my grandmother worst of all. She says she'll probably be dead before we get back. And of course she may. She begs me to leave Nancy with her but I can't.

Yes, I'm glad you didn't arrive during the cold spell. It was fiendish. But that weather was abnormal, nothing like it ever known here before.

Spring is bound to come now. We've already had several days of almost summer heat but it is a little cooler now.

I have, thank God, a cook—an Amazon, youthful and good tempered whom I pay three dollars a week to do all the work including the washing. Isn't it amazing?

Allen's "secondary anemia" is improving. His blood count has gone from forty five to sixty in two weeks. He eats raw eggs, take iron pills and even eats spinach and raw cabbage without protest. He was really scared and I've been worried about him too. I've gone from 130 to 118 but beer will put it all back on me. I'm rather glad to lose weight. I was getting hippy.

Must get back to work. When are you coming? Make it soon.

Love, c.

1. Written along the margin: "Baltimore Mail Line."
2. Ford's wife.
3. *Poems, 1928–1931.*

Clarksville, early spring, 1932
To S. W. in Rochester

Friday night

Dear Sally:

You are probably sitting there waiting for a telegram from me but damn it, the office was closed by the time I had finished amassing some information I wanted before wiring you. Allen thought I ought just to have wired you the bus schedule and tell you to come on. You doubtless have my last letter by this time, though, and know that we are giving up the house April 15. I thought at least I ought to find a place you could board before wiring you. (I haven't the least idea whether you are interested in boarding in these parts, but I thought I'd find out.)

Cloverland is the only available place. It is within walking distance of Merry Mont—a lovely walk through the woods. Forty dollars a month, Clyde said, but hesitantly as if she thought that might be too much. Perhaps it is. It could be arranged, I'm sure. She's never taken a boarder before.

I explained didn't I the difficulties about your coming to Merry

Mont? Miss Carrie would be delighted to have you—she thinks you're grand, but things are pretty primitive there. I doubt if you can survive unless you were born there. (Allen after a somewhat intensive training is now practically a Meriwether and ought to be able to stand anything.) If Ma would only let me do the housekeeping but she won't give up any of her routine which after all is her life so each meal is sort of sent down from God and of course an eighty year old woman can't cook for four or five people even if she thinks she can. I don't know [how] she'll stand us till June, though she's delighted at the prospect.

You could have one of those wings to yourself at Cloverlands. They used to be slightly ha'nted but Clyde has taken all that out of them with her improvements. (They took the darling dormer windows off of the house.) There's [a] bath on that side of the house. You could be most private and Clyde is really a nice soul, still Radcliffish after all these years among the kin.

I had looked forward so to your coming. Damn it, I wish we hadn't had to give up the house so soon. But Paris will compensate us somewhat for missing the spring here. Do come on (if the boarding idea doesn't appall you and isn't too expensive.) And don't weaken on the idea of going over with us. I think the trip in the car will be fun. Let me know what you decide. I do wish I'd known about the motor trip a day ahead, or if I had just been able to telephone Clyde but they have no telephone and I had to drive out there which threw me late getting back. I could have made it but I had no idea the western union office closed so early.

Love, c.

[added as a postscript]

It's been cold here—swimming, my God, no! This whole winter has been freakish, jonquils and hyacinths blooming in January then very cold weather in March. It is warming up now but is not nearly as warm as it is usually this time of year. It ought to be pleasant from now on, though. We've had just one or two days of summer heat. We're still having fires, though.

John Ransom wrote today wanting to know if Allen wanted his teaching job at the University College or whatever it is at Exeter. Allen is anxious to get it—it would give up a small, but regular income and relieve him of some of his reviewing jobs that irk him so. I don't know that he can get it. We thought we might go to France first then to England in the fall. Would you consider Devon? It's not so cold there, is it? It might be rather amusing for some months. John, his wife and two children pay ninety dollars a month for their rooms and board! Starcross, I believe the village is.

Clarksville, April 8, 1932
To S. W. in Rochester

Dear Sally. The Rev. J. M. Gordon oft remarks that when sorrows come they come not single spies and right he is as usual. I now have appendicitis and God knows what the morrow will bring. . . .[1]

We have also just gotten many advices from steamship companies. It seems that all the companies are cutting their rates almost in half except the Baltimore Line. Allen now thinks we'd better go through New York. We'd love to have you in these parts but it seems pretty silly to come down just to drive back. I though I'd better let you know how things were so you could shape your plans accordingly. Please don't give up the idea of going abroad with us. I have a feeling that all our difficulties will vanish once we set foot on board ship.

I have always thought appendicitis was such a silly affliction. I TUNED UP DAY BEFORE YESTERDAY WITH A FRIGHTFUL PAIN IN MY STOMACH. (Caps unintentional.) It deserves caps though that pain. Allen thought it was a large dill pickle which I ate under his disapproving eye but Ted says it's appendix. I had been working like a hound trying to finish that cursed fairy story and had left myself just a week to pack up and clean the house for the new tenant whose wedding date depends upon our movements. Ted said if I was better today I might put the operation off a week which would give me time to pack. I shudder at the thought of going abroad with only the things Allen considers necessary. One of his brightest ideas last move was to pack all of the articles which we use every day in a trunk belonging to Andrew Lytle and ship them to Andrew at Huntsville, Alabama while we drove to Clarksville. I simply could not make him see that it would be bad to be in Clarksville with your toothbrush in Alabama.

I'm sure you must be about to give up by this time. We seem to have a new complication every time we write. However we'll get through them I'm sure and make the boat whichever one it is.

I expect to go to the hospital next week. After which I shall repair to Merry Mont and let come what will. I wrote the Cloverlanders will be pleased to board you and it would be a great pleasure to have you in the neighborhood but I feel like a pig urging you to come when I don't seem to be able to lift my hand in your behalf. We will do our swimming in Spring Creek and West Fork instead of the river. Social life will be largely picnics. I plan to discharge my social obligations by several picnics at Marion Henry's creek with what the papers call "the Nashville group" in attendance.

By the way if you should be minded to ride Mister Rob who has fallen quite a victim to your charms would furnish you a pony, I am sure, and you could amble over to see us.

Love. Sorry to have to write so many contrary advices, caroline

1. Added in top margin: "I don't have any pain now but am rather weak from starving two days. Ted is letting me have liquid food now.

Clarksville, April 14, 1932
To S. W. in Rochester

I wrote you a letter but it got sent out to Merry Mont with some fruit jars or something. Your last letter has just come. Allen didn't refuse to take the telegraphed money from any prideful feelings but because the WU man said that was the simplest way to send it and he regarded it at that moment as a loan which he didn't think was necessary. As for me I accept the gift with heartfelt thanks for I do remember those hellish moments, hours, rather of wanting to be catheterized and not getting it done and I am really tired of aches and pains and won't mind at all treating myself tenderly for a while. You are a sweet angel to think of it.

What I'm worrying about now is the possibility of our European trip going agley, your part, I mean. We won't go to England unless Allen is offered that job and if he is I guess we'll have to go as the stipend is so ridiculously inadequate. Allen would have to go in time for the college's opening, I suppose. John arrived there in October last year but he probably went in late and happened on this job by accident. And alas, I don't believe we can move up our date of sailing. My fellowship isn't available until July 1 and Allen and I both have engagements to lecture in Monteagle July 15. Everywhere this tiresome lack of money handicaps one. If we don't go to England wouldn't it be worth your while to come with us? We are still waiting to hear from John Ransom about the job. I'll let you know the minute we hear from him. He ought to reply soon. We cabled him but I fear he is off on some between terms vacation and so may not have got our cable or more likely may not have been able to get hold of the dean who'd decide on Allen's fitness for the Egyptian tutorship, whatever that is.

We are winding up the last of our packing and will leave for Merry Mont right after a scrapped up lunch. I'm rather sad at the thought of leaving. The place is getting that lush green look and the dogwood is just out in the woods. And I simply can't bear to think of "the little girl" as her fiance calls her lolling about on our porch. She is a Montgomery Ward bookkeeper and he is a German tobacconist. And they are going to paper my bedroom, with paper, doubtless, from Montgomery Ward's. I think, too, that chaste Benfolly will be the scene of an outrageous charivari Saturday night for the young bloods of the town plan on following the happy couple out and preventing to the best of their ability Wagschal's enjoyment of his wedding night. Well, thank God, he's fond of dogs so Freda ought to be happy.

Allen will let you know how I get on at the hospital. Ted is off fishing at Reelfoot Lake this weekend so he evidently doesn't regard my condition as serious. Still I will be thankful to have it over. Something is playing havoc with my digestion and it must be appendicitis though Ted says it may be a cystic ovary.

I must return to the packing. I don't do any bending or writhing— just decide where every damn thing goes. Thank God it's most over.

Love and many thanks for the gift, caroline

Clarksville Hospital, Clarksville, April 25, 1932
To S. W. in Rochester

Dear Sally, I'm using your money to stay at the hospital a day or two longer than I would have; can't "void." But Ted's examined my urine &

there's nothing the matter with me but stubbornness. Bound to happen in a day or two.

Last night at two o'clock the place was suddenly full of gay voices of young people. I couldn't imagine who'd be so gay coming to [a] hospital for an emergency operation. I never thought of a baby. The voices went away, then I heard that terrible stertorous breathing after they gave her something and that table clanked up to take her to the delivery room. It was a Caesarian—she died just as the doctor was taking off his glasses. Poor doctor! A year or two ago he operated on her husband's first wife—some trifling operation so she could have a baby. She died—nurse left sponges in or something. Everybody is saying Poor John Ross (the doctor), instead of poor husband. It was strange those gay voices in the night.

No letter. Paper wiggles so. I'm eating anything. Getting along fine. No complications whatever.

> *Love,*
> *C.*

Trenton, Kentucky, April 28, 1932
To S. W. in Rochester

Dear Sally:

Here I am neatly installed at Merry Mock as Nancy used to call it and most pleased to be here. I am still staying in bed but sitting up a good while mornings and afternoons. Going to town tomorrow to see Ted for the last time. I certainly am thankful this business is over.

Our present plan is to sail on the Stuttgart July 21. Passage, tourist third, round trip is $156. Amazingly cheap, isn't it? We are still waiting to hear from that hound, John Ransom, about the teaching job. Can't imagine why he dallies so unless he's been out of touch with his mail—like William Faulkner who wrote Allen yesterday in the most affected hand I ever saw that he hadn't opened his [mail] for three months and therefore couldn't contribute to the Southern number of Poetry which Allen ill advisedly edited.[1] W. F. is a piece of cheese. I do not say this because he spit on me that time; he just is. Too bad. He sure can write.[2]

Don't believe I will ever write anything again.

The tobacconist and his bride are doing well at Benfolly. You know I like being here so much better than there. God, it's a relief not to have to keep house! I always did love being here in the spring. The fields are unbelievably green and there is a light veil of dogwood bloom all through the woods. The country is really heavenly. Miss Carrie, by the way, issues you the most heartfelt invitation to come down—most every day she says, "Now if Miss Sally was only here . . . . ." It's only me that tells you not to come.

I didn't have any ether dream at all this time. I usually have some terrible metaphysical dream that involves infinity and it comes to me piece by piece over a period of a year or so, but this time I was just telling John Ross to give me the ether a little slower and the next thing I knew Ted was grinning at me like a Cheshire cat beside the bed and I couldn't realize that it was all over. It was just a section of time dropped out of consciousness. I suppose your physical condition has a lot to do with your reactions to ether. Allen says I already have a much better color and I notice I can drink coffee now without ill effects. I guess my appendix had affected my digestion for some time.

You cannot stand any more of this typing.[3]

love, caroline

1. The issue of *Poetry* was Vol. XL, No. 2 (May, 1932). Allen included poems from Warren, Davidson, Bishop, Fletcher, and others, besides his own.

2. Faulkner did not share the Agrarians' feeling for the South. His was different. Years later Caroline reviewed *The Portable Faulkner* favorably in the New York *Times*. He sent her a box of roses with his card.

3. The typewriter ribbon was worn, and the letter was becoming increasingly faint.

Trenton, May 3, 1932
To S. W. in Rochester

Dear Sally:

I now sit up and perform a little on the typewriter—I assure you it entails no abdominal strain. Your letter, just arrived, sounds rather forbidding. I hope to the Lord I don't have any adhesions. Perhaps I won't, being rather rugged.

I really am taking things easy—have been in bed most of today. Yesterday—I suppose you will say it was imprudent—I attended a birth-

day party, Cousin Kitty's eighty ninth anniversary. The honoree who
looks like a little brown witch could not reconcile herself to the fact that
she was eighty nine and had all those grandchildren. Otherwise it was a
pleasant affair. She bore up well during the onslaught of the first eight
grandchildren but when seven more appeared she said "Now whose children are those? Sweet little things, aren't they?" Finally she sidled up to
me and whispered "If somebody would just give me the name of my
oldest son I could say the names of all my children" and sure enough she
did when I had started her off with "Robert Tutweiler." It must be rather
a happy state—no memory, no regrets and it's rather reassuring to think
that four sons and two daughters and all their progeny can slip off the
mind so easily. It was rather annoying to Miss Carrie who being still in
possession of all her faculties sat grimly beside Cousin Kitty saying at intervals "That's your son Henry's boy" and so on. "And who is Henry?"
Cousin Kitty would query brightly.

We expect to hear from John Ransom almost any day now. He was
waiting to take the matter up with the principal who had not returned
from vacation.

If you don't go abroad with us you *must* come down, and I have
decided now to let you come to Merry Mont. One great difficulty is in
process of being removed—the flies descend in swarms, the screens being
very casually arranged. But Allen is fixing the screens in a fairly workman-
like manner and I believe we'll be able to keep 'em out when he's finished.
This leaves only one difficulty—the uncertainty of Miss Carrie's temper
but as a matter of fact she rarely gets annoyed at her favorites—and you
are one of 'em. Allen, too, is in high favor just now on account of his
putting locks on all the doors. It is so long since even a minor repair has
been made at Merry Mont that she is as pleased as a child over her new
locks. I really think she will bear up nobly under the invasion. She bore
up last time and we were here two or three months. Her only disapproving remark was to the effect that it was strange that people with good
blood in them could keep a room as dirty as I did. But I myself have often
marveled at how dirty I can keep a room so I wasn't hurt.

I really think you could stand Merry Mont pretty well. After you're
here awhile you sort of settle into the place. The dirt which appalls at first
comes to seem an advantage. One simply picks one's way about over stacks
of old magazines—and it is a relief never to have to think of cleaning up.

I am really quite addicted to the place—I much prefer it to Benfolly.

. . . .

      Allen is ready to go to the mail.

Love,

C.

      [added as a postscript]

      "Summer Dust"[1] is being translated into the German. I think it will be a scream. Paul Rosenfeld & one or two other New Yorkers told me they found it quite incomprehensible—and what could a German make of it?

      Hart Crane jumped overboard from a steamer going from Vera Cruz to New York.[2] Malcolm telegraphed that he did it in a fit of despondency. He left a note saying the world had no place for poets. Poor Hart! It was the inevitable end to such a life as his, I suppose.

      Here's a piece Bandler wrote about Penhally.[3]

    1. A short story of Caroline's dealing with relations between blacks and whites. Only years later did northerners begin to study these. The story is more understandable now.

    2. Crane committed suicide April 27, 1932.

    3. Bernard Bandler, "Land and Tradition," *Hound and Horn*, III (1932), 493–98.

Trenton, May 4, 1932
To S. W. in Rochester

Dearest Sally:

      A cablegram has just come from John Ransom. He says the Carnegie foundation is sending a professor over so it seems there's little chance for Allen to get the job. This means then that we spend our time in France. Now can't you come since the summer can prolong itself indefinitely.

      Our plan is to go to Toulon. I had a letter from Ford the other day. He and Janice expect to go to New York in October or November so we'll probably take over their place as we did once before. He says in the meantime we'd better have him make reservations for us as every farmhouse is filled up by July. Let us know if we are to make reservations for you too.

      Our party has been growing while we've been dallying. We're driving up in the Ford and are taking it over. Chink and Lyle Lanier and possibly Marion Meriwether are coming with us to stay until September when their jobs call them home. We also have in tow a jeune fille of sixteen who is going to school in Switzerland next year. However she will be no encumbrance—we are to ship her to Switzerland as soon as we land in Paris. Then we intend to drive down to Toulon. I had been saving a place in the car for you when Manny suddenly decided she might go. She hasn't had a vacation in God knows when and leads the most desolate life in that girls' school and hates the whole thing so thoroughly I jumped at the idea of her going. However it isn't at all sure that she will.

Now as to reservation we have two cabins, the whole lot of us on the Stuttgart, sailing July 21. We got them minimum rate ($164 round trip, including port taxes) by crowding up like this. There are six and a half of us (including Nancy) and eight berths. If you want to get in on the minimum rate you can take one of the berths in the female cabin. Otherwise it will cost you something like $190. We will be delighted [to] have you share our quarters if you care to do so. Needless to say this is tourist third.

The reservation is already made for you automatically (they can't put anybody else in with us, you see). If you decide to come along and share our quarters let us know and send a cheque for forty dollars to

The Travel Department
Nashville and American Trust Company
Nashville

Or send the cheque to Allen and he will forward it to them. If you write them direct address Granville Bourne and tell him you're joining our party.

Allen says tell you we're getting cabin class staterooms at tourist prices by engaging them early.

Do let us know if all this sounds alluring, You really must come. We are going to Toulon, first because Ford and Janice are there and second because I don't want Allen to spend another winter in Paris but Toulon would be all right for you too, I'm sure. Ford says it is delightful except when the mistral blows and that he assures me is very good for your health. However I think I shall just lie low those days—I loathe wind. Only they say it comes down the chimney and seeks you out.

Love and let us know that you're coming along, caroline.

I'm feeling pretty good. Can't stand up straight yet but so far no trouble at all.

I wrote yes, I would go with them. I naturally wanted to be with the Tates, and I was still being advised to spend the winter in a warm climate. I vastly preferred the south of France to Florida.

Trenton, end of May, 1932
To S. W. in Rochester

Dearest Sally:

I am certainly glad to know that you are really going with us—something final about that cheque for reservations. It's the Norddeutscher Lloyd, don't know why I didn't think to mention the line, thought you'd know by the name but the truth is I have very little sense these days. Anyhow I hopes we'll all get off July 21 and as they say in the advertising literature "leave all care behind." There is something about putting the ocean between you and your relatives. I do not think there will be many Meriwethers along. Manny has about given up the idea of going. She is the only one whom I'd consider taking. There'll be room for you in the car going down, that is, there'll be Allen and Nancy and me on the front seat and Chink and Lyle Lanier and you on the back or some other arrangement. We'll have to send the luggage, except small bags some other way.

I had a long letter from Ford the other day. He had been too depressed to write for some time, having his usual troubles with publishers and then setting out on a vacation and having all his five hundred franc notes blown away from him rounding a corner of the castle of the good King Rene at Tarascon if that's where it is. He and Janice talk of going to New York in the fall. In that case we might take over their place, though I hate the thought of housekeeping. They have a good femme de menage he says.

I am so glad you are going!

Allen liked what you said about his poems—and why shouldnt he?

But he thought it was all very perceptive, aside from the nice things you said about the poems. He is up to his ears just now, trying to write two articles (memorial) on Hart Crane. He has been asked to write a poem for the Confederate Veterans reunion at Richmond in June and is appalled at the idea of writing a poem to order.[1] The Ode to the Confederate Dead is the best poem he ever wrote—they ought to use that but they want some[thing] new. I don't expect the veterans will like it much after it's written.

I must get to work. I am completely demoralized by these months of semi-invalidism. My side feels quite whole now and I can stand up straight but my bladder keeps acting up in a very trying way.

Your letter is lost in [a] vast tangle of letters. I can't remember if there was any other information I ought to give you. We sail from New York, of course.

I *must* get to work. Love, caroline

[added as a postscript]

I am going to ask—in desperation—what is probably the greatest favor I've ever asked of you. I've asked it in vain of Allen. It's to read the ms I'm sending. Allen's tried it twice and each time breaks down and says he simply can't. It's a fairy story which I've contrived and concocted purely with the idea of making some money. I've tried it out on Nancy and she shrieks with joy at what seem to me the most horrible spots. Now I can't decide whether to try it on Perkins of Scribner's or not. He is enthusiastic about the idea of a fairy story by me but I think he really expects something. What [I] want to know is whether you think sending him a thing like [this] wouldn't injure my standing with him. It is so dull. If you find you simply can't go it why don't try but if you do wade through tell me what you think. I simply can't decide whether to send it on or not. Of course I hate to think of throwing away all that work. My idea, too, was that I might avoid starving if I could only learn to write a juvenile, say one a year. Nothing else I write brings in anything and I've got to do something.

I've just discovered that I left the carbon copy at Benfolly so you get out of the ordeal of reading it.

1. "Hart Crane and the American Mind," *Poetry*, XL (1932), 210–16; "In Memoriam:

Hart Crane," *Hound and Horn*, V (1932), 612–19. The poem, commissioned by the Richmond *Times-Dispatch*, became "To the Lacedemonians."

Trenton, June 1, 1932
To S. W. in Rochester

Dearest Sally:

I enclose a letter I've just received from Ford. Write me what you think of his various proposals? Shall we take a villa together or shall we just get lodgings? If we got a femme de menage I suppose the housekeeping wouldn't be much trouble. The villa at the bottom of his garden *might* be as cheap as the others when you take the garage into account. We'll have to have a garage for the car. I suppose we might wait till we get there and look around. Anyhow let me know whether you favor taking a villa or just getting lodgings. Of course there's no reason to make a decision just now. We may have to stay at Cannes a week or two with our friends, the Laniers, who have come over for a vacation and don't fancy Toulon much.

Another idea has just struck me. If we decide to take the villa at the bottom of Ford's garden (sounds like a poem of Humbert Wolfe's) we might let the Laniers crowd in for the short time they'd be there. And not go to Cannes, I mean to stay.

Still another idea: if we wanted to stay in Paris longer than they did we might let them take our car and go on down to Cannes which they feel they must see, then bring it back to us when they got through with it—if the authorities aren't too strict about driving licenses and so on. I believe, though, they are.

Oh well, most any way suits me.
                                        Anyhow write,
                                        love C.

Trenton, June 15, 1932
To S. W. in Rochester

Dearest Sally:

I have been wanting to write you every day but I have been up to my ears in odd jobs and have had to lend Allen my typewriter besides.

I wish we could come by Rochester but it's impossible. We'll just make it to NY in time for sailing as it is—that is, we'll be there two nights and the accompanying day and a half before sailing but both of us have to see our publishers and as many other people as we can work in during that short time.

My aunt, Margaret Campbell—she lives in Chattanooga—has been trying to persuade us to leave Nancy with her. I hardly know what to do. Living conditions would be better for Nancy, doubtless—it is rather difficult to arrange things so she has her school, her friends, proper food and so [on]—but I have to consider my aunt a little. Her youngest daughter is eleven. I suppose Nancy would fit into their routine fairly well. They live on Missionary Ridge with a lovely garden for her to play in, a good school near and so on. Pidie,[1] my aunt, is horribly sentimental about Nancy, as she considers her her grandchild but a little spoiling wouldn't ruin her. I would feel as safe about her as I possibly could. Still it is hard to put the ocean between us. On the other hand I could do a hell of a lot more work. If we do leave Nancy I suppose Allen and I had better take pension. God, I'd love to get out of the cares of a menage for a year!

I reckon we'll just have to wait till we get over there to see what we'll do. . . .

It is certainly fine you have all those clothes. Please bring them along if they won't weight you down too much. I haven't bought any clothes and don't intend to—for what Bonrod calls the main and simple reason. I'll get what I have to get on my second Guggenheim installment, so I won't have much baggage, and can help you convey your wardrobe if you're overladen. About bags. There'll be four of you in one cabin, perhaps. I've told the jeune fille, Dorothy Ann, to try to have only one bag in the cabin. She seems very obedient to my orders, calls me Ma'am and Allen Sir. Let's hope she'll continue so amenable. She's really a sweet child, very Spanish looking, descended from hardy Scotchmen, don't see how she gets that way.

The party will consist of:
Allen and me
Chink and Lyle Lanier (man and wife)
Dorothy Ann (aetat 16)
Sally Wood
Maybe Marion Meriwether

Maybe Nancy Tate

I'm used to sharing quarters with Lyle and Chink. I suppose I'll stay with Allen and Lyle and either Nancy or Chink and you gals in the other cabin. You may regard Manny as a nuisance not knowing her, but I know you will like her. She is a darling sweet creature and needs this outing horribly—if only we can persuade her to take it.

Will you be coming up to New York any time before we sail? If you do and *are* staying at a hotel would you mind letting the jeune fille stay at the same place? All of the people who have been down here to see us have offered to put us up when we come to NY and as we'll be short of money we'll probably take them up if the offer still holds good. But they'll probably all be out of town. I wouldn't consider staying with Stark Young for a moment. He is full of antique sofas and cabinets that used to belong to countesses. I wouldn't trust myself among them, much less Nancy.

I have just read somewhere where Zelda Fitzgerald has a novel coming out this fall. I thought she was in a sanitarium with a complete nervous breakdown. How do people get the work done that they get done. I certainly hope you'll get that book off your chest while we're over there. I imagine Toulon will be a good place to work. This Merry Mont is no place for *me* to work. Poor Ma has had a regular house party all summer. Her two daughters and the Tates and last week Dad came up from Florida and spared us a week before going to Estill Springs. He was in spendid form. We had a great time sitting on the porch all day and talking. I fear Allen would have been completely demoralized if Dad had stayed longer. He was getting that care free spirit to a pronounced degree. They went fishing every afternoon. We could not even get them to attend Aunt Molly Ferguson's funeral. Allen would have gone but Dad instilled the spirit of rebellion in him by announcing grandly: "Cousin Molly Ferguson is no more kin to me than a catfish. Why should I go to her funeral? No, I am going fishing. I haven't many more years to live and I have already preached four thousand funerals and some of them were the very devil." When I pointed out that Allen could go even if he didn't he put up a pathetic plea for Allen's society—"We hold high concourse on that pond," says he, "I am starved for intellectual companionship. Down in Florida I never see anybody but niggers"—as if he didn't prefer the society of niggers!

It was a great blow to Dad when Allen received a hundred dollar prize from the Poetry Society of South Carolina the other day. He took Allen's book and pondered over it all one morning, then announced "He couldn't write a poem if he was going to be hung for it" and recited "Hail to the Chief Who in Triumph Advances" as an example of pure poetry. By the way Allen did get the poem written for the Confederate Reunion. I can't imagine why they asked him! It's pretty good too. I'll enclose a copy if he has one.

Nancy is eight pounds over weight. I have lost fifteen since January but I am really feeling pretty good now. Margaret was doubtless impressed by my posture when she saw me. I couldn't stand up then and did look very queer.

There were many other things I had to say but they elude me. I am writing hastily on Allen's typewriter while he fools with the car. He is dividing the morning between the car and Elinor Wylie whom he is trying to write about for the NR.[2] When he gets stuck on Elinor he goes out and works on the car. I am trying to make Nancy enough clothes to last for a year if I do decide to leave her. It takes me two days to make a dress. They really look right sweet. I made a little blue one with puff sleeves the other day and now I am working on a lavender one with a bertha and after that I tackle a blue organdie. I love to sew but you can't sew very well and have any kind of prose style.

We'll bring all our sweat shirts and woolen stockings.

Marion Henry's father has had a stroke of some kind—he went to sleep driving the car. His mind is affected and he is terribly broken physically. He looks like a man of seventy five. They have to have an attendant with him all the time and may have to send him to a sanitarium. I feel so sorry for him. Marion is trying to farm—a thousand acres, two different farms. It is a big job. But I think it is good for her to have something to do. She takes it very seriously.

I must get back to my sewing.

Next time you write send me Ford's cable address which is in that letter. I forgot to take it down. I might have to cable him.

I'm getting rather excited over going now that the time draws near. I am so glad you are going with us!

Love, c

[added as a postscript]
If Dorothy Ann stayed in the same hotel you wouldn't have to

pay any attention to her, of course. We'd look after her except for the sleeping.

1. *Pidie*, the Negro abbreviation for pie dough, means sweet. It was the right name for this aunt.

2. A short review of her *Collected Poems*; it appeared in *New Republic*, September 7, 1932, p. 107.

Trenton, June 21, 1932
To S. W. in Rochester

———————————————————————————————————

You are quite right about its being better not to make any decisions till we get there—Allen and I had both come to the same conclusions, especially if we leave Nancy. God knows I loathe a menage. It would be grand to get up in the morning and go to work without even thinking about dishes.

I, too, would like to be on the shore awhile before settling down for the winter. The Laniers are amenable, amiable creatures and of a most economical bent. They'd as soon go to Cassis or any other place we went —only they do want some bathing.

Allen says it's time for you to send the rest of your money for the passage.

The steamship agent informs me that he has received a deposit on Manny's fare but we've had no word from her. I rather think she's going but am not sure. If I had had any idea of her going in the first place I'd never have hooked up with the Laniers. Dorothy Ann, I must say, was wished on me while I was too weak to resist—you can't lie flat on your back just after being catheterized and say "No, Madam, I will not take your daughter to Europe and futhermore I have always thought that you were a complete mess and should have been bashed in the head long ago." Ah well, it will all arrange itself, more or less satisfactorily, I feel sure.

I do hope you're better now. I think the winter on the Riviera will probably be good for you.

· ·

The two main hurdles I have to clear now are leaving Nancy at Chattanooga—it will take manoeuvering to go off gaily with her approving—and that damn lecture at Monteagle. They say the old ladies all wield palm leaf fans and never change their expression no matter what you say—I'm chiefly afraid of being left entirely without voice.

Ma, Loulie, and Margaret Campbell had a nice day with Margaret Meriwether Mc(Gilli)Cuddy the other day. We consider that Ma is bearing up nobly when she doesn't voice her disapproval. Really, I think it's Loulie (her daughter) gets on her nerves worse than the Tates. She dotes on Allen and me too, me being named for her. But Loulie tells her she is too old to do this and that and cannot cook mutton when all her life she has been renowned as a mutton cook and all that sort of thing. I really sympathize with the old lady. It looks sometimes as if Loulie had her down, but she nearly always rallies. She observed the other day: "Loulie would be a bonanza to a feeble minded person but she ain't much comfort to me."

I will let you know definitely about Manny as soon as I possibly can. The poor child can't know herself for a day or two now. Her mother had an operation this spring—a small skin cancer removed. It has healed all right but she fancies there is another small one coming. John Ross whom I took her to yesterday can't say. She goes this afternoon to Nashville to the skin specialist who operated. If this is another cancer I'm afraid Manny just won't go. It is not the kind Mother had—the doctor says it is not diffusible through the system. Still if another one just keeps coming they will feel sort of hopeless. I'll know about this in a day or two, though.

Allen now informs me severely that if I'm going to lecture on Southern novelists I ought to know something about them. What do you, for instance, know about Charles Egbert Craddock or George W. Cable? Not a damn thing, probably. Well, neither do I. I can read up on 'em, though, while I'm at Chattanooga. Anyway I have the right dress to wear —as my aunt says it looks like you had better clothes in your wardrobe, and that is enough for me to aspire to.

I think we are going to stay with Bernard Bandler in NY, the awfully nice, serious and learned young man who is one of the editors of the Hound and Horn. I want you to meet him. He says he wants to throw some sort of farewell party for us which will be all right, only there won't be many of our old cronies in town—and some of the cronies, alas, are cronies no more. . . . I never could abide Louise Bogan and now she's written this venomous review of Allen's poems I shall take advantage of it.[1] She's always getting tight and saying to me "Caroline, *why* don't you like me?" Heretofore I've never had anything to say.

Your friend, Larry Kohn fancies that I made him a gift of a copy of Penhally. Deluded lad. Shall I undeceive him or you? I don't even have a copy myself—he flatters me.

I'm sorry Little May's renter is such a hell hound. They nearly always are, of course. I expect she'd like Penhally. All the people who are the kind of people I thought I was panning so hard tell me they love the book and find it such a true picture of life in the old South.

Have to give Allen this typewriter for a while. Courage. We'll soon be aboard the lugger—thank God there is nobody in France whom I can call Cousin,

Love,

C.

1. The review, of *Poems, 1928–1931,* appeared in the *New Republic,* March 30, 1932, pp. 186–87. It was snide about the parochial Fugitives and condescending towards Allen's "genuine" talent, too often, Bogan said, lamed by "determined incoherence," perverse ostentation, and sterile vocabulary.

We met in New York. The jeune fille did not stay in a hotel with me. I think some relative was with her. Neither did the Tates stay in Bernard Bandler's apartment. Another one, big enough to contain me too, was offered them. It seemed strange to be in Greenwich Village again.

Bernard Bandler did give his party. Lincoln Kirstein, the other editor of the Hound and Horn, *was there. Malcolm Cowley came, I remember, and a young man from Rochester who wrote for the* New Yorker, *Robert Coates. The discussion became so interesting far into the night that no one wanted to leave.*

When we had completed our rather dull crossing on the Stuttgart, *we were thankful to feel under our feet the solid streets of Paris, and they led almost immediately to the Closerie des Lilas. What was our surprise to see at a sidewalk table Bernard Bandler and the girl who had been with him in New York! They were there to continue the conversation.*

Television and radio have made it seem impossible that talk could be so interesting that people had to cross the Atlantic—by boat then—to go on with it. But so it was. I believe we even stayed in Paris a little longer than we had planned to finish this conversation.

Allen enjoyed driving in France because, he said, the French system was like his own. There were very few rules. "You just do the best you can." One had to be quick and intuitive, especially in Paris.

*Our goal was Toulon, where Ford and Janice had a villa, and somehow
we all arrived there and set up housekeeping in a rented villa called Villa Les
Hortensias, quite near Ford and Janice. We had a Corsican femme de ménage
who paid much more attention to monsieur la poète than to Caroline and
me—as did our landlady. The plan was for the three of us to take turns getting
meals. Allen didn't mind his turn, but abhorred loneliness while about it, so he
had to be accompanied.*

*Every night either the Fords came over to our villa, we went to theirs, or
we all visited a restaurant together. The talk was constantly about novel writing. Henry James took the place of Jefferson Davis and Robert E. Lee. Referring
to Galsworthy as "poor Jack," Ford said he was only interested in country weekends where the host gave all his guests candles to go up to bed.*

*(Ford was highly regarded by the French because he considered the bal-
anced sentence, the sound of words and phrases, important. My friend in Vence,
Monique, wrote prose as if she were composing music. There were exceptions,
though—Proust, for example.)*

*It is not remarkable that Allen, surrounded by all this, turned to fiction.
He wrote a short story, "The Immortal Woman,"[1] which Donald Davidson
found "repulsively Jamesian," and he began a novel, "Ancestors in Exile," which
was never finished, though he used parts of it in* The Fathers, *his only novel,
published in 1938.*

*Caroline wrote "Tom Rivers," one of my favorites among her short stories,
there. She believed that with serious fiction one should not be able to tell whether
the writer was a man or a woman. "Tom Rivers," however, on account of its
subject and the way it was handled, gives the impression that it could only have
been written by a man. Caroline did a lot of writing from the man's point of
view, and one could not tell the sex of the author, but "Tom Rivers" seemed
different to me. Quite a feat.*

Ford was engaged in writing his autobiography, It Was the Nightingale, *published in 1933. I was still involved in World War I and the way it had
changed the life of everyone caught in it. Malcolm Cowley was the only one of
the Tates' close friends who had experienced it firsthand.*

*People who received Guggenheim awards had a hard time of it really.
They were supposed to go to some interesting foreign place and then largely
ignore it while writing English, not the local language, about something already in their minds. Being at a distance from one's subject helps to get it in
focus, but it can also prove distracting. Allen was having a hard time with
Robert E. Lee.*

During the summer, the Tates and I went to a beach to swim. Ford said that it was a plage populaire *and that we would catch germs from the people who went there. But the Mediterranean proved to be antiseptic.*

Ford received an invitation from someone he called "the hope of British painting," Sir Francis Rose, to visit him in a village above Cagnes. He naturally wished to take Janice and the Tates, and Caroline decided we should all go. The house we visited looked simple, but it was obvious that no expense had been spared and also that men keep house better than women if they wish to. Not being used to England, I did not realize at first that Rose's Lime Juice played a part; the connection became clearer when we realized we were also staying with a Guinness, married to a South American painter, and then met Miss Hennessey. It became a special milieu. The Spanish painter, Picabia, arrived the following day, very talkative. But the special guest that evening, besides Ford, was a Bourbon, who had some rather distant hope of the French throne, and his much older wife. When she turned out to be a Hapsburg, Ford simply withdrew. Caroline said, "Look at him. He thinks you mustn't talk to a Hapsburg." This ancestral scruple left the old lady alone, for the younger people were amusing themselves elsewhere, but Caroline and Allen, whose southern manners made them take quite the opposite view, leapt into the breach.

Allen bowed and said, "Madame, your relative, the Comte de Paris, was right about the Battle of Gettysburg." And then he explained it to her at length. Whether she had ever heard about the War Between the States or not, the Hapsburg lady was pleased. We chatted with her for some time. At one point, the august personage, glancing around and observing a fat lady in slacks, remarked, "The pyjama does not do for everyone."

When we returned to Toulon, Caroline said, "I accepted the invitation because I thought it would amuse you." It did.

However, in Toulon everything was fenced in, and I began to crave the prettier country around Vence, where one could take walks across the fields. Allen had said that he needed the library in Paris to go on with his book on Lee. We decided to give up the villa.

I had been given a very small puppy, half Cairn and half Jack Russell terrier, who made the Villa Les Hortensias more amusing. One evening when we were all sitting around the fireplace, our drinks on the floor beside us, the puppy moved around quietly, trying to get his head into each glass. Caroline said, "He's just like the little boy in Sanctuary,[2] *who went around finishing all the ladies' drinks. You'll have to call him Uncle Bud." That was his name thenceforth, in two languages, for the fifteen years of his life.*

When our rent at the villa expired, Uncle Bud, my typewriter, and I took off for Vence. The Tates packed everything in their car and started north. I think it was just before this that Ford organized the famous picnic at Cassis, which inspired Allen's poem "The Mediterranean."[3] *Caroline's letter about it has been lost.*

Since the Tates had no apartment in view in Paris and had to live cheaply, I gave them the name and address of the concierge of my brother's former studio on the Rue Daguerre, which had indeed been cheap.

37 Denfert-Rochereau, Paris, November, 1932
To S. W. in Vence

Your M. La Person[4] is a charming man, just the man I'd like for my landlord though a trifle perfidious, I fear. Just as we got in the Ford to leave Cap Brun—in the midst in fact of the affecting farewells of Madame Lamure[5] and Allen—comes a letter from M. L. P. saying one of the small studios is vacant. I was so charmed at the thought of having some definite place to go. The thought sustained me all the way on the trip which was hellish but when we got here the renter had decided to stay another month. We spent one day hunting in the drizzling rain—it is that petite cuisine that is so difficult to find. But rents have fallen amazingly. You can get the same salon and little bedroom that we paid 700 for at the Hotel de l'Odeon for five hundred with privilege of cooking a bit—on the first floor, too. We can find you a place easily when you come up. Or we can put you up here as long as you can stand the cramped quarters. Big bed in the studio and small bed in the bedroom (balcony). Allen fell in love with this place—five hundred a month—and says he is sure he can work here so I thought we'd try it a month. It really is a nice place. Lowenfels,[6] real estate agent in his off moments—wants us to turn it over to him when we leave and let him rent it for seven hundred. It's a studio—you simply can't find that little kitchen unattached to a studio, it seems—a long good sized room with the tiny kitchen and a balcony bedroom. Unfortunately the last tenant has left a large mural but you get used to it in time. His other canvases are a problem but we sort of step around them. We're in a back court; the house in front has been done over and is pretty swell but this back part is quite unimproved—no running water and one of those stand up affairs for cabinet. There is a gas stove, though, thank God. We may get in at Daguerre later—I fell in love with the neighborhood.[7] All those wonderful shops! They really are grand. In the meantime we're trying to feel enough settled here to get out the old manuscripts.

. . . .

We wished for you on the trip. It was marvelous—as far as Valence when a cold fog took us by the throat and hasn't yet let us go. (No, you couldn't stand Paris now.) I have not seen the sun since we left Valence. But the country coming up was incredibly beautiful. We stopped at Arles, and Tarascon and spent the night at Avignon—at your Louvre hotel which certainly is fine. Have you ever seen those Roman tombs at Arles? An alley of poplars, the ground covered now with bright yellow leaves, milk trucks and everything else thundering through and those rows of tombs on either side. And you can almost make out the inscriptions. It is somehow much more impressive than the arena. That was really the last fine day we had, at Arles and the next morning at Avignon when we saw the Palace of the Popes. The fog got so bad a little farther on that we had to crawl along at ten miles an hour, almost a whole day. It is not at all cold here now, just that usual feeling of a light drizzle about to set in.

I must write to the Fords and Mme Lamure and perhaps take a look at Ote Mortimer[8] who seems rather remote by this time.

Write and let us know how things go. Love, c.

1. *Hound and Horn*, VI (1933), 592–609.
2. William Faulkner, *Sanctuary* (1931).
3. See Radcliffe Squires, *Allen Tate: A Literary Biography* (New York, 1971), 118.
4. M. La Personne, concierge at my brother's former studio.
5. Owner of our villa in Toulon.
6. Walter Lowenfels (1897–1976), American poet, newspaper editor, and Marxist critic.
7. Mme. La Personne called it *mi ouvrier mi artiste*.
8. A character in Caroline's novel *The Garden of Adonis* (1937), which she had begun writing in Toulon. It was interrupted there by the short story "Tom Rivers" and later, in Paris, by "Old Red."

rue Denfert-Rochereau, Paris, November 23, 1932
To S. W. in Vence

I was just sitting here thinking uncharitable thoughts about you when the concierge brought your letter in. I had been really worried over not hearing from you, divided between fears that you were sick and hopes that you were sunk into your book so deep you didn't note the passing of

time. I'm relieved to know you haven't come down with bubonic plague
or anything.

But business before pleasure as Willy said on that immortal occasion when Allen asked her to take the trash out in the yard and burn it.
. . . .
Vence turning out a good place to work I believe you can get the whole
thing done before March 1. It's going to be a long weary winter. I feel it
settling down—I have hopes of getting my book done before April.

It's funny—here we all are, each in his small corner—K. A. writing
in Bale waiting to know where they are going,[1]—you in Vence and us
here. Our corner here is rather a hole but I like it. The studio itself is
charming, rather imposing. The petite cuisine is terrible, the dank balcony
bedroom impossible except as a dressing room. You can take baths in
great comfort; the heat all goes up there of course. The dirtiest place, the
whole thing that ever I saw in my life but we really like it. We're paying
too much, of course—five hundred. Allen advanced the usual arguments
—you can work better in a room that suits you and so on; you save
money not going to cafes—for once it all proves true. We are both working like hell, have settled down into one of those routines in which people
do produce books. It's funny. God—or the devil somehow creates these
islands about once a year for us, the only time you seem to get anything
done. There is not one soul in Paris I feel even a passing interest in. It's
marvelous. Allen works here at home in the morning. We have lunch. I go
out to the market—a swell market round the corner—come home, sleep
till two o'clock, get up and go at it again, till five when I walk briskly
around the court eight or ten times, come in and get supper. After supper
we work some more and so to bed. If it will only last! We spent one
evening at the Closerie with John Bishop,[2] had dinner at the Falstaff one
evening with the Bishops, had dinner with Ruth Harris;[3] Ruth Harris
and Stella [Bowen] came here to tea and that is the extent of our social
life in Paris. Oh yes we had Thanksgiving dinner with of all people the
Lowenfels. The Pilgrim feast would have gone unnoticed by me but the
Lowenfels suggested we chip in on a turkey so we did. Lillian cooked a
grand dinner. George Davis[4] was there and a professional (lady) cousin
of Proust's. I've met several of Proust's lady friends—they are invariably
incredibly vulgar women. This woman wrote a very nice article in Harper's once: My Cousin Marcel Proust. Some journalist must have put it in

shape for her. George Davis says he will come to see us if we will send him a pneumatique the day we want him. He'll wait a long time for that pneumatique!

I wish I could see Uncle Bud's spots. They must be charming. I am regretting now that I didn't bring Cinders along as Cecil wanted me to.[5] She could run in the courtyard here and accompany me to market. Give Uncle Bud eighteen kisses on his wet nose. I miss him so much.

The weather has been mild, that gray rainy mild weather of November up till this morning when it turned very nipping. The shop keepers all had their rabbit shoes when I rushed out a minute ago to buy some coal.[6] We get sun when there is any sun through our enormous window and it is nice to be able to step out in the court any minute for some air but it is like being in another world from Toulon—I don't even feel that I am in Paris. The Communists have their meetings in the back of the Bal Bullier right across the street. We stepped out last night to the corner and found the street swarming with policemen, two I should say to each comrade.

I must now get back to work. I wrote nearly three thousand words yesterday. The glow of conscious virtue persisted even this morning. I probably won't get anything done for another day or two. However it is a relief to be able to work again.

Allen sends his love. We miss you. . . .

       Love, c.

[written as a second letter and mailed with the preceding]

Your second letter has just arrived. For heaven's sake don't worry about Mrs. Biddleston and Ruth Wilde.[7] You can't do anything. Mrs. B. would have had cancer no doubt if she'd stayed with her husband. Ruth Wilde is the one that can sink you. Don't let her.

We are getting along all right. The resourceful Lowenfels kept insisting that we could get money ahead on our letter of credit. He took us to his bank yesterday and they advanced us some money if we opened an account—I never dreamed you could open an account with a shoe string. I paid the Fords some money I owed them and sent Nancy some money, long overdue, and kept just what I figured we could get along on till Jan. 1. . . . I am so anxious to get my debts paid. At the same time we've decided on a plan that will cut us down a little. Allen has just written one NR article ($50) and thinks now he won't write another one till he has finished the book. I believe it is best, even for the unfortunate debtors, for him to do that. He will have a clear stretch from now till spring and if he gets going he can write that book in three months. As soon as he is through he will have to haul off and write some articles. He can always do that but he can't do it and write the book at the same time and this next few months—before the Guggenheim runs out—seem to be the only chance he has to write that book.

Don't worry about our health. Of course there is no telling when flu will lay any of us low but we are getting along fine so far, eating very well on very little. The market round the corner is marvelous. I save a few sous on everything I buy and as I get my exercise walking around looking the stalls over I figure it's all to the good.

1. Katherine Anne Porter's husband, Eugene Pressly, was in the diplomatic service.
2. John Peale Bishop (1891–1944), American poet and novelist and close friend of Allen's.
3. A girl whom we had rescued from a certain amount of trouble in Toulon.
4. Perhaps the best-selling novelist (1906–1957), later fiction editor of magazines such as *Vanity Fair* and *Harper's Bazaar*.
5. Cinders was Uncle Bud's mother, a pure Cairn. Caroline was a trifle lost without an animal. Cecil Wright, our British painter friend, had been living near Toulon.
6. These studios were always heated with coal stoves. One bought coal in little stores labeled Coal and Wine, always kept by an Auvergnat.
7. English friends of mine from Vence.

Hôtel Fleurus, Paris, December 1, 1932
To S. W. in Vence

Dearest Sally:

It's just dawned on me that Joyeux Noel is almost upon us. Well, I wish you could be in Paris for say two nights—Katherine Anne and Gene [Pressly] and Allen and I have decided to splurge ourselves at the Cochon au Lait Christmas Eve. But with Nancy off my mind Christmas seems very simple to me. She is to have a rubber doll—a new kind that you can wash in a tub and as she wrote Santa "a rakin chair" (Rocking). All bought in Chattanooga. Since this is Uncle Bud's first Christmas don't you think he ought to have an extra nice bone?

Speaking of dogs we were taking a turn in the gardens the other day and I saw streaking towards us an oversized white French poodle and one of those Mexican toy terriers—chi—what do you call them? "My God, look at that" said I, meaning the remarkable pair of dogs. Allen having an eye more for the ladies said "Yes, it's Gertrude Stein" and so it was.[1] She stopped and had a chat. The toy terrier proved to be "Lord Byron," brother to Francis Rose's "Squeak." Gertrude was surprised to hear that it was me and not Allen who had the Guggenheim this time. "You?" she says "And what can you do?" "I'm trying to write a novel" I rejoins meekly. When you come up I do want to take you there. She will treat you with great contempt on account of your sex but you can see her Picassos and it will be worth going. She never addresses a remark to the women and it is rather nice, you can just wander around and look at her pictures. She is putting her money on Francis Rose by the way—the whole top row of her studio is Rose.[2] She must have twenty of his pictures. One portrait of her is to say the least remarkable.

We are now moved into the Hotel Fleurus, thank God. We have a fine large light room and pay sixty five francs a day for everything for the two of us. Don't you think that is remarkably cheap? I found that I simply couldn't run that apartment as cheaply and God knows it is a relief to get out of the housework. I used to start doing the housework at four o'clock in the afternoon the minute I finished writing and I hardly got through before Allen came in ravenous for dinner. Then I had to get what air and exercise I got after dark. But here I can run out in the [Luxembourg] gardens for a turn while it is still light. It makes a lot of difference.

. . . .

The Fords say they are coming up January 15. Janice is very outraged with Victorine who hangs on to her job with them and charges a franc more than other people pay a day. Janice blames it on the children. "People rush around having children" she writes "and then their friends have to support them. I would not feel that I could afford a child." Speaking of children that people have rushed around having poor little John Untermeyer[3] has been quite ill at the American Hospital. He had a fever of 105 or thereabouts for four or five days and the doctors had no idea what the trouble was except that they eliminated appendicitis and pneumonia. Poor Virginia has been frantic, of course. His fever went down yesterday to nearly normal, which encouraged us all a good deal. I haven't heard this morning. Must go down now and telephone. I went out there yesterday, may have to go today. She seems to have no friends here and rather leans on us. She has a cousin here. She came to the hospital, took a look at the child and fainted so she was no help of course.

From Toulon came the other day a fine knitted scarf, "Mon cher

Monsieur Tate, I send you a big birthday hug, Gisette" was the inscription.

The Fords are taking the studio we had. I have to go around there today and make some more arrangements about it. What with that and little John sick and the moving and looking for pensions and all I have got so tired I can hardly stand it and am getting no work done to boot. However I hope to settle down as soon as Christmas is over anyhow.

I am bargaining with the Guggenheims and have hopes of getting some more money. Moe[4] wrote me the other day a reproachful letter asking for my budget and so on. I wrote him up a fine budget, adding that I didn't include laundry in it because I did all the laundry myself or clothes because we bought no clothes. But he is a hard hearted devil. He may not come across after all.

Nancy has read her first book by herself, "Happy Surprise" by Mme de Segur or something. I am real proud of her. I *must* go and see about that child. I do hope you are feeling better. I don't know whether to wish you pleasant company for Christmas or not. It seems to me the more people you know the more complicated life is. Ruth Harris, for instance, all right in Toulon but a bother in Paris. Much love and do take good care of yourself and let me hear from you whenever you can. I still miss Uncle Bud! Don't you think they'd take him in at the Fleurus when you come up in the spring? How could they resist him? The Fleurus by the way turns out the best and cheapest pension and God knows we've investigated enough of them. K. A. and Gene pay much more for demi pension at the Malherbe than we pay for full pension here and have horrid dark little rooms. I found one pension run by Jamaica niggers, remarkably cheap and scrupulously clean and most appetizing odors from the kitchen but Allen balked at the niggers. Most respectable looking niggers they were too. Another place we went the white haired patron slapped himself on his prominent stomach and said "The cuisine. My God, it is I the chef of the Marquis de So and So who make the cuisine. No more to say." Meanwhile the odor of burnt meat from his cuisine was almost overpowering us—but enough of our sufferings. Looking for places to live is always just hell and that is all there is to it.

Love, c.

[added as a postscript]
. . . But just after I wrote you a thousand things turned up. I sold

Tom Rivers to the Yale Review and had to spend two days revising it, then the moving and finally John's illness. I have not had time to catch my breath till I hope this afternoon.

1. Allen had been a frequent visitor to her salon in rue de Fleurus during their previous stay in Paris.
2. Gertrude Stein had a weakness for any man whose name was Francis. This explains her partiality for Picabia, who annoyed Picasso.
3. Son of Louis Untermeyer (1885–1977), American poet, anthologist, and editor of the *American Mercury*. As Virginia Moore, Mrs. Untermeyer had written an admiring review of *Penhally* for *Nation* (October 7, 1931).
5. Henry Allen Moe, president of the Guggenheim Foundation.

Hotel Fleurus, Paris, January 13, 1933
To S. W. in Vence

Dearest Sally:

I was just lying here cursing God when your letter arrived. I have grippe and have been reduced to reading Simenon, having read everything English in the room, and French is no good for me when the old bean is as feeble as it is now. All of which is to say your letter was extremely welcome—but I wish you had given a few more descriptions of Toulon social life—the ones you did give were so diverting.[1] You didn't say much about your Christmas—I judge it wasn't very hilarious. Ours wasn't either and for diversion on Reveillon night we went over and made a few last minute preparations at Denfert-Rochereau for the Fords who had to arrive here Sunday morning at nine o'clock. We set the alarm at seven thirty and then got to the damn train with half an hour to spare. We had all been saying darkly—including Miss Porter (she insists on being called Mrs. Porter but I can never remember), well, Miz Porter having a touch of grippe and being pretty crabby kept saying that if the Fords were in a difficult or complaining mood she for one was going to see little of them, a statement concurred in heartily by Col. Tate, and Miss Gordon, I must say, was wondering how much she would stand for—but they arrived most cheerful and we all went to lunch at the Pate D'Or and got very tight and then they came here to dinner at the Fleurus and praised the cooking, saying how unlike it was to the Mon Reve, a remark hastily passed over in the general good fellowship.[2]

They are pleased with the studio but won't be long, of course. I wrote them that it was very primitive, no confort moderne, that I ran out in the courtyard or along the hall for buckets of water.[3] They were surprised to find it had no toilet—how can you have a toilet without running water?

. . . .

If you get a picture of the Villa Agatha out of Cecil you mustn't by any means give it to me. You must keep it for yourself. I would find the gesture exaggerated. I, by the way, have a healthy geranium plant stolen from the villa that last day.

I am sorry about the portrait. I suppose it must have rattled him, our picking up and leaving so suddenly. The more I reflect on it the madder our ever going to Toulon seems. It was sheer stupidity in me to think Allen could write that book without a library. He has written one page and a half so far but he is sinking into the period a little deeper each day. Reads absorbedly all the time and has made one or two discoveries about colonial Virginia that are interesting to him. I inadvisedly took some time off for the festivities, then yesterday just as I was settling back to work I was stricken, with grippe I am certain. I could hardly believe it because I never have it, but I have fever and ache and my chest is congested. I have been in bed two days now. I expect I'll be better tomorrow. Allen turns out to be a splendid nurse—to my surprise. He never had a chance to nurse me before; he always got sick first. He gives me splendid inhalations and pours hot grogs down me at night. I get quite tight and so get through the first half of the night comfortably. . . . It is too silly. I never felt better in my life and then I was just laid low. New Year's Day K. A. Gene Allen and I went to the Jardin des Plantes and walked around admiring the animals. It was a wonderful day—we have had four days of almost Toulon weather. I think I must have caught a germ in the elephant house which was to say the least fetid. All Paris was there, of course, with its gorge wrapped up.

Allen now turns on me and demands fiercely if I am sweating and says I must have an inhalation.

You must stop in Paris in the spring. It will be lovely then. Love. Forgive this stupid letter. Lots of love, C.

[added as a postscript]

Two days later, couldn't tell the day of the week. I am getting up and going downstairs to lunch today, haven't had any fever for two days and feel pretty good. Katherine Anne is up too, Janice took the count as soon as she got here and was still in bed yesterday. Ford was reported by K. A. to be "lumping around, wheezing." Allen so far remains miraculously sound.

Allen says this is Friday.

I'd like very much to see Cecil's head of you. Your mother will naturally hang on to it but maybe she will lend it to you sometime to bring down our way.

1. I had gone to Toulon to meet Rochester friends, Walter Blair and his wife, Elizabeth Hollister Frost, a writer. We spent New Year's Eve sitting in a café watching small boats from the French fleet pick up sailors who had been on shore leave. One out of every three or four fell into the water, either out of drunkenness or the awkwardness of the launches, and they had to be fished out, dripping. Fortunately, it was a warm evening.

2. The Mon Rêve was a restaurant in Toulon where we and the Fords used to dine. The remark was passed over because Ford had persuaded us to come to Toulon, and it was not a success, not even the restaurant.

3. There were two water faucets in the courtyard, one labeled *Eau Buvable*, the other one *Eau de la Seine*. This had reminded me of a line from Baudelaire.

Hotel Fleurus, Paris, late January, 1933
To S. W. in Vence

Dearest Sally:

I was so glad to get your letter. I'm glad the work is progressing whether in long, short or staccato sentences. It doesn't matter what kind of sentences they are, I'm sure, as long as one follows after the other. You're quite right about showing things to people. Whatever they say it takes the wind out of your sails, K. A., for inst. telling me my manuscript sounded like somebody trying to write like me—why didn't she say it was just plain rotten?

This, so help me, is the first day that a glimmer of light has stolen through the Old Bean. The grippe has knocked me out of almost a month's work. I was sick only a week but the germs must have lingered in my system, there were two weeks when I would wake in the morning, drink my tea and then just turn my head over on the pillow. I am horribly lazy but that isn't natural for me. Perhaps it was partly because the illness coincided with a problem that had come up in the plot of my novel. Anyhow I took ammoniated quinine[1]—as an aperitif Janice said—and went through the motions of working until a few days ago I began to feel like something human and today I at least know what my next chapter will be

like. It is maddening to lose so much time. I am anxious to finish before
we go back but hardly expect to. We think now we'll go in April, soon
after we get our last Guggenheim installment. Allen wants to do some
more of that damned documenting in Washington.

Nancy has had the grippe, once rather slightly, then a relapse which
kept her in bed nine days with fever. She was just up last time I heard. I
am watching anxiously for mail. I don't know how I'd have done any
work if I'd had her along but I am never going to put the ocean between
us again, work or no work. It's been better for her but it's hell on me.
Every night when I go to bed I am convinced that she will die before we
get back. In the morning I'm not so sure but I feel so rotten after lying
awake half the night that I don't get much work done.

. . . .

The *petit cercle* has reassembled itself here in Paris—and there are
the usual rancors, at least they don't seem to make as much difference in
a city as they do in the country. Perhaps it is because you just see somebody else the next night if some friend has bored the hell out of you. The
Fords, to my amazement, continue to like the Denfert-Roch studio.
Janice, here a few minutes ago, complains that she has no luck. The first
time she's ever had a real professional studio in her life but Julie,[2] spending the time from half past ten till two each day knocks her out of work.

. . . .

K. A. and Gene, still much in love, are at the Malherbe—they do most
of their drinking in their room. We go mostly these days when we go
anywhere to the Cafe Flore—next to the Deux Magots it has inherited
all the clientele etrangere of that place.

. . . .

I can't think it would be a deprivation to anybody not to see the
Tates in their present low condition but we will be charmed, of course, to
see the Blairs. As for her elegance it will be a pleasure to see some fine
feathers.

Janice gave me the Castle of the Good King Rene for Christmas.
And Stella presented us with our family portrait or did I tell you all this
before? I certainly have been lucky in the way of art, not having had a
cent to buy a picture with. I certainly will try hard to sell some of Cecil's
drawings, though God knows who'll buy. I'll ask the Bishops. John liked

those drawings he gave us very much. Maybe they may know somebody. I had an idea he was having some sort of hard time. No one of us has heard a word from him.

It is cold as the devil here, skating in the Bois and all that. We've had an open fire here the last two days and it's been marvelous. Before that we were so cold we could hardly typewrite. But this bitter cold kills grippe they say. It's been a terrible epidemic here, two or three varieties. Allen has escaped so far—I can't understand it unless it's that Riviera sun.

. . . .

I finished my story about Allen and Dad.[3] I'll enclose a copy if I can get around to correcting it up enough to have it make sense. It's not one of my best, just a kind of trick. Oh, O'Brien is using The Captive in Best Short Stories this year but of course he doesn't pay a cent for it.

I hold my breath as I write it but Allen really seems to be started this time. He wrote five pages this morning, his best day's work so far and he has the whole book pretty well plotted by this time. It's a fiendish thing to write, half a dozen people telling their life histories and the problem of varying the style comes up of course. If he can just get this book written maybe we can get out from under this cloud that has hung over us, for three years now.[4]

Moe wrote that he might allow me some money but I haven't heard another word. I'm hoping a letter will come in each mail.[5] I wonder if you aren't needing your fifty dollars?

There isn't much news here. We are all trying rather desperately to get a little work done, come together moodily in the evenings for a little beer or hot grog and then back into the depths. I've been lower this last month than I've been for years. I never dreamed the flu could affect me like this.

I must get back to work. Love and write when you can.

[added as a postscript]

I went prancing into one of those little musee shops the other day to get a print of that Gaugin Le Cheval Blanc for you but the man just laughed at me, said it hadn't been reproduced and might not be for another fifty years. I don't see why; other Gauguins have been. There are two pictures of Toulon that I like very much in nouvelles acquisitions at the Lux.—I never get far enough from the Fleurus to see anything anywhere else—one is the Rade and the other might be a view from that mountain we drove up one day.

Janice is painting a picture of K. A. which Allen & I call—privately—Battling Porter. A stout, washerwomanish woman sitting in a corner, her mitts poised almost as if for action. If there were only another figure with a sponge and a towel it would be perfect.

. . . .

Sunday, January twenty eighth I think: Your card just came. I have been so no account that I just haven't gotten round to mailing this letter which will apprise you of our state of health and whatever of plans we have. Oh, God, how I do wish we could drive down there again before we go home! We could take the Fords down and bring you back and all cross together if you are ready to go home by that time. I'd love so to see that country again. If Moe would only allow me some money but no word from the scoundrel as yet. I'm afraid, though, we couldn't make the trip. Whatever money we get will have to go on our debts.

I've been worried to death about Nancy as I hadn't heard from her since the first day she was out of bed but last night a letter came saying the whole family had recovered. Nancy is now reading Sara Crewe!

I've had a nasty pain in my ear which keeps me indoors—I'm sure it's not going to be an abscess but it's annoying enough to keep me from working. It's been bitterly cold here. We've had a fire in the room which has been pleasant but I get pretty tired of this room when I can't work. This stretch from Christmas till March is terrible in Paris. I'm thankful you aren't here.

. . . .

I seem to keep adding to this stupid letter. I've been all day, two days, three days trying to get a few letters off but they don't seem to get in their envelopes.

Rem's poems: I don't know what "Where lilacs were Lovilla"[6] means exactly but I *like* it. I believe I like that one best of all. Allen likes 'em too—says they are well written but his mind is not on poetry these days. He is bringing his great grandfather and train over the mountains and has got them only as far as Bean's station.

Thanks for the drawing—and for the magazines which arrived today. Scribner's made me pretty sick. I can see why they turned down Jenny Wiley after reading that "Hill Idyll." "At long last he closed his eyes etc." But the dialogue is awfully good. Knowing how to write seems to be a hindrance. I didn't like that story of Jim Boyd's, although I saw in it here and there flashes of whatever it is I've liked so much in Long Hunt. This story hardly seems to be written by the same man. He evidently has only one thing to write about. He's *really* good in Long Hunt.

I haven't done a damn thing today or yesterday or the day before or for nearly two months. Consequently I have insomnia and am very bitter.

How are the detective stories holding out? You will be glad to know I have had to take to French ones.

Ford's publisher has eloped to the South Seas with his stenographer and fifty thousand dollars of the firm's money. I think they are going to quit sending Ford his money and say he can sue the errant member of the firm if he cares to. Ford, faced with privation, has got very hoity toity— poor devil. Janice told K. A. he walks the floor at night and pictures Julie starving. It is at times like these that it is very difficult for his friends to rally round him.

Esther Murphy has come back from Amerique with some good stories of election times. She went all over the country with Roosevelt, having nothing else to do and having got a taste for politicking while married to a Strachey⁷ whom she's divorcing this week. She reports that the country is on the verge of an agrarian revolution. She says the politicians even realize that something has to be done for the farmer and that Roosevelt is just waiting for something to take a stand on, that he really has the matter at heart—which is hard for me to believe. She had one good story. A young Englishman who had been listening to some of Edmund's nonsense said of the Democratic and Republican parties that they reminded him of the following limerick:

> There was an old man of Khartum
> Who kept two black sheep in his room
> They remind me he said
> Of a friend that is dead
> But I cannot remember of whom.

. . . I'll mail this tomorrow, so help me.

1. A southern habit Caroline was never able to get rid of.

2. Ford's daughter.

3. "Old Red," which did prove to be one of her best.

4. This sounds like "Ancestors in Exile," a novel Allen began under the Toulon influence but did not finish; parts of it were later used in *The Fathers*.

5. The banks had all closed after the crash, and the assets of Americans abroad were frozen, but the Frenchwoman who ran my pension let me have money. We were far from understanding the depth of the Depression in the United States.

6. Lovilla is the name of our grandmother who was brought up in the country near Rochester. Every farmer's wife around here used to plant at least *one* lilac bush near her house. Many houses have disappeared but the lilacs remain.

7. John Strachey (1901–1963), English Marxist author and lecturer.

Hotel Fleurus, Paris, February 10, 1933
To S. W. in Vence

Dear Sally:

God moves in a mysterious way his wonders to perform. I had just heaved up myself and was on my way out to purchase a tonic after some debate with Allen—he preferred copper and iron pills and I was on the point of trying Biondonimine recommended by the fat Boston lady at the next table, not knowing the name of your tonic (naturally I would take Old Doc Wood's tonic by preference) when I found your imposing package of ampoules. I was also looking at some rather anaemic looking pills given Allen by Ted Ross last spring—he said when he prescribed them that they were more for the mind than anything else as they were really no good so I had little faith in them. These fine, red-blooded ampoules enchant me. I am sure they are full of red corpuscles—I like a *dark* tonic, makes you feel there's strength in it. Swamp Root, Black Draught etc. I shall take one in exactly thirty minutes. Really, it was angelic of you to get them for me. Such wonderful reading along with them too. My God, it is a relief to know what I have—I have been trying for weeks now to tell people how I feel but they won't listen. They will have to when I say I have *anaemie banale*, for of course they've always known it.

Yes, it really was time something was done. I got the proof of "Tom Rivers" this morning from the Yale Review. Miss McAfee wrote that she had taken the liberty of revising the manuscript in three or four places, inserting quite a lot of her own writing. I was just sitting down to thank her for doing it when Allen glanced at the letter and said that he thought it was unwarrantable insolence. I realized that my own reaction was not quite natural. Perhaps I shall be able to give her hell after a few of these ampoules.

I am delighted to think of you dancing in crinolines and curls to violin music by candlelight. I wish Uncle Bud could be in the number with a flounce perhaps about his middle.[1]

. . . Not a word from Moe yet about whether he's going to let me have more money. February is the month in which I should apply for an extension. I think he is waiting and will probably allow me a few hundred *if* I don't apply for an extension. It would be cheaper for the Foundation as an extension would give me a thousand dollars—but it would mean another half year here anyhow. Allen says he cannot finish his book without getting hold of some Lewis letters in the Congressional Library, and I suppose we'd better concentrate on getting that book done.[2] I don't think I can make fall publication on my book now as I am wasting all this time when I ought to be writing. As you say, though, it's early to make plans. People like us can't ever make plans anyhow—they can just emulate the poor, benighted Hindoo.

It was stupid in me not to tell you to not to send [*sic*] Old Red back. I had another copy. Much obliged for the criticism. I believe you are right. I know that there isn't enough action. Ford thought so too and so did John Bishop. I was really more interested in rendering the character of the man than I was in the action of the story and that always betrays you. I will revise it later. Just now the mere thought of it is too much for me.

. . . .

Monday: I had to stop and rassle with Miss McAfee as she wanted the proof sent back immediately. I felt like crying when I saw what she had done. She had asked me to cut the story and I had cut it liberally. Then she had taken the revised manuscript and cut again, going with unerring aim to the heart of the story. You remember that paragraph where he reviews his past life reliving it as Tom Rivers. (You helped me with that.) She had simply cut that in half so that it made no sense at all. It is strange. They seem to have a real instinct for ruining a story. I am sure she hadn't the least idea what the story is about. . . .

We went yesterday to Esther [Murphy] Strachey's for tea. Esther rushed over to London last week to get her divorce but rushed back without it for some reason bringing with her her mother-in-law. Mrs. Strachey, a lady of sixty five or so is writing a novel about Paris in 1848 and is over to get a little atmosphere and details for the work. When one has a son going Communist and the usual trials of any mother of a family it must be fine to be able to sink into a period as she is doing. A very nice old lady. She drank Perrier while we drank champagne and said at intervals "I want to prowl around!" We are going to prowl over to Lamartine's house which seems to have been—to be—on the rue Tournon.

I don't know any news, cheerful news, that is. Ford's publisher has stopped payment which leaves them in a hellish fix, of course. We wired to Perkins and sold an article Ford was writing. Galsworthy having just died and it being on Galsworthy it was saleable but God knows what will happen in the future. After all the supply of publishers is limited and Ford has almost run through them.

I hope you will get up to Paris a little while before we leave anyhow. I'll let you know as soon as I myself know anything definite about our plans. Moe has really acted badly—he doesn't like Allen and is taking it out on me. But he'll have to write me soon.

The weather is preternaturally spring-like. One of the mildest winters ever was I reckon except for those few days of bitter cold.

I must get to work or at least go through the motions. I am taking the tonic most faithfully and am fancying of course that I feel better. Most substantial tonic it is. I feel a little like Dracula after a few swigs of it. Love, c.

[added as a postscript]

Oh, Allen wanted me to ask you what was now the status of Cecil's portrait. That is is there any danger of Cecil's destroying it? He wants it preserved and says he will contribute to its purchase as soon as he can get his hands on any money. So if you're writing Cecil do see if you can't make his business instincts override his artistic conscience. I was crazy about it and I hate to think of it going out of existence and since you say you'll leave it to Nancy it's only fitting that we should help pay for it.

1. On account of my friendship with Monique and Toinon (Marie Antoinette) de Ladébat, I had become a member of the *jeunesse* of Vence, even though I still belonged to the very small foreign (mostly English) colony. Our social life was simple but amusing and did not interfere with writing, being conducted in the evening.

2. The Lee biography.

Hotel Fleurus, Paris, early February, 1933
To S. W. in Vence

Dearest Sally:

I have some news of our plans sooner than I thought I would. We got American mail last night, three or four letters, each one a little more depressing than the other. The plumbing in the upstairs bathroom at Benfolly has burst owing to Wagschal's carelessness in not turning the water off. We had thought we could let the taxes run till June but either we were mistaken or they've set the day of grace up—anyhow Jess Staton the county trustee or whatever he is [is] a-suing of us or about [to] be a-suing of us. These are the major calamities. Anyhow after thinking it over we decided last night that we'd pick up and go home where we can deal with these things a little better. Also I want to get there in time to set some hens and raise some garden against what is going to be another hard winter. Benfolly is rented till June. We'll go to Merry Mont which suits me just as well. I can raise a much better garden there, the soil not being composed of rocks as at Benfolly.

Allen is going down to see the steamship line this morning. If we can get our tickets transferred to one of the big boats we'll do so. I don't imagine you'll want to go so soon. I myself shudder at the thought of the winter sea. But I'm letting you know right away in case you are ready to go home.

I hate to leave Paris but it will be a relief to get home in a way. If this inability to write continues there will be other things I can do. Sheep. My God. They begin to lamb in February, the coldest, wettest spell usually. Chickens. Stirring up the niggers if all else fails. I am afraid we will have a devil of a time at Merry Mont. They are making the new road now. It runs through a corner of Woodstock land and cuts off a corner of Merry Mont right by that cabin. It is impassable now except on horseback they say but we can keep the Ford at Woodstock and wade through the mud in boots. I guess we'll leave Nancy at Chattanooga till school is out. I hate to jerk her about so. She will probably be very much annoyed when she knows her fond parents are coming.

I must get to work. Love. Sorry to be so sudden. c

Later: . . . I'm damn sorry we won't be crossing together or won't even be in Paris together this spring but I'm sure it's best for us to get home as soon as possible. We can live at Merry Mont for practically nothing and the money we'd be spending here can go to pay debts.

Katherine Anne is at the Malherbe on Vaugirard when you do come up. We're leaving here Saturday, driving to Havre, sail Sunday.

Must dress and go to the de Lanux's for dinner. What a life this is!

The Tates returned to America, but I stayed in Vence. My dog's having to get over distemper was the excuse. Actually the Pension Mourre was a perfect place to write—out in the garden much of the time. Walking and swimming were available, and there were plenty of friends for the evenings.

I also had the happiness of the French language. This turned out to be useful during World War II. The Resistance poems of Louis Aragon came into my hands, and I translated several for Malcolm Cowley, who had known him, and for John Ransom for the Kenyon Review.

Trenton, May 20, 1933
To S. W. in Vence

Dearest Sally:

I often think of you—as a man plunged into a rushing mountain stream might tread water and think of absent friends—if he was man enough. Life at Merry Mont is that rich and strange there isn't time for concentrated effort. Anyhow we are here and what you might call settled down. Benfolly is rented till October so we've decided to stay here through the summer. Ma says she may not be here next winter and I think she really enjoys having us in her way.

We stopped two days in Chattanooga. Nancy's school was just getting out when we arrived. I think it embarrassed her horribly for her wandering parents to turn up just as the children all streamed out. However she recognized us. Her first remark was "This is an easy old school. I don't have to study at all." When Allen could not repress a snicker when she said "Okay" she observed "I say Hot Dog too." She has grown a great deal and is touchingly polite at home and gets a book to read from the library every week. I couldn't get used to her reading so fluently. She read me a long and very dull story of a husky dog, stopping only at words like "Antarctic." She has read Sara Crewe too by herself. We left her there to finish the term and came on to Merry Mont with a two night stop at Chattanooga.

We had two parties with the agrarian brethren and sistren. We played charades. A great hit was Tippecanoe with a street scene from Paris—Andrew halting behind an upturned card table for a cabinet d'aisance tipping his hat to passers by with sonorous M'sieu, dames. The Ransoms laughed heartily at this—they all seem to have mellowed up a good deal. The chief topic of conversation was Brother Lytle's latest amorous fiasco. The gal up and married another man the other day. It seems a repetition of the Colonel's daughter affair. She wrote Andrew a thirty page letter—one of those letters—which Mister Lytle mistook for a legal document, relating no doubt to the mortgage about to be foreclosed on the farm. He opened it and read it then laid it on the shelf and she was married to another man by the time Andrew got home three weeks later to find the letter.

Well, anyhow we are here at Merry Mont—and I feel as if I'd never been away. The pile of dusty magazines is a bit higher. The great problem now is Uncle Doc. We left him lying on the bed moaning a little and saying he would probably die before night. We come back to find a changed man. He is charged with energy, got up the other night and milked the cows at two o'clock. (This seemed to enrage everybody, though I can't see any real objection.) He also plunks the guitar all night and croons. It's very soft and rather lulling. That also enrages. Another offense was getting all the negroes drunk at hog killing time. We got here, thank God, just after the hogs were killed. Cath says we missed the strangest sight of all—every tree on the lawn with an enormous pink carcass hanging from it in bright moonlight!

Day before yesterday we started out in the Ford and visited several of the kin. We collected two horses and two saddles and bridles. Cath and I rode them home in the moonlight. It was grand. I had forgotten how I love to ride. Yesterday Allen and I and Cath were preparing to ride to Guthrie to meet Red and Cinina. Uncle Doc was superintending the saddling of the horses and suddenly he said "I wish I could go too." Whereupon Nick says "The ole gray mar is out in pasture." They saddled up the

old gray mar, and off we went, Allen on a twenty year old saddle mare of
Cousin Lucy's, Cath on the spotted pony and I on Brownie. We were a
strange sight, affording the whole countryside much diversion. Niggers
came rushing out from cabins all the way to look at us. It's fourteen miles
there. We let the horses rest all afternoon and came home by moonlight,
Uncle Doc singing "I'm up from Alabama with a banjo on my knee."

I have a fine idea now for your summer. There is not a vacant
cranny at Merry Mont and anyhow the life would be too hectic to one not
of the blood but you could board at Cloverlands—for twenty five dollars
a month, private suite with bath in fact. Last summer they said that they
would take you as a favor for forty—but this summer seems very different.
I know Clyde would take a boarder because we had a scheme to get Uncle
Doc off on her and she said she'd take him for twenty five but we couldn't
get him to go when the time came. Sure enough, do come! It's a half mile
walk through the woods, a mile by the road. I will get you a horse to ride
if you will. In fact I have her now, Flora, a little on in years but a smooth
saddler. Then when we got to Benfolly in October you could stay with us
till it got cold. Do consider this. Could you live much cheaper at home?
There'd be nothing to spend money on here. The main diversion would
be swimming—the creek would be two miles away. These ponies we have
to ride are the sweetest things you ever saw. Brownie is the best saddler
but Lillian is good enough and adorable to look at. All curves like Nancy
she is and with the loveliest little Arabian head. . . .

Truly you'd be most comfortable at Cloverlands. It's the loveliest
old house and Clyde and Henry are awfully nice. Clyde, poor child, is a
Radcliffe product hurled suddenly into the midst of the kin some ten
years ago and still a bit bewildered.

Allen has one whole long chapter of that damn book finished and is
starting again. I believe he is really going to get off this time. I sold Old
Red (as was) to Scribner's. And now I'm afraid they wouldn't take it if I
made the changes I had in mind. It's a fact that they have never taken any
story of mine that wasn't inferior.

We have a cook, thank God. Uncle Doc who has the next room to
ours wakes us in the morning with half a dozen loud twangs on his guitar.
The first morning I thought I was on the SS City of Norfolk where re-
veille was played on a gong.

I must get to work. Let us hear from you. When are you coming home?

Love, c.

. . . .

I stayed in Vence most of the summer, then returned to Rochester and missed the chance to stay at Cloverlands. Malcolm Cowley stayed there while visiting the Tates in May, 1933. In 1965 he published an article based on his very pleasant visit in the Southern Review. *The article, entitled "The Meriwether Connection," is included in Cowley's* The Dream of the Golden Mountains *(New York, 1980).*

Allen had said on one of my visits to Benfolly that Caroline felt she had to look after all the Negroes in Montgomery County. Responsibility of this kind is not understood in this country. Feudalism existed here for only a short time, in the South. The Tates used to go off to the jail when one of the blacks was locked up. Years later I thought, What a contrast to Attica! Maybe this was the only way in which poor blacks could be sure not to be abused in jail.

When Caroline's father visited the Tates at Benfolly—only briefly as I remember—all the typewriters stopped clicking. People just sat around, on the floor if necessary, to listen to him. He was the best raconteur I ever heard. With the first sentence one was caught and simply had to stay there to find out what happened. He was always artistic enough to leave while the literary people still wanted more.

Perhaps he tired of them rapidly. When I had been there about three days, he suddenly put both hands on the table and said, "Miss Sally, are you a Yankee?" When I said yes, there was silence, due only to politeness.

Guntersville, Alabama, June 6, 1933
To S. W. in Vence

Dearest Sally:

I have been sitting—lying, rather—looking for the ms. day after day but it hasn't come. I will read it, make notes and send it on to you immediately when it does.[1]

I reckon I must have three letters to you lying buried in my ms. No use in sending them now. The truth is I have been in the throes of a minor nervous collapse for some weeks. I'm sure now it is minor. I am feeling almost myself again. It's that wretched back of mine. I will confess to you what I've concealed from the family so far. I hurt the damn thing pulling up some enormous weeds in the garden. The ache lurked about for a while then transferred itself to my knee just as it did the time I had that three months' break down in Chattanooga. But my nervous system is evidently in much better condition now than it was then for it didn't really get involved. I coddled myself very seriously for a good while and have got over it. But I just somehow haven't been able to write letters or rather to mail them. I have written you many.

Going to Merry Mont was a mistake, I reckon. It is just too hectic and the place has a very bad influence on me and through me on Allen. The family responsibilities kept getting heavier and heavier. It is not only routine, niggers to get out of jail, turkeys to run in, and all that. It is the moral pressure that my uncle constantly exerts on me to take care of my grandmother in her declining years. She is failing fast now, almost blind and fell down three times the other day. Of course he keeps wishing Allen and I'd stay there till she dies but I have told him I won't do it. We get Benfolly August 15, thank God.

Pidie, the aunt who kept Nancy for me, arrived from Chat. the other day, took a look at me and said "You need a vacation." I knew I did and with her help Allen and I got off to spend the next three weeks in Alabama with Andrew.[2] We packed in two seconds, the family, all except Pidie, in full pursuit, saying finally "Well, you won't leave before dinner." "Yes," I said through my teeth. "I am leaving this very minute." And leave we did.

I don't suppose you realize how wicked a woman my grandmother has been. She has carried it to such a pitch that she is a real moral influence. And now that this implacable nature has a little mellowness overlying it she is much more sinister. Dad takes a theological view of the matter and says "Mrs. Meriwether ought to have a chance to repent her sins before she dies." Well, I was a fool for going there.

You were right about Allen's library spasms. Violent attacks, of course, all summer. But I was so glad to get him out of the house I was rather glad he had them.

. . . .

But we, thank God, are in Alabama. Wish you were here. You'd like this place, I think, at least you'd like it for a while. It's an old dog run cabin, fixed over just enough to make it livable. A house run by men. Even the cook is a man, George, he moves about the kitchen, attended by several henchwomen who are humble because they don't know the mysteries of cooking. We go bare foot, all of us, including George, who puts on a white coat to serve dinner—more formal he is than the rest of us. We have an aperitif before lunch—a bottle of sherry Andrew stole from his grandmother—but drink raw corn before dinner. We go swimming in a lake or the river and Mr. Lytle lures us out occasionally to look at some crops. The plantation is three thousand acres—we walked five miles the other day to inspect two fields of corn.

Mr. Lytle secluded himself in the kitchen the morning before our arrival and made chess pies in our honor. He put meringue on them, though, in spite of his nineteen year old daughter's disapproval. He also makes something he calls "Charlotte Roosh."

Tell Uncle Bud I dote on his picture. Such a noble look to that profile, rather like his father. I am so sorry those two dogs are dead.

I have not written K. A. one line since leaving Paris and have written the Fords once or twice. God knows what has become of all of them. . . .

Yes, I suppose we feel pretty pure. At least I do, though my gm [grandmother] has been rather worried because Hob Mallon comes out from Clarksville and takes me to the movies. She confided to Pidie that "That man appears as soon as Allen leaves the place." Malcolm and I were going to Guthrie one night for beer and supper and she forbade me to go. "You run around too much with married men" says she. To my own surprise I said meekly, "Well, all right, Ma, we won't go." Malcolm was rather dazed. These little sallies are not the reason why Merry Mont is sinister; in fact they've given a little spice to life.

Malcolm departed the other day, his book almost written.[3] An interesting chapter on Rimbaud, taking Wilson's *Axel's Castle* pronouncement as his starting point. It's all well written and acute at times but the trouble is that the ideas of his generation so often turn out to be the ideas of men like Matty Josephson.[4]

George says dinner is ready. I know this is a poor letter. It is just that putting anything into words seems almost beyond me, until I've rested a day or two longer. I had insomnia for a week or two till it just got me down. That damn ache would keep on strong after four aspirins.

Will write again right away. I am feeling so almost like myself now. This place has rested me. Dearest love, c. Address Benfolly, Route 6, Clarksville.

[added as a postscript]

I told you, didn't I, that I mailed the book to your English friend immediately after getting your letter. So seldom I do anything like that on time I want to get full credit.

I am not stuck on my novel but I am in no shape now for very difficult work and have hit on a book to write that will be relaxation and a sort of labor of love. I am going to call it "Green Springs to White Oak."[5] It will be written in collaboration with Dad if I can ever get hold of him long enough to take two or three weeks dictation. I think the germ of the idea came to me from something you said once, that those stories were evidently works of art for him. It will be more like Siegfried Sassoon's "Memoirs of a Fox Hunting Man" than anything I can think of, though no doubt people will find resemblances to Hemingway's bull fighting book in it. Anyhow it is to be [a] history of a life dominated by a passion for fishing. It will at any rate be an interesting experiment in prose writing for me. I hope to make the action very rapid. The first chapter will be called "The Green Springs," then there will be other place names for headings and a lot of detailed information in it. One chapter will be "Game Fish are Ground Nesters." Another: "The Spell Is on 'Em." The action of the book will be chopped off arbitrarily at some place like White Oak, some place that he hopes is the perfect spot so long sought for. I noticed when he was here the other day that he often in conversation starts off a chapter, thus: "Sometimes the Black Bass strikes from natural pugnacity . . . . ."

Allen is yelling time to go to town. I've learned to drive. Think of that. Maybe that gave me the nervous break down. Anyhow I've learned so next time you come down we can rush hither and yon independent of Allen. Love. c

1. The reference is to the book I had been writing, which I now call "The Education of Nancy Calkins." Then it was known as "The Mental Voyage." It was a personal memoir on the model of *The Education of Henry Adams*, a sort of preview of feminism. Clifton Fadiman

approved the first chapters of the book but didn't like the rest of it. He was always trying to get me to turn it into a novel. Now that women's lives have general interest, the story might be popular. My agent once told me, "Never mind, it will make a good posthumous work."

2. At Cornsilk, the Lytle family plantation, Guntersville, Alabama.

3. *Exile's Return: A Literary Odyssey of the 1920's* (1934).

4. Matthew Josephson (1899–1978), American critic and biographer.

5. It turned out to be *Aleck Maury, Sportsman.*

Trenton, August 14, 1933
To S. W. in Vence

Dearest Sally:

Just back from Alabama and found your manuscript had been here several days—Miss Carrie wasn't equal to the feat of mailing a manuscript. I am in the very throes of moving back to Benfolly and haven't mind if I had the time to read it. I hope you don't mind my keeping it a few more days. It won't take long to get settled there as the furniture is already in place. In fact I hope to spread my papers out and at least sit down to my desk by Thursday or Friday. I have peeped into Nancy ["The Education of Nancy Calkins"] every now and then and have read the first chapter. I am impressed by the ease and lucidity of the style. It seems to flow right along. I am anxious to see what impression the whole book will make. You are already too late for fall publication but ought to make spring.

I wrote at random to Curtis Brown (agents) the other day and was surprised to be answered by a man I know, Raymond Everit.[1] He used to be at Harcourt, Brace, read and turned down "Penhally" but I remember bullying him into advancing K. A. P. another five hundred on her novel.[2] I hope he doesn't hold it against me—I fear that novel will never get finished. Anyway he is alert and as intelligent as any of them—it might be a good idea to send your book there. As soon as I have read these chapters I'm going to tell him about it anyhow.

I canned a dozen cans of beans yesterday and a dozen the day before in preparation for what looks to be a hard winter. I am writing an expatriate story from what I suppose is a Southern slant, niggers, or rather one nigger in Paris.

Benfolly is looking lovely these days. Actually grass in the yard. Daisy Miller wandering around, giving three gallons of milk a day. The crops in the bottom are miraculously green and flourishing. We will be very glad to get back.

I must return to the packing. This is just a note to let you know I'm not as negligent as I seem. I've just had my hands full the last few days. I rested myself very seriously in Alabama and quite got over the pain in my back. I gained seven and a half pounds down there!

Give Uncle Bud eighteen kisses and tell him I know he still misses me. Love, c.

[added as a postscript]
This is Monday, Aug. 14. We move tomorrow.

[inserted in top margin]
Just got your letter saying you are coming home. Well. Well. It's good news about Saxton.[3] I'll have Allen drop him a line before you get there.

1. Charles Raymond Everit (1901–1947) was at Harcourt, Brace between 1924 and 1929, then manager of the Curtis Brown Agency, 1930–1935.
2. The novel, then called "No Safe Harbor," was finally published in 1962 as *Ship of Fools*.
3. Eugene F. Saxton (1884–1943), one-time editor of *Bookman*, then head of the book department at Harper's. He and Maxwell Perkins were known as the best editors of the time.

Clarksville, October 4, 1933
To S. W., c/o Mrs. Paul McGhee, 7 Beekman Place, New York City

---

Dear Sally:

Well, here you are in the land of the free. I can't even visualize Beekman Place, so unreal has New York grown to me—it will probably seem as unreal to you, fresh from Vence. No, Cannes,[1] I see that bar proved alluring as you moved close to it.

I have been on the point of writing every day but things have been pretty thick, of course, what with moving in and all. We are all settled, even to the new hen house (the old brick smoke house remodeled.) Daisy Miller, our Jersey cow grazes on the lawn and duly scatters manure which I pick up on a dust pan and place carefully around the petunias. Yesterday I canned five cans of corn and four of beans. I have also finished a short story called "A Morning's Favour," the delights of sin in the woods triumphing over religious ecstacies.

. . . .

I have also read the manuscript of your book at a sitting, two sittings, in fact. It seems to me to get right along. The war chapter is best, emotion in it, I suppose. But the chapter right after the war is almost as good. Fine. I can see now what you were driving at and how hard it is to give anybody else an idea of what you're trying to do in a book like this— I don't know any other book like this one. Malcolm's isn't.[2] Experience doesn't enter into his book as it does into yours.

I'm writing this late at night, rather tired or perhaps I could say these things better. I'm leaving tomorrow to spend a week with Dad in East Tennessee—to get the data I want from him for that book. He is showing signs already of giving us the slip on his promised visit so I thought I'd better take time by the forelock.

. . . .

Goodnight and love, c.

1. I had moved briefly to the tiny fishing village of Cagnes on the shore for swimming. It was the Mediterranean that proved alluring for swimming in the hot weather, though I thought of it, much as Allen did, as vastly inferior to the Atlantic. There were no tides, and its color was not "wine dark."
2. *Exile's Return.*

Clarksville, mid-October, 1933
To S. W. in New York City

Dearest Sally: I have just read: "He fixed her with two stern unwinking eyes that looked as if they were made of glass . . . . ." and *then* you go on and add "they had so little expression in them." You do this all the time. Why in the name of God do you do it???? If the man's eyes looked as if they were made of glass only a fool would think they had expression in them. It practically amounts to telling your reader every second paragraph that he is a fool, or at least that he hasn't got enough sense to have a reaction to the picture you've given him. You make the picture and it's always good, then you tell the reader how to react to it. So does Galsworthy, so does Harold Bell Wright, so does every second, third, fifth class reader [writer?]. I don't know why you do it. Wellesley, I suppose. You have got to quit it. It perplexes and enrages me.

Well, thank God, you didn't explain Harold Stearns' remark about a dog not being able to live on his own vomit.

I should perhaps have mentioned first that your chapter on Bohemia as Culture is exceedingly well done. Held me,, really, with only that one burst of indignation from start to finish. You are writing awfully well, these days, Old Thing. Yes, what you needed was to do was a book. Pulled your style together.

. . . .

. . . I am now doing a series of stories for a Sunday School periodical. They pay me six or seven a story and I can write them when I can't write anything else. I hope I can get that fifty dollars to you before the family throws you out.

I got back from Caney Fork yesterday, found I could do the work in two days and a half after all. We worked all morning then Dad fished till four o'clock, then we worked till dinner time then we worked from dinner till bed time. Dad complained that it upset his mind. In the night he was heard to yell out: "Take this down." I shall model the book on the autobiography of Davy Crockett.

I found the cook gone when I got home, Uncle Doc was drunk— had stolen all the cream and sold it for liquor so we had no butter as a consequence of his debauch. He is, however, penitent this morning and we're all pulling ourselves together. I shall go out to Merry Mont this afternoon and pick up another cook if I can and hope to be back at work tomorrow.

What is New York like these days?

Go to see Malcolm and Muriel [Cowley] at 360 West Twenty Second Street if you have time.

. . . .

The Methodists are calling for the next installment of the adventures of Dick and Margery. Let us hear from you. Love, c.

Clarksville, October 22, 1933, mailed with the following letter
To S. W. in Rochester

Dearest Sally:

I have been wondering how you were making out in N.Y. and
whether you were home yet.[1] Of course it's too soon to tell about N.Y. In
a way I think Harper's suggestion is rather good. At least I kept thinking
every now and then "these people ought to be in a novel." And that is no
reflection upon the organization of the book—it is simply that the people
move through it so vividly. Since you mention "The Testament of Youth"
another idea comes to my mind. I don't believe you have just the right
title—The Mental Voyage, now that I consider it calmly, having sort of
grown up with it I never really considered it before, or at least I considered it so many years ago that it, the title, had sort of settled itself in my
mind—but I say now that I examine it anew I believe you ought to have a
title that does just what the Testament of Youth does. Think one up and
write [and] tell them about it. The Mental Voyage is too intellectual, puts
people off. I'm glad you were able to tell Perkins in two words what your
novel was about. Don't see how you did it. It should have impressed him.

Allen is away and I am no good at judging distances but Maysville
cannot be far from here. I hope Pickett[2] will come with you but if she
won't you must come anyhow. But we would love to have her. I wish you
all were arriving now. The weather is gorgeous, the leaves more wonderful than I've ever seen them. It's been very mild. We lie in the sun on the
slope and think of the Riviera.

Allen's father died suddenly, yesterday and Allen left this morning
at two o'clock for Cincinnati.

I wish we could come to see you. But it is more than usually impossible. There is a chance, however, that we might do even such a wild
thing as that in the next year or so. At least it seems to me that there is a
chance of us throwing off the shackles that have bound us now these three
years. It is a great secret. Allen doesn't want anybody to know it. But he
has written Balch that he cannot write the book he has contracted for.[3] It
had got to the point where neither of us could stand it any longer, the
nervous strain, aside from the unpleasantness of slowly starving to death
while Allen tried to write a book he never wanted to write. He has been

tied up now for three years by this book and has made less money than he did before. He has offers all the time for magazine work he hasn't time to do—I believe he can make more writing articles than he will on this book, the way Balch will handle it. Anyhow we have decided to assume the debt. It's a great relief.

You sent too much money for the books. I'm not sure exactly how much till I go upstairs and ask Allen the price of his first book. A dollar and a half I think.

No, I never went in for Saki extensively. Read one, maybe two out of Mr. Brooks' library. Pretty British and whimsical as I remember him— maybe I didn't really get him.

Just been reading Graves' "Goodbye to All That."[4] He certainly does write well. I don't really like the book, though.

Love to Little May when you see her. I heard through Pidie now at Merry Mont that she'd had a sort of breakdown and was in bed. I'm so sorry and do hope she's better.

I neglected to state that our family at Benfolly has been increased by two: Manson Radford and his wife, Rose.[5] Manson's mother, Kate, is May's dear friend, made me think of it. They're sweet creatures. Live in the cabin which we've moved into the locust grove. Rose paints—seriously to my surprise—and Manson mostly shoots crows. I believe, however, he is thinking about writing something if he ever gets around to it. We enjoy having them here.

And did I omit the big news which is that Manny's mother, Loulie, is living with us this year and keeping house. It's too heavenly for me. She says she's going to see me through my book but I don't believe she can stand it that long. Anyhow it's grand while it lasts. Lucy,[6] (colored) in your room completes the collection (Uncle Doc resides in the garage). The interior reminds you somehow of Van Gogh's bedroom. Don't ask me how. Pulled together by a fierce will, anyhow, both of them. You might think from this roster that we haven't room for you. But not so. We have elastic resources which we will disclose when you arrive. Plenty of room for Pickett too.

I'm dead sleepy and am going to bed. I do five pages of the autobiography a day come what will—it makes me very stupid but I've vowed to get on with it.[7]

"Old Red" is in Sept. Criterion and will be in December Scribner's—two versions. Take your choice. In the Scribner version I lopped
off the ending, finishing it up with the fox taking to earth. You won't like
it but I always was worried for fear I had an anticlimax there. Too late
now, anyhow, to speculate about what's wrong with it.

Sunday: I was interrupted by the arrival of Pidie on her October
visit to Merry Mont.
Allen has just got back from Cincinnati. I'll send the order for the
poems this very day.
Are you going to Florida this winter or is it too soon to think of
going anywhere? You'll come by, won't you, if you do go? We're having
the most wonderful, balmy fall.
. . . .
I met a man from Rochester the other night. Bill Vaughn, former
Nashvillian, works at the Eastman Kodak Co.[8] He knows Rem and Rosa-
lie[9] and likes them very much.
Well, I must get to work. This is a poor letter.
Love and do write. You haven't as much to do as I have. How are
you feeling these days? Me, I feel swell, physically, but I can't seem to get
any work done which keeps me in a peevish mood, c.

1. I was starting for Florida again to finish my book, visiting friends along the way.
2. Elizabeth Pickett, my college friend, whom I was about to visit.
3. It was the book on Lee, about which Allen had a real block, the causes of which
students of his work have debated. Perhaps if he had let the book go and written something
else, he would have been able to return to the book with renewed interest. But Allen was very
conscious of the financial security that had come from his other biographies and was trapped
by this. The escape offered him at last was teaching.
4. Robert Graves (1895–1978), the English poet and novelist, whose autobiography,
Goodbye to All That, was published in 1929.
5. Friends who were living in the tenant house.
6. The new cook brought from Merry Mont.
7. *Aleck Maury, Sportsman.*
8. William Vaughn, a student at Vanderbilt under John Crowe Ransom, who encouraged him to apply for a Rhodes Scholarship, later became president of Eastman Kodak
Company.
9. My brother and his wife.

Clarksville, fall, 1933
to S.W. in Rochester

Dearest Sally:

I got home from Nashville last night—I went because I wasn't able to work and now today I'm not able to work because I went—and here is your letter. My answer to your other letter I was ashamed to find on the table in the dining room. I hadn't got round to mailing it. I enclose it now.

. . . .

Harper's has everything classified, it seems. I sent them a story the other day and they wrote back that they'd had enough stories of "the hit war" type of people. We evidently strike the permissible extremes. Emotion on the Riviera[1] is tawdry and the emotions of the Hit Wars is just too sub-human to even read about. We must win our way to middle ground. Hold the White Collar man as the norm and then range a little on either side of him, but not too far. By the way was your letter from an ass named Frederick L? Allen. He's a journalist who has written a bad jazzy kind of book heaved suddenly into an editorial seat. I was really tempted having his letter to write back and say that the Hit War people whatever their shortcomings, didn't speak in an advertizing jargon unbecoming a respectable publisher's office. But this butters no turnips.

I try to visualize the novel you'd write . . . [about your early life]. You certainly could disguise the coal fields stuff so that it wouldn't be embarrassing. As for the rest, it certainly seems to me that it would go. But whether it's the thing for you to do now I couldn't for the life of me say. The truth is that that period of your life (that sort of period in anybody's life) is good for three or four books. It seems a life and death question now which one you shall do and it is. But looking back on it later it will seem just a question of which book you did first. I don't believe, either, that you'll get worn out with any material as deeply felt as this. I wrote Penhally from two or three angles before I finally hit on a version that at least kept me interested till I was through.

I have been troubled all along by the neither fish, flesh nor fowl aspect of your book. You remember when incidents involving human beings first came in I wanted you to keep them within the tone of the book, rather than play them up for whatever they were worth as you did.

God knows how this is to be done and yet some people contrive to do it. Ford did in his Return to Yesterday, has evidently done it again in what must be a continuation of his autobiography, "It was the Nightingale"—I haven't seen it yet, just judging from reviews. I am being slowly run crazy by the same problem in the book I'm trying to write now—my father's autobiography.

I don't know yet whether you haven't managed on the whole though, to solve this problem. Harper's reaction tells me nothing, really. Certainly the book as it stands is worth going on with. But you know that yourself. On the other hand if you can't bring yourself to go on with it in its present form this [other] idea . . . may be God-given. You could use an awful lot of the stuff. I suppose what I want is for you to do both books.

I try to simmer down my conclusions but it's very hard and I may be saying exactly the wrong thing. I don't feel the slightest confidence in any reaction I have to my own or anybody else's book. But I do feel and always have felt that the note should be struck more clearly in the auto-biographical book—either it should be really a mental voyage, in which case one asks why all this wasting of time with people who obviously aren't worth wasting time with. (The same incidents, that is, but a slightly different perspective.) What I'm trying to say is that the emphasis must be put one place or another, either the mental or the emotional adventures of this person. God knows how you'd record intellectual adventures or how separate them from emotion—but as I say it seems to me a question of emphasis. I can see how all these problems would fall away if you really were doing a novel. It may be significant that people reading your book say why don't you do a novel. The people you have in there move as people do in a novel. Their emotions may be tawdry but they move in a very clear, authentic light—the thing, whatever it is that makes a novel have reality. Of course I'm anxious to see you do a novel. . . .

No, I haven't anything of Cecil's except two pastels, one he gave me and one he gave Allen. I'd be glad to send them up, though, if you think you might sell something else for him on the strength of them. . . .

We had one cold spell but it's mild again, very spring-like. We had a month of the most gorgeous Indian summer I ever saw. I wished you were here then. The woods were more beautiful than usual. One place you sit and the yellow beech leaves came falling down continually, like rain. There is still a good deal of color but the leaves are going fast now. I

think I have made the last bouquet for the table, zinnias and marigolds.
I've planted ivy all around the house but Daisy Miller keeps biting off the
leaves. We have finally got rid of Uncle Doc, thank God and now get
three gallons of milk a day instead of the two quarts he let us have. It was
an exciting contest while it lasted, our whole thoughts were bent on milk.
He got up in the night, milked the cow secretly and sold the milk. Anybody coming along would have seen a strange sight in the moonlight one
night all of us out to bag the cow. It was the cook's idea. We solemnly
fastened a pillow case around that noble bag then secured it by tapes that
ran up over her back, tied the knot in a way known only to Lucy and
there she was. I thought this was Lucy's brilliant invention but she says it
is a common practice, a sort of chastity belt for cows. It was too much for
poor Uncle Doc. He gave up. But he couldn't bear to live here without
stealing milk so he went off to live at the Wolards.

We have solved another guest problem—drink—with homemade
sherry. It is really pretty good and comes nearer seeing you through a
long winter than anything else I know of. We have twenty gallons on
hand now and are trying hard to let it get a little age on it.

I am still pegging away at the Life and Passion of Alex. Maury. I am
running into all sorts of problems that I hadn't foreseen, of course. Have
six chapters in very rough draft. Hope to finish it this winter, anyhow. I
found myself absolutely unable to go on with my novel, but hope to get
back to it after taking this rest.[2]

. . . I'm going to haul off and write some short stories or rob a
bank or do something. I am trying to get some reviewing to do now.
To date my earnings in that line have been three dollars but the Nation
answered my first request with a book and Malcolm[3] will send me something from time to time and the Yale Review too I think. So I really
ought to be able to earn a little extra money that way. I'm reviewing
Roark Bradford's new book for the Nation now.[4] Reviewing isn't as hard
as I thought it would be. I never thought I'd be able to do it.

Nancy and Lucy, the cook, make so much clatter, playing dolls I
can't even write. I hear Nancy say "Lucy, you ought to read Oliver Twist."
"Whar is it at?" is Lucy's response. She is a gem, young and strong and
good natured and old fashioned. I find myself thinking I own her. She
really is more like slavery time niggers than any of the modern variety.
Needless to say she came from Merry Mont where she has been under
Miss Carrie's stern tutelage for nearly a year.

When are you coming south? Please come as soon as you can. And you have got to stop here. We can keep you warm with roaring fires.

Have you read Sigrid Undset's trilogy?⁵ I was sunk in it last week. Very good, the most impressive thing is the authenticity of the details of mediaeval life. You can see and smell those feudal halls.

Love. Forgive this poor letter. I haven't been able to write letters all fall. I feel fine now but there's been a sort of mental let-down which persists. Not being able to finish that damned novel, I suppose. Anyhow we are all well and all send love, and pay very little attention to anything I say about writing, your book or anybody else's for I really know nothing about it, C.

1. *Tender Is the Night*, published by Scribner's in 1934, after being serialized in *Harper's* was not appreciated until later.
2. *None Shall Look Back*, which was then called "The Cup of Fury."
3. Malcolm Cowley, then one of the editors of the *New Republic*.
4. Bradford (1896–1948) was an American author of psuedo Negro folklore. Caroline reviewed his *Kingdom Coming* (1933).
5. *Kristin Lavransdatter*.

Clarksville, January 9, 1934, mailed with the following letter
To S. W. in Rochester

Dear Sally:

Andrew is sunk in a swound on the dining room couch, Allen is reading Belloc's Charles I and Nancy is writing you a letter. You might think she did not appreciate the tea set—I looked over her shoulder and observed the somewhat violent transition she makes. But it has just receded into the background since the puppy arrived. She and Lucy May set tables all over the dining room for one solid week—it, the d.r. is now referred to as the Deux Magots for as you observed when you were here it does get a cafe like look and feeling. The parlor is doubtless the Closerie des Lilas.

I wish you could have stayed on for Christmas. We did have a good time—now that it's over I feel as if I'd been in a violent storm; Manny, Red and Cinina arrived first and spent the whole holidays. Cinina took to her bed after the first three days—Manny said the strain of bearing with us was too much for her. We had a party last Saturday night—the Ransoms, Laniers and Owsleys¹—we had to send two couples into the Mallons to sleep and Allen and I slept in the bed with Manson and Rose, quite cosily. Anyhow everybody seemed to have a fairly good time, what with dice and poker and charades. The charade hit of that evening was Lyle stripped to his shorts as the human fly diving into the black mantilla—or perhaps Manson as the bull being worn down by Andrew as the toreador. They have all gone home now and we are settling down to our usual routine.

I am not vain enough to think that Fate sent you journeying down here for my especial benefit but I don't know where I'd be now if you hadn't come. I knew I was on the wrong track but didn't know how to get off it—your comments set me right somehow. (I refer you may by this time have gathered to my book.) I worked right up till the day before the party and hope to have five chapters to send Perkins by the end of this week. I don't believe I can finish the book for spring publication though. Anyhow I'm going to dive in and work as hard as I can for the next two or three months. I was just getting wound up when Christmas came along as I might have known it would.

Thanks for sending The Wings of the Dove.[2] I managed to get through it before Christmas. It's certainly a lesson in construction for any aspiring writer. The way he piles up all those unwieldy parts of the narrative before he sets them clanging off together—it reminds me of the wheels of a locomotive when he once gets it going. The scenes in Milly's palace are magnificent, aren't they? I may plow through it again.

The puppy which Nancy has probably described by this time is a perfect darling. We found two of them abandoned in the middle of the road. Doug took one and we the other, both girls of course. I think she is going to be on the collie order—she has a lovely little white ruff—but I think Uncle Bud will like her anyhow. Nancy has named her Tony but I can't resist calling her Cousin Sis.

Nancy now curls her hair at night. It doesn't really suit her, makes her look rather ordinary but she loves it and it impresses the little girls at school so I let her go ahead. She had a fine Christmas, with the tea set, Just So stories, perfume, a lovely doll and various useful gifts from Santa Claus. The green candles were grand. We had several dinners by them. And the picture frame fills a long felt want in my life. I used to stand and admire a window full of them on the rue Vavin. Little did I think one would ever come to me out of our own ten cent store.

I regret to report that my Aunt Loulie passed out New Year's day after two glasses of eggnog, not cold but rather limp—she, not the eggnog. She said it was from sitting too near the fire and the next day to show that she didn't have a hangover she got up, or rather started ringing bells at six o'clock. I fear Christmas was pretty hard on Loulie.

I must now go back to copying my third chapter. I hope Mac[3] got married all right and that Christmas was all it should have been for the Woods. As for me I'm glad it's over. Love and write, c.

1. Frank L. Owsley was professor of history at Vanderbilt and one of the contributors to *I'll Take My Stand*.
2. The novel by Henry James published in 1902.
3. "Mac" was the nickname of my younger brother, Horace McGuire Wood, who graduated from Antioch College in Ohio and later taught at Black Mountain, N.C.

Clarksville, January 9, 1934
To S. W. in Florida?

Dear Sally: (Excuse the headpiece[1]—only piece of paper left downstairs and you know our stairs.) I had just written you yesterday when your letter came. I am so sorry to hear you had grippe. You ought to have stayed here, you would have had nothing worse than a hangover.

My father has removed himself to Leesburg and hasn't confided the name of the hotel, only one in the town, probably. He was staying at a small place, Clermont, at a most splendid hotel, entitled Lake Highlands. He paid seven dollars a week for everything as I recall. If Mac doesn't mind being what Andrew would call chinchy on his honeymoon he could probably get good rates by telling them he was an intimate friend of the poor old broken down preacher—of course Dad always establishes himself on a long time basis as a member of the family which helps make things cheaper. He fished in lakes both at Clermont and at Leesburg. He is interested, you know, only in catching the same kind of fish he'd be catching on his native heath—he doesn't want to catch big fish.

. . . .

I am going to write at least one sentence today or die trying,
Love, c.

[added as a postscript]
Did I tell you Nick Dudley's remark on the occasion of leaving

Merry Mont—he is taking a Sabbatical year on the next farm: "I sure did hate to get rid of Miss Carrie."

I have told Cousin Sis that when she gets grown a fine Yankee gentleman of Scotch descent will come down courting her and she is much pleased with the idea. Nancy says "All those children will have such fine fur coats." She really is an angel of a puppy. Loulie has completely succumbed to her. She has taken charge of her and calls her to her meals in a piercing affectionate voice. When C[ousin] S[is] hears that voice she tumbles over herself getting there.

1. A chapter outline of *Aleck Maury* was typed at the top of the page.

Clarksville, mid-January ?, 1934
To S. W. in Rochester

My dear Sally:

I am sure you have the flu, possibly with complications. Ford romantically calls these January days "between dog and wolf" and God knows they are hellish to live through. I do so hope you are not sick.

The cold spell, I see by the public prints, was wide spread over the nation but maybe you didn't realize it was a cold spell in Rochester. We register these spells at Benfolly. This one coincided with other major events. First I left the key in the car and ran the battery down so that it, the car, required four strong men and gallons of hot water to get going. Second, the Radfords who had been complaining about the enervating spring weather decided to go to New Orleans. Third, Mabel, Lucy's successor, took a vacation lasting the whole of the spell. With things in this state Allen of course went to bed with flu. It was a mild case and he is up now, playing the violin. Loulie and I really didn't have time to worry about him much we were so busy doing the chores. I packed coal, three rounds a day and I even succeeding in milking the cow. I always thought it was like playing the piano, you either had to learn or have the gift but it seems if you just yank hard enough and rhythmically enough the milk flows. The only problem was keeping your hands warm enough—if it had lasted much longer I was going to drive her into the dining room for the operation. We lived through it, Loulie and I, but we did feel a little bitter to think of Manson, Allen and Mabel lying around here for days and then all being hors de combat at one fell swoop. Allen says it will make us appreciate him more. But I hardly think so as I feel sure he will be in bed with flu again the next cold spell. The pipes froze too, of course. I fear I impose on your sympathetic nature by relating all these untoward events.

Well, for good news, I have one hen setting and I get sometimes as many as nine eggs a day. It interferes with my work, some, wondering if the blue hen has got that egg out yet. But it's such a joy to retrieve your own eggs out of the nest. I have two hens setting! One just started. Other good news: The jonquils were budding and would have been in bloom now if it hadn't turned so cold. And all the shrubs I planted last fall are living. Today is really marvelous, the loveliest hazy light over everything. Scribner's are very enthusiastic about Aleck Maury. I had the funniest letter from Perkins about it. "This book" said he "is about a man doing what he wanted to do. People ought to do what they want to do, not what somebody else thinks they ought to do etc." It was quite touching. I am firmly convinced that I have got myself published on the strength of Perkins' prejudices. First he is crazy about old places and now it seems about doing what you want to do and I happened to make two lucky hits or Penhally would even now be reposing in the bureau drawer.

Nancy, like Perkins, is very crazy about doing only what she wants to do and made forty six in Arithmetic in her mid-year exams. She had absorbed the public school attitude towards education a little too fast but Allen is giving her hell about it and she is doing a little better. She is taking violin lessons from Vratislav Mudroch who thirty years ago was concert-meister of the Prague Symphony Orchestra—he, with Jan Kubelik was [Otakar] Sevcik's most promising pupil in those days. He now resides at Adams, a suburb as it were of Guthrie. I don't know what's happened to the man. I doubt if Nancy will ever do anything with the violin but Allen enjoys Mudroch very much. He is very dark and very Bohemian, which in itself causes him to be looked upon with suspicion in these parts. And he is a very exacting technician which causes him to get few pupils—they say he destroys the love of music in the infants of Clarksville! He came one day, bringing his violin and played something for Allen. God knows what it was but Allen said it was very difficult and he just tossed it off to show what he was capable of tossing off. I rather wish he hadn't come around. He works on my sympathies too much. He makes the leetle ladee hold her stomach in, which is a blessing. He congratulated Allen on our first meeting on his "scientific attainments." He really is a darling. "Adams" he says "is a leetle hole. I am ashamed to live in such a leetle hole."

Speaking of violinists Cinina's brother, Peter, aged thirty four, who has been running a dance orchestra in Indiana or somewhere threw up his job and appeared at the Warrens the other day. It is a good thing you were not here with your impressionable nature. You would likely have fallen for him. He really is a charming creature, awfully good looking and not at all like Cinina except for a family resemblance. He has been driving a hundred miles a night between orchestra engagements and sleeping in his car and so on and says that he is now going to be a dentist and keep music for his own pleasure. Thirty four seems a little late to be starting out on a medical education but he seems quite undaunted. Allen says he's a very good violinist, sort of natural musician, though of course not in Mudroch's class.

Spengler's[1] new book: "The Hour of Decision" is the most exciting thing I've read in a long time. He says that this is the grandest epoch, not only in the Faustian civilization, but in all world history, greater and more terrible than the times of Caesar or Napoleon. And all of us "pale faces" says he have a universal dread of reality. He's very illuminating too on the period from 1861 on. He says it was an abnormal condition that never existed before and never will again—being an "expert" he never hesitates to say what will or won't happen. But now we are back to a normal state, a "life in danger," a mighty age says he relishingly. It's peace that's done us in. Nobody can stand a long peace. We are now "covetous, void of under-standing and incapable of bearing misfortune." All these Utopian concep-tions and Workers' paradises etc. are due to too much peace. But history will take care of that. We now have "one of those incalculable great catas-trophes that are the normal form in which history takes its major turns." You'd like it.

He's very good on the tragic view of life too.

I am alternating Spengler with Pickwick Papers. Before that it was Dracula. Allen and I both think The Dutch Shoe Mystery (Ellery Queen) almost the best detective story we ever read. The only flaw—well, you may not have read it. It really is a jewel.

You don't have anything quite short, say two thousand words? I sold a chapter of Aleck Maury to The Magazine,[2] California thing that's just started, and might be able to sell something for you. They paid me twenty two dollars for the story. It was an excerpt from that possum hunt chapter. It's absurd, or course, to limit short stories to two thousand words as I have told them but [Fred] Kuhlman, the man who runs it has no sense at all.

How is No Saturday Night coming?[3]

I am so afraid you're down with flu. I believe Spengler wastes his worry over the western world. Steam heat and flu will wipe us all out soon anyhow.[4]

Andrew has been quite ill with it [the flu] and writes mournfully from Murfreesboro that youth has gone. He used to recover right away from a bout of flu but now ten days afterwards he is still "deef" and has to get his uncle to read to him and his uncle is drunk and half blind. I fear his romance is not progressing well either. In a military communication issued before he got flu he spoke of treason and spies having been at work and the miscarrying of supplies.

Cousin Sis is quite well except for a rash on her stomach caused from over eating. And Miss Loulie washes the vital oils out of her too.

The cabin got on fire the other night but we put it out. I guess this is all the news,

Love, c.

[added as a postscript]

Nancy appeared on the stage for the first time the other night. She exclaimed "What?" in unison with thirty other children. She wore a blue bastiste that was very sweet one night and the next night her old blue organdie dyed rose color which really looked better than the new dress. . . .

1. Oswald Spengler (1880–1936), German philosopher whose major work, *The Decline of the West,* caused great controversy in the U.S.

2. Edited in Beverly Hills, 1933–1935. Among others, Tate, Blackmur, Winters, Warren, and Williams were published in its pages; the Tates' friend Howard Baker was also closely associated with the magazine.

3. A short story called "There Are No Saturdays Without Sunshine." The title was the first part of a Provençal proverb that concluded, "and no women without love."

4. I did get the flu while alone in the house in Rochester. The furnace stopped working in zero-degree weather, and Uncle Bud ran away—all at the same time. Larry Kohn arrived on the scene and coped with everything. Uncle Bud had never learned English, but Larry spoke French. Neither of us intended to see much of the other, but the little dog did love to ride in his car.

Clarksville, May 22, 1934
To S. W. in Rochester

Dear Sally:

I have written you no less than three letters in the last month. They are all buried in my manuscript—I cannot find a damn one of them. I do hope you are feeling better by this time, what with spring coming on and all. It is lovely here now. The iris is all in bloom, and the Rambler roses and zinnias and nasturtiums and so on would make quite a show in the beds around the house if Fidelia would not prance on them. Daisy Miller has a new calf, Primrose Ann has kittens, chickens hatch apace—all is very fecund at Benfolly, all the lower orders of creation, that is. Me, I am half out of my mind—as usual you will say, and I suppose this crisis will go by like any other. Only I cannot get a cook and Perkins keeps writing me that I must get the novel done as soon as possible. They actually talk as if they might advertize it and then I might have some chance of pulling out of this hole of poverty if only I could get it finished. But the business of cooking three meals a day, churning and so on is too much for me. I am so exhausted by afternoon that I have to get in bed and stay for hours and I can't think of a word to write. I am starting off fresh tomorrow with a little gal, a friend of Beatrice's whom I picked out of a tobacco field. She is sweet and willing, though, and makes right decent biscuits and tomorrow I plan just to leave the lower floor to her. God knows it doesn't matter much what we eat.

I didn't start off to give you a list of our domestic trials though but to tell you to send Sunday Morning Breakfast to Fred Kuhlman The Magazine, 522 California Bank Building, Beverly Hills, Cal.[1] They turned down Karl but they may take this. Anyhow they've changed their policy and are taking ordinary length stories. Do this right away. I am mailing same time I mail this a letter recommending the story whole heartedly and telling him what to think about it. If I can't keep this girl or she isn't adequate I'm going down to stay with Dad a month at Caney Fork. I've got to finish his book or my name is Mud.

In one of the letters I wrote you I gave you a full description of what we refer to as "our accident."[2] We were going to Nashville to a party when a nigger came out of a side road at full speed and crashed into us. It was very odd, the amount of time it all seemed to take. Allen says he debated whether to swerve and decided he'd hit a telephone pole if he did. He said aloud "He's going to hit us" and it seemed years before he did. Our car turned over and over and we were pinned in it but it didn't catch fire. All the glass was shattered yet none of us were cut though my hair was full of broken glass when I got out. The little knob that turns on the ignition was driven deep into Allen's leg but it healed quickly with no trouble. We all took anti-tetanus shots which was unpleasant. (Nancy wasn't with us, thank the Lord; she was very disappointed and said "Next time I'm going to be in the wreck.") I got my shoulder caught between the two seats—I would—and twisted so that it was painful for me to use my arm for nearly a month, and turning over in bed was a feat to be approached very carefully. It set me back nearly a month in my work but we certainly felt lucky to have escaped without any real injury. The car was mashed in like a tin can—we'd have been killed, I suppose, but for Mr. Ford's all steel body. We sold the wreck for three hundred dollars—we got nothing out of the negro, of course—his property was in his wife's name!

. . . .

Loulie has gone—she stood us as long as she could. Do write and let me hear how you are. I'll be a better correspondent if I ever finish this book. Love, c.

1. *The Magazine* took this story, which I called "Breakfast in the Country," and as a result, Clifton Fadiman wrote to ask me if I'd write a novel. This started a long correspondence between us.
2. On April 1, 1934.

Memphis, Tennessee, October 1, 1934
To S. W. in Rochester

Dearest Sally:

About a month ago en route to Benfolly after a hurried trip to New Orleans I spent a night in Memphis. It was too hot to sleep and I read P. G. Wodehouse most of the night and at intervals looked around and reflected that while I had had a hard life and many blows I had never yet had to live in a bungalow such as the one I was then in. A month has passed and I am now installed in a slightly uglier bungalow six blocks from the one I was in that night. It is Red's fault. He was offered a job at

Southwestern, then when a better job came alone he turned this one over to a slightly dazed Allen so here we are.[1] I don't think Allen can stand it more than a year. He takes it very hard and God knows there is enough work for two men. But if we can stick it this year—and we'll have to— and live on little or nothing we may be able to pay off some pressing debts and thus something will have been accomplished. Anyhow that was the idea in coming. The bungalow—the Hamburger House, A[llen] calls it—has a good Confederate address: 2374 Forrest Avenue. It is right by the park too, which is nice. "Third largest free zoo in the world"; I find, though, that the seals are the only animals I can watch with any pleasure. It may be nervousness that makes them play all the time, but they do look happy. It is so sad to stand by the black panther, though, and watch his eye light as he gazes past you and sees a bird on a bough or a plump little boy. The bungalow: thirty dollars a month (have to furnish your own heat etc.) for one large living room, one large dining room, two large bed-rooms papered in morning glories, strong enough our landlady says to crawl down and get in bed with you, one large kitchen, one large pantry, one small bath and one small, dingy though ornamented with a willow tree back yard. And all, thank God, on one floor. The packing up at Ben-folly nearly finished me, being done on three floors as it was. It wouldn't have been so bad but all the company who had been threatening to come all summer came those last two weeks. Virginia Moore, pretty as ever and as much concerned with the finer things of life, though a little upset because Louis [Untermeyer] since his third—or is it fourth—marriage has concealed all his assets and professes to be unable to support their little boy. Little boy awfully cute and precocious and a perfect demon, the kind that runs through the kitchen and slaps the cook every few minutes just to keep things going. Next batch of guests, Herbert Agar and his wife, Eleanor Carroll Chilton (Agar).[2] (That's the way she puts it.) I was very much prejudiced against him because he wrote a sonnet sequence about his marriage to Mrs. (Agar) called "A Year's Burden" concluding with the lines "Pain without ending, sorrow without cease." I was all prepared to defend Mrs. (Agar) against him while he was there but found it all the other way. He's one of those charming, tall, rather saintly men— oh draw Cecil Wright out to seven feet and give him a large nose and you have him.[3] Mrs. A. is at heart an "Oh God the pain girl" but she went to Smith. Nice girl, dresses awfully well. While they were here she got an advance from Bobbs-Merrill of twenty five hundred bones on her next novel. Yep. I read the first page of it that she left on the floor in the guest room. It was a description of her own figure, very well done too.

All this and I haven't mentioned your story![4] It was quite a shock to me when I saw it in The Magazine. They hadn't deigned to write me about it or indeed about one of mine that they've had six months so I thought it was all off. A change has come o'er the spirit of their dream since the demise of the Hound and Horn. They used to write me flattering letters urging me to recommend people etc. Now they are not quite sure whether I can make the grade or not. And they're always announcing that they will not become the organ for any literary party. I imagine Blackmur and the other Hound and Horn relicts have made an effort to capture them. I imagine, too, that B. and the others think the Agrarians are trying to do the same thing. As a matter of fact all the agrarians are too busy keeping the old bean above water to care what literary party they represent. I'd send them some more stuff, something with a labor slant might just hit them, show them you aren't tarred with [the] same brush as me. I'd send them, by all means, some chapters from the book. And right away. Before they have a change of heart.[5]

Memphis is hot as hell and very dull but there is one thing—it has the most wonderful niggers. Cinina said you could just walk out in the street and hail the first one that passed and get a jewel and it's true. The English department are all very nice, all suffer frightfully from boredom except one young man who has devised all sorts of nice ways to amuse himself. He records his own voice and his friends reading Chaucer or singing Frankie and Johnny on the Victrola and copies modern paintings on cardboard, having devised some treatment to make them take paint like canvas. At odd moments he paints still lifes and photographs family portraits and God knows what else. Anyhow he still has plenty of joie de vivre after seven years. The head of the department is a melancholy Dane but awfully nice. His wife is so lonely and bored that she cries out with joy when you take her to a picture show or suggest a steak dinner down town. However Benfolly is not so hot in the winter. I guess we'll make out, if Allen can only stand the work. There's far too much. One Freshman course, a Chaucer course and a seventeenth century lyric course, which isn't such a lot in itself but they have the tutorial system and there are endless conferences with students. The place is lousy with Rhodes scholars. It's in the process of being turned into another Swarthmore.

I hopes very soon to be able to send you fifty bones which you should spend on your rr fare to New Orleans, stopping here en route. No, I can't go to N.O. or anywhere else—unless, of course, Aleck Maury should make money in which case we might do almost anything. It ought to be out in October. I don't see how a book called "Aleck Maury, Sportsman" could possibly sell. That was the title the salesmen finally decided upon. I'm really sick over it. I am thinking of writing a horror story next.

I just got a cook this morning. I tried doing the work for a week myself. I could manage all right and have plenty of time left to write but as Hart said "it constricts my imagination." When I get through the ideas that seemed so hot in the morning aren't worth fooling with.

It's lunch time and I've a million things to do. Do send some more stuff to The Magazine and let me know how it comes out. I thought the story looked swell.

love from all of us, c.

1. Warren went to join Cleanth Brooks at Louisiana State University.
2. Herbert Agar (1897–1980) was a poet, historian, and editor of the Louisville, Ky., *Courier Journal*. He won the Pulitzer Prize for history. Mrs. Agar wrote children's stories.
3. Wright was very frail and thin.
4. "Breakfast in the Country."
5. Improvident as always, I did not follow Caroline's advice on account of the letter I had had from Clifton Fadiman. Would that I had.

Memphis, late October, 1934
To S. W. in Rochester

Dear Sally:

You'd better not bring Larry down here. Allen will certainly go for him. He can never see much in the men his lady friends propose to marry and always says so.[1] I, having a few match making tendencies hate to see him probing into the vitals of a romance so don't do it.

I am glad to hear about Mr. Raushenbush divorcing his wife. The first sensible action of his'n I've heard of in a long time. Don't see how he stood her this long.

I ought to be working this morning but here I go writing to you instead. Aleck Maury is here and looks on the outside pretty good. But it always gives you a sick feeling when you see a book you've written in print—at least it always does me and Allen says it does him too. I reckon everybody is similarly affected. Scribner's, however, cheer me with their advertizing. Their blurb says "A warm hearted human book, shot through with sunlight and the ripple of mountain streams!" And they have put out a circular for the trade advertizing Maury alongside of William Lyons Phelps, Philo Vance and Queen Marie of Roumania,[2] so maybe some money will come out of it. I ought to know by Christmas. By the way I'm ordering your copy today so don't buy one.

Yesterday comes a letter from Ford and Janice saying they will arrive in New York on All Saints' Day, can you beat it. I rushed to the telephone and sent them a cable remembering Ford's weakness for being cabled to then found when it was gone that I had misread the letter and they were already on the boat. God knows whether they ought to have come, probably not. I don't think Ford has been away long enough for his misdeeds to die out in the public, or rather the literary clique mind, and Biala as she now signs herself is not going to help things along.[3] Still it will be nice to see the two critters. I only wish we were at Benfolly and they could have landed at Norfolk.

The Bishops who were to have arrived here today—they have shut up their chateau and have been in this country almost a year with only one French maid, imagine it, have decided to spend the winter in New Orleans. We have been reading John's novel in proof.[4] It ought to be a sensation. The story told by a little boy is the detailed account as presented in court and when I say detailed I mean detailed of a rape—of a gentleman by a Southern lady. It's a brilliant technical feat. I still don't see how he thinks he's going to get away with it.

This leaves us with only Memphis society for perhaps a long stretch. However I like it. It's just dull enough here to afford sufficient diversion and yet not distract you from your work. And the few people we do know here are fine. Childe Jones, for instance, proves quite a treasure. His account of his examination at Oxford at the hands of J. A. Clement Webb and some other old whoozis is a classic, worthy to go down in history beside Brother Micajah.[5]

Those Magazine people are awful. They've still got my story and not a word out of them. I didn't know there was a lynch wave. I've a mind to write my experience at one of our Saturday night lynching parties and send it to him. Bet he'd print it like a shot. It takes shape in my mind already (Hemingway style, not Faulkner, would be best): "It was dark when Bill got to the house that Saturday night. I went to the door myself. "Naw," I said, "I ain't going. I got a cramp in my leg." He didn't say anything for a minute. I could see he felt pretty bad. "Aw, Tom" he said, "you better come. You ain't missed a Saturday night yet."

"Who you going to lynch?" I asked.

"Aunt Sally's Joe."

I knew the nigger he was talking about, a big yellow buck nigger, with gray eyes, my third cousin once removed by my great uncle Lionel.

"All right," I said, "I'll come" and I went in the house and got my rope and we started down the path."

I could do better than that if I took time. Still, I claim the idea is good. You could work up some right pretty stuff about the lynchers, those who were afficionado and those who weren't. It tempts me but I will to work instead.

Have you sent your ms. to Fadiman yet?

We dined night before last with General De Saussure, of the late C.S.A. I've seen and been bored by many a Confederate veteran in my day but this old man is really a gem. His mind clicks right along and it is actually possible to have a conversation with him; he really listens to what you say. He spoke rather disparagingly of the Battle of Bunker Hill, "a mere skirmish" and as for Paul Revere's ride: "The fellow was scared and didn't know what he was doing." He had just flown up to Ohio to meet "my friend, the Commander of the Grand Army of the Republic." The two of them dedicated a tree on some one of the Dawes' estate. Gen. De Saussure said the aeroplane ride was "swell."

Ford's new book—he has another one on top of Henry For Hugh—is about Provence and illustrated by Biala with drawings of a bull fight at Nimes. They might be very good.

I must get to work. Nancy is having a Halloween party tonight and I have to finish a witch's costume and cut out black cats and orange moons to pin on the curtains. I had sworn we wouldn't have even a pet cockroach this winter and here we have an Angora guinea pig. He is really quite sweet, the Angora hair takes away the ratlike look. The children adore him. I'm afraid he won't last long they pet him so much.

I'm certainly distressed to hear you have another operation hanging over you. Are you sure you ought to have it? I'd get two or three opinions anyhow.

The weather that has been so heavenly has at last turned a little cold. But the leaves in the park are still quite brilliant. We are thinking of going to Benfolly this week end. I rather dread it, not knowing how we'll find things.

MUST GET TO WORK. love, c

1. Caroline exaggerates about our plans. Nothing had yet been settled.

2. Phelps was a professor at Yale and a critic; Vance wrote detective stories, and Queen Marie enjoyed talking about herself.

3. Ford had married Violet Hunt, daughter of Alfred Hunt, the Pre-Raphaelite painter, after leaving his first wife, "Mrs. Hueffer," before World War I. Unable to get a divorce in England, he had gone to Germany for it. Ford and Violet Hunt were widely received and entertained before the public discovered that his divorce was not legal in England. At this news, Violet left him and wrote an emotional book about the experience—*The Flurried Years* (London, 1926). Ford had been brought up as a Pre-Raphaelite; his grandfather was the painter Ford Madox Brown. The Pre-Raphaelites were unlike modern Bohemians. They disliked industrialism, but instead of advocating something new, they looked with favor on the Middle Ages and admired saintliness, although it accorded ill with their own tendencies. In charades at Benfolly, the scene of Dante Gabriel Rossetti burying his poems in his wife's casket as a sign of grief and remorse (he had been unfaithful to her) was frequently acted. Then the actor representing Ford as a little boy, wearing one red stocking and one blue, was made to go and steal the poems back.

4. John Peale Bishop, *Act of Darkness* (New York, 1935).

5. Andrew Lytle's joke about the poor white baby who was nursed until, a grown boy, he would tip his hat before beginning.

Memphis, November 27, 1934
To S. W. in Rochester

Dear Sally:

A highly important technical point occurs to me in connection with what you say of page 224 in my book.[1] I will get it down while it's in my mind. I don't believe the term "under writing" or "over writing" applies to points like this—I realize, however, that you were speaking of them in general. You are right in saying that it is hard for me to come out and say the thing as I did there. It's one of my faults as a writer. One reason is because I am afraid. I too often see inexperienced writers thinking that they have done the trick because they have come out and said it when it isn't done at all. And always I come back to the conclusion that it can't be done that way. The only reason I could state the meaning of his life as I did on page 224 is because I had implied it over and over again in all the rest of the book. This was not a statement of fresh fact but a summing up. This is true of Henry James to a much greater extent. In your "Wings of A Dove" which I have obediently read and pondered over, the thing when it is said, comes to you with a cumulative effect, a sort of rounding off of something you've already been brought to accept. It's really as if you'd been knocked down with a sledge hammer and then given one final tap.

I'm glad you approve of Aleck Maury. I read it over once in print and got that sick feeling in the pit of the stomach and laid it aside. I don't think myself that he got enough personal hell—would have made the book more dramatic. Neither of my books so far has been rounded off enough. It was damn careless of me to forget about Dick's eyes.[2]

About cutting the cord. Since you are interested in the psychology of these matters 't'was not I but fate that did it. Half way through I got one of those body blows (metaphors mixed here a bit) that necessitate to say the least sitting down and getting the wind back. But before I got the wind back along comes said fate and gives me the kind of kick in the pants that leads to action of some kind. Aleck Maury is a sick book, like Sassoon's Fox Hunting Man.[3] If I was to work at all I had to work through somebody else's mind as my own had been rendered unendurable to me. Even so it should have been a better book.

*   *   *

We went this weekend to Nashville, Merry Mont and Benfolly. Sixty miles an hour in a cloud of dust all the time. Party at Chink's and Lyle's Friday night. Feature of the evening exhibition of young son by proud Papa Lyle. (Yes, I think his insomnia is already better.) The baby is awfully cute, two months old now. We call him Little Rip. Chink in describing the experience said "Well, I felt a little ripple." If he'd been a girl they could have named her Undine[4] . . . . . Allen stayed for the football game and I went down to Merry Mont on the bus. Pidie and all of 'em had been writing me these letters about something must be done about Ma. I found her much the same, hardly any feebler and just as hell bent as ever on staying at Merry Mont. The weather was fine.

We drove over to Benfolly in the afternoon. Everything seems as all right as you could expect it but the house even on that warm day had the chill of the grave. You could hardly stand to go in and jerk out objects you felt the need of.

Do you really think you'll come down? It would be grand. I can't think of any attractions here except our somewhat enfeebled society and the park. You'd love the park. It's really lovely. I take a walk there every morning before starting work.

I'd better give you our Christmas schedule now—no, I don't suppose you'll be willing to absent yourself from the Wood festivities then. We're leaving here, anyhow, soon as school is out, will spend Christmas Day and one or two others at Merry Mont, then circle back to Memphis, leave Nancy, take on the Johnsons[5] and go to New Orleans to visit the Warrens and Radfords.

I got the second O'Henry prize.[6] It melted, of course, like mist before the debts. I'm beginning to feel very proud of our achievements since coming here—over five hundred dollars worth of debts paid off since the middle of September. I really think the end of the school term may see our heads above water—you have to be deeply in debt to realize how exciting it is to contemplate such a prospect.

Nancy and her friends are playing I Spy all over me and the type-writer. I can't collect my thoughts, anyhow, so I'd better quit. I wouldn't have the heart to send this incoherent letter to anybody but you.

As soon as you have any plans let me know. Of course to speak truth we'd both love to see Larry. Make him drive you down.[7]

love, c.

[added as a postscript]

When speaking of attractions I forgot the walking club. We really have splendid walks, young Jones, Frances Arthur, the Davises[8] and I. Allen won't walk, of course, but attends the tea-supper that follows the walk.

The Magazine kept my story eight months and returned it with a rejection slip.

Brother Micajah's fame seems to have penetrated even to "Esquire." I saw an illustration the other day: three black bearded mountaineers sitting on the porch of a cabin. One says: "I wonder if Maw's through having her baby yit. I'm powerful hongry."

1. *Aleck Maury, Sportsman.*
2. I had reminded her that his eyes would have been open after he drowned, not shut tightly as described in the novel.
3. These books were not sick; she meant that she and Sassoon were trying to escape their present by writing about something very different.
4. Undine is the spirit of the waves or water and also the name of the fairy romance by De La Motte Fouqué, which is read by Lucy in *The Strange Children.*
5. A. Theodore Johnson had come to Southwestern in 1926 and had become professor of English and dean.
6. For "Old Red."
7. Caroline did not recognize the lack of free time of a doctor in practice. In any case, we had not decided about our feelings for each other. Caroline was the only person to whom I had spoken freely. I did visit the Tates on my way down to Florida.
8. Faculty members.

I visited Elizabeth Pickett in Maysville and the Tates in Memphis on my way to Florida after Christmas. Allen looked tired with all the teaching, but Caroline had somewhat grimly recovered from the burden of her debts and had more confidence in her work. Nancy was happy, being near so many children her own age. The bungalow was a very alien setting after Benfolly.

Memphis, February 15, 1935
To S. W. in Delray Beach

Dear Sally:

Your letter just arrived. I was glad to hear from you and glad to know Florida is even better than you thought. I reckon it was the right move after all. There's really nothing can compare with that sense of well being you get from all that sunlight. To make your lot seem brighter even I will report that practically every member of the faculty here thinks that every other member is on the verge of a nervous breakdown. Sam[1] is conceded to be in a bad way, but it is Ted Johnson who seems the worst off. Last Sunday night when the reading of "The Country Wife"[2] finally did come off and what a damn funny play it is Ted stammered so he could hardly read. He had the same symptoms once before just before a break down. I went to tea at Mrs. Jett-De Saussure's yesterday,[3] with Marie and Ponny. We all agreed that it was the weather had everybody in such a state.

Well, this is just a note to let you know that if you don't hear from

me in some time it will be because I am up to my ears in The Cup of
Fury. I looked at the calendar this morning and got scared, realizing that I
have only three and a half months left when I can be sure of a chance to
work. So here goes.

That Scribner advertizing man was here last night. He had a letter
from Webber, ad. mgr. of Scribner's saying Aleck Maury to date had sold
1300 copies which is not at all cheering. I signed the Eng. contract yesterday but haven't got any money yet.

Nancy is still thrilled over her dancing lessons.

Allen returned from Cincinnati with reports of great goings on.
Ben is thoroughly committed to the project and has found what they have
always needed: a young man aching for something to do with plenty of
money and already converted to the cause.[4] Allen goes back in March for
a banquet and some more conferences. Now that it begins to look like it
will go through we begin to wonder how we can stand living under Ben's
nose—the mag. will have to be in Cin. if they put up the money. Allen
dreads the idea more than I do though I can see how it would be a good
deal of Tate to have around.

Well, that bridge doesn't have to be crossed yet. Must get to work.
Will send you Act of D[arkness] soon as I get through. Have torn my hair
for days over the review which turned out rotten.

Dixie Lee is pretty sick. Cold I think but I can't help thinking of
rabies. There's a scare over it in town now. I've dosed her with argyrol,
Vick's etc. and am trying to tone her system up with raw meat but she
doesn't get much better. I think what she needs is Florida.

Poor Hauptman[5]—I think he is innocent.

The liquor came the afternoon you left. It would, of course. Well,
since you've a bar rail to park your feet on I'll keep it with pleasure. Still
raiding here.

I am sorry your visit was so short but I suppose it would always be
like that. I don't think we were in a very bright state ourselves.

Four of the jonquils transplanted from Benfolly are blooming in
the back yard amidst the grime.

I have talked the Nineteenth Century Club out of a plan to
"honor" us with a tea. Mrs. Myrick keeps coming.[6]

The black panther at the zoo is dead, got in a fight through the bars with the puma that looked so sick. The man at the pavillion comes and brings me all the zoo news when I sit there for my Coke now. One of the lions, raised on a bottle used to be such a pleasure to him he said. They led him around on a leash and used to bring him to the pavillion every afternoon for his ice cream cone which he ate, the pavillion manager says "very nicely." But as he got older he lost his taste for ice cream and got savage so had to stop his visits to the pavillion.

WILL NOW GET TO WORK.

I had the grippe last week—mostly I think as a result of losing sleep while Allen was away. I really was scared and took a hair brush to bed with me, thinking to use it as a Dillinger pistol if any invader came. I was really sick only two days—it was rather a relief to have something quite definite the matter with me. I feel swell now I'm over it. Fortunately neither Allen nor Nancy took it from me.

Will NOW get to work, Love and have as good a time as you can. c.

[added as a postscript]

Thomas Wolfe's new project is called: Of Time and the River, or The Hunger of Man's Soul in Youth.

The grippe came to the relief of my figure. I have just weighed at the grocery—130 pounds with my coat on. It must weight 2 lbs. at least. I'd believe the scales wrong except that a dress I've had to quit wearing now fits me perfectly.

1. Samuel H. Monk had come to Southwestern in 1924; later he was professor of English at Minnesota, where Allen finally received a permanent appointment.
2. The play by William Wycherley, dated 1675.
3. Wife of the Confederate general.
4. Allen and his brother Ben were planning to start a little magazine in Cincinnati.
5. Bruno Hauptman, convicted of kidnapping Lindbergh's child.
6. A woman Caroline was tutoring in writing. A small beginning of her later teaching.

The next letter also was written to me at Delray Beach, Florida, then a small, almost completely southern resort. I was spending all my time writing or swimming—no social life. My younger brother and sister-in-law were also there, but they lived in a house of their own, not very near me.

Memphis, March 6, 1935
To S. W. in Delray Beach

Dear Sally:

Your letter has just come. I fear you are suffering for books. I am
a worm not to have sent you Act of D[arkness]. I finally finished reviewing it, wrote a rotten review, and should have got it off days ago. But
have been in bed with flu for five days now. Being in bed for five days is
so unusual I can hardly believe it's me. It's grippe, of course . . . . . Yes,
I realize I might have rabies. In fact Robin Mason is coming out this
afternoon to see about me. He really is sweet, just my idea of a doctor.
He came out once before and gave his opinion on both Dixie Lee and
me. He was sure D. L. didn't have rabies but she continued sick so long
and seemed to suffer so I took her to the pound where she was put in a
lethal chamber. Poor little devil. She was gay to the last, always wagging
that absurd tail. I discovered that Rastus next door had had a bad case of
distemper. She must have caught it from him.

There has been an epidemic of New York visitors. Louis Untermeyer lectured here and we had him to dinner a few nights ago. Louis is
worse than ever. He refers now to "my practically permanent wife." Allen
says her picture looks like a tough jazz baby. On Louis' heels comes Nathan Asch[1] who is really terrible. Allen never could endure Nathan and
I've invited him to dinner Sunday night. I imagine he's down here spying
around on some Communist agitation.

I made borscht for Louis and it turns out that he himself is a great
borscht maker—of course he would be of the sour bread school.

Notes from Merry Mont: Bill Gordon,[2] after years in the city has
forgotten the way of mules. He went out at dusk the other day and passing the barn saw the men taking the mules out. Went up and started to
help one of them, took hold of a trace chain then slipped the ground
being very muddy. The chain being suddenly tightened made the mule
kick. He struck Bill right on the temple. He was knocked unconscious.
Poor old Ma had just closed the blinds for the night when they came
bringing Bill in. I suppose she thought he was dead but she stood up to
things with her usual courage, got a drink into him and bathed his tem-
ples and so on. They took him to Clarksville, still unconscious. The

doctor says there's no concussion or broken bones and thinks he's perfectly all right. But it was certainly a miraculous escape. We're still a little
worried about him, of course.

Allen has had an idea for a poem with Dracula as the basis but can't
get the proper framework. He has been able to do a little work, meaning
writing, lately, which causes great rejoicing in the household. The other
night when the play readers were here he delayed coming in to finish an
article. I remarked that this was the first day's work he'd been able to do
since we came here. They all turned on me, of course, with "What do you
think he does every day?" and I was hardly able to explain that work to
me means typewriter.

This is no letter. I've been lying here for five days with nothing to
read but Henry James. The Portrait of a Lady is marvelous. It took care of
two days of my invalidism for me. I was really so excited towards the last I
didn't mind having the grippe. But that Sense of the Past—try that sometimes when the inside of your head feels like it's made of mud, anyhow.
Honestly, those Midmores and that Ralph are too much. I swear to God,
I have come to a conclusion about Henry—it may be the delusion of a
fevered brain—but I believe he's like the little girl with the curl, when he's
bad he's really awful. I must read S[ense] of [the] P[ast] some time when
I'm well and see if it really is awful.

. . . .

Mrs. Myrick still comes, still full of hope.

We went to supper the other night at the funniest place, people
named Lake. Old Mrs. L. one of those peculiarly offensive, peculiarly
Southern women, filled with wind. Always talking about "Uncle Andrew"
(Jackson). Offended Allen who says you might just as well, say Uncle
George (Wash.) or Uncle Napoleon.

Really no use sending this letter. But it will let you know we're all
extant. . . . I really am better. Expect to be up tomorrow.

Love. will send Bishop,

c

[added as a postscript]

Didn't get this mailed when I wrote it and now I'm up, for the first
time today and enjoying very much being out of that bed. The weather's
lovely, forsythia and jonquils in bloom everywhere.

1. A Polish-American writer (1902–1964) and one of the "lost generation." His best-known novel is *Pay Day*; he also wrote reviews and did script writing in Hollywood.
2. Caroline's brother.

Memphis, March 23, 1935
To S. W. in Delray Beach

My dear Sally:

How are you bearing up? I imagine you on the last stretch, perhaps, of your book. Your grim silence seems to promise great works at any rate. I hope you haven't just been taking time off to have grippe. It would be positively indecent of you in that climate.

We have managed to wear through the last month and it has been a hell of a month too. I had grippe till I really forgot what normal life was like. I couldn't really believe it could take me like that and popped up and down for weeks. It was all a little complicated too by fears that it might after all be rabies. In fact my doctor's wife called off a dinner engagement one night for the protection, I'm sure of her two Scotties. I am all right again now—feel like a stream that has been ice bound with congestion all gone from my chest—and quite chipper. It was a wonder Allen and Nancy didn't take it.

It is really spring here now, forsythia in bloom in the park and plum blossoms showing white through the woods. Red bud is out too and willows, of course, and everything looks pretty swell. Makes us homesick for Benfolly, of course.

I have in the last three of four weeks fought a great fight and conquered. I have written a story concocted and executed with my eyes on the Saturday Evening Post and yesterday after repeated goings over with Buckingham[1] we got the damn thing out of the house. I really thought it would kill me before I got it done—I know my coming down with grippe was just a ruse to escape from it. But it was waiting for me when I got up and I just waded in and finished it. If I do say it myself it is a pretty neat article—full of the real dope, supplied by Buckingham—lousy with expressions like "he blazed into a point so hot it smoked" and all working up to a swell finale in which Falcon's Speed Boy by Speed Merchant out of Ensley's Flirt wins the National stake, thereby enabling his master to marry The Girl. Buckingham particularly admired the way the "love interest was handled." "No gooey, morbid love making" were his words. The Girl needless to say, fulfilled Dad's cardinal requirement—pure as the driven snow though just a little doggy. Now that it is out of the house I wait with absolutely no curiosity to know its fate. If it sells I am perhaps done for—I would have to do others. If it doesn't sell I am sustained by the thought that Clarence Budington Kelland himself couldn't have put forth greater effort.[2]

But damned if that Buckingham didn't turn out and come out with another idea—a story to be called Wild Goose Bill. I have thought about that Bill for several days now and I just don't believe I can face him. There are limits.

More important news that I haven't mentioned is that Allen is at last working again. If a paralytic had suddenly thrown away his crutch to take dance steps we couldn't be more pleased. It has considerably lightened the thick murk of gloom that has hung over this household for two years now. He has written an essay on the Profession of Letters in the South and is now revising his whole book of essays.[3] He has also indited an admonitory poem to his whilom friend, J. G. Fletcher.

One night, it is now two weeks ago, we were waked about eleven o'clock by the arrival of a special delivery letter. From Fletcher. He said "I am through with you"—he was offended because Allen published an article in the Va. Quarterly Review which he has quarreled with. Since then we have had on an average of a letter a day explaining why he is through with Allen. One had a note appended to the effect that Allen must tell me that our friendship was at an end also though he valued it highly etc. The poor creature is off his head, I think. He also told Ransom he was through with him. Ransom came back with a rather un-Ransomian "Who do you think you are to be giving me orders?" The Ransoms, by the way, are having a baby in April. I haven't got over the shock yet.

The Cincinnati deal is still on[4] though nothing definite has been done yet. Allen and Andrew go up there next week. Speaking of deals how about yours and Larry's?[5] Is it still on? Or have you been too much occupied with your book to decide yet whether you'd get married?

Well, I thought most kindly of Larry the other night when consuming the last of his liquor which I so basely kept—it was base though how when it is so hard to wrap up an ordinary parcel can one bring oneself to send good liquor out of the state? By the way we expect to have legal liquor the 23rd—across the bridge in Arkansas. Everybody is quite excited.

It seems months since you were here—in fact it hardly seems that you were here at all we were all so low in our minds during that gloomy stretch from January to March. I have come to dread it. I seem to have a sort of moral collapse every year at the same time. Perhaps one escapes it if one goes to Florida.

The faculty are all pretty well recovered from their nervous break downs though Sam Monk staged an extra one last week. He didn't get the Guggenheim. I think he'd counted on it subconsciously to release him from an intolerable situation here and it has gone hard with him.

We go finally to tea tomorrow with the poetess whom Allen has so fought knowing.⁶ She came to call herself—after I had met her daughter somewhere and liked her—and turns out to be one of the nicest people we've met here. A woman, however, of decided charm. One feels a little sorry for the daughter to always have to be a foil to it.

I must fall to and do my evening stretch of reading. Hard day. Mrs. Myrick in the morning. Tea with lots of ladies and a singer in the afternoon. Mrs. Myrick, thank God, has just about finished her book. We delivered the baby, shot the villain and reworked a passionate love scene, all this week. The funny thing is that she actually has learned a few simple things, like showing two people sitting in a room. The awful part is that she says she wants to dedicate the book to me.

I suppose you are by now surrounded by your family. Love to your mother if she's down there,

love from all of us,
caroline

1. Nash Buckingham, an expert on dogs, who collaborated with Caroline on the story "B from Bull's Foot," *Scribner's* (August, 1936).
2. Kelland was a banal popular writer at this time.
3. Allen's book was *Reactionary Essays on Poetry and Ideas*, published in 1936. The essay appeared in the *Virginia Quarterly Review* (April, 1935).
4. Ben Tate's offer to buy a magazine with Allen.
5. Larry and I were extremely partial to each other, but not to the idea of marriage. We were putting it off.
6. Probably Anne Goodwin Winslow.

During the winter of 1934–1935 the Southern Tenant Farmers' Union, backed by Norman Thomas and the Socialist party, had been trying to organize the sharecroppers suffering in the social and economic distress indirectly caused by the New Deal attempt to curtail cotton acreage; the big plantation owners and town businessmen tacitly encouraged violence and terrorism to frighten organizers and union members, evicted troublesome tenants, and generated hostility to the "Reds," coming in to destroy the "southern way of life." Marked Tree, then an Arkansas Delta village of two thousand people (half black) forty miles northwest of Memphis, was in the center of the violence. This area of the Delta had been covered in virgin timber until recently, and lumber companies still owned most of the land, now in cotton. The largest landowner in the county (seventeen thousand acres) was the Chapman-Dewey Lumber Company, whose resident manager was A. C. Spellings. The Reverend J. Abner Sage, pastor of the First Methodist Church, was a close associate of Spellings and preached against the "shiftless poor." Fred H. Stafford, also a close associate of Spellings, was deputy county prosecutor and defined himself as an authority on the "Red menace." The mayor was J. E. Fox, owner of a small store. On April 15, 1935, the New York Times *began a series of articles on the situation by F. Raymond Daniell that ran through the rest of the week.*

Memphis, Spring, 1935
To S. W. in Wrightsville Beach

Dearest Sally:

I think after this you could tell practically anybody to go to hell. I've been anxious about you, wanting at least to know where you were and it was a great relief to get your letter. You're quite right to finish the book, I think. Katherine Anne is the only person I know who can afford to leave things unfinished and even she complains that the jagged ends of 'em sometimes wake her up at night. By the way she writes that she is coming to Benfolly in August—I think she really will land in America this time because her husband on leave is paid three times as much salary if he goes to his own country for vacation—neat way the consular service has of keeping up the home ties.

Allen is toying with the idea of summer school—it's a temptation of the devil and he recognizes it as such. He'll only do it if he gets enough students to make up four hundred dollars.

This morning a handsome black and yellow hand woven rug arrived from Norris, Tenn. I can't think who sent it unless it'd be you or James Rorty.[1] Hearty thanks if it was you but I rather imagine you're too occupied with your book to go around buying rugs for friends. I believe it must be James—a conscience gift as 't'were. He left us the other day in a most horrible mess. We picked him up at the Southern writers conference at Baton Rouge a week or so ago. There is always a New Englander at these affairs—the next one will go ungreeted by me, though I'm fond of James in spite of all. He, like so many of them, is roaming the country—since last October. He's more thorough. The others usually devote a few weeks to the grand tour—well, James has been a-roaming this country in search of material for a book. His thoughts turn, of course, to Marked Tree and the trouble with the share croppers' union there. He stopped over in Memphis to investigate and stayed with us. We had many talks around the fireside in which we stated our various opinions. It's quite evident, of course, that we differ from him on several fundamentals but he asked Allen to go over to Marked Tree with him. I hated dreadfully for Allen to go. In fact Cassandra-like I foresaw the whole damned show but there was no way I could get the vision across to either of them. Well, we went. We interviewed the district attorney and the riding boss of the plantation where most of the trouble has been. The d.a. was a belligerent fool. The riding boss is one of the smoothest articles I have ever seen. It was a pleasure to see him work. James was a child in his hands. I do not believe that James in his interrogation scored one single point off that man—everything was parried, covered beforehand, doubtless, and all the information was given with a detached, casual air—he might have been talking about something a thousand miles away. Everything would have been all right if James hadn't decided he must see the preacher, the Rev. Abner Sage who runs a cooperative association—organized against the union. We stopped the rev. on the street. The rev. said he didn't care to be interviewed. James proceeded to interview him anyhow. "Who put me on the witness stand?" says the rev. "Well, why aren't you willing to be interviewed?" says J. "See here," says the rev. "if any more of the fellows come in here asking questions there's going to be trouble and if you don't let me alone there's going to be trouble for you right now." At which point James concludes the interview and we depart thinking the preacher is pretty awful. We were a little embarrassed by James' method of questioning—he is pretty belligerent and neither Allen nor I believe northern agitators ever do anything but harm in the south. Still we didn't think much about it till we get home when that evening Dr. Diehl[2] calls Allen up and asks him to come to a conference in his office. The preacher, the plantation boss, the mayor of the town and the filling station operator who heard the conversation are all there. The preacher and his cohorts threaten that if any story is written they will give a story to the A.P. saying as how this northern agitator accompanied by a Southwestern professor stopped him on the street (blocked his passage on the street) and questioned him against his will. Some of James' questions when repeated by the other side do sound pretty insolent. His tone of voice didn't help 'em any either. The college was just on the verge of a drive for funds to carry on with. There isn't anything Allen can say of course except that he doesn't think James will write a story. He comes back and reports the whole matter to James. James expresses a great deal of compunction. I'm sure it was genuine too and wonders what he can do to smooth things over. It is so obvious that the only thing he can do is not to write a story—he was there for half of one day and didn't discover one fact that Daniell hadn't set forth in his Times articles—that we didn't even think it necessary to ask him not to write a story. After he had left something told me that he was busy writing a story—I could just hear the click of that Rorty typewriter. We pursued him by telegram through Nashville to Knoxville. He sent a carbon of the story he had written, three pages saying merely that things were in a pretty tense state at Marked Tree— there was absolutely no news in it and I don't know why the Post would want to print it. But he stated that he was accompanied to Marked Tree by Allen Tate and Caroline Gordon "who strongly disapprove of northern interference in Southern affairs . . . . ." Of course the question that leaps to the mind is why then are they such fools as to take a Northern agitator in there? I'm damned if I know but it's been a lesson to us, one that was needed probably.

. . . .

      . . . they [poor whites] live in the most desolate huts with not a tree to shade them, hard baked ground all around. Their situation is not any worse, perhaps, than that of the share cropper on any delta plantation but God knows it's bad enough. The Socialists seem almost inspired, though, in their mishandling of the situation. They have refused to adapt the union to the country in any way whatsoever. These plantation owners who are bleeding the people have been shrewder. The union refuses aid to any non-union member but the plantation co-op aids all alike. Neither Allen nor I quite realized how bad things were over there or we'd never have taken James over—we did so very reluctantly because we knew that it was impossible for him to do any good there and very likely that he would do harm which he promptly did, of course.

. . . .

He's really an awfully nice fellow—I got to like him very much. I just don't think you can trust a radical because where the revolution is concerned they can't have any personal loyalties. He is positively rabid on the subject that the Agrarians must develop a field technique eventually which is certainly true. But adopting the present radical technique which is really what he demands of us won't get us anywhere and besides as I have tried in vain to make him see Allen and John Ransom and Don Davidson would make damn poor field workers. And I don't really think it's up to them—they've formulated the doctrine. Somebody else will have to put it into practice.

. . . .

We all went to Red's Southern writers conference in Baton Rouge, being as our way was paid by Huey,[3] and had a grand time. Ford came down for it, but Janice didn't. Ford and Allen went back by train but Polly Lytle and I drove over to New Orleans and stayed four or five days, a-pleasuring ourselves as Andrew would put it. (His health was not yet recovered from the Christmas debauch so he couldn't attend.) Manson [Radford] is working on relief interviewing niggers. Rose is working steadily and has done some fine things—I never saw anybody's work show such rapid development as hers has in the last year and a half.

The convention was really quite interesting. It was divided quite neatly into two armed camps, the Agrarians and those who thought there were far too many Agrarians present. The Agrarians having the confer-ence in a sack, as it were, through Red's being presiding officer, started out discussing the Southern tradition in relation to literature. Lyle Saxon[4] and Roark Bradford, the only real big shots there, listened in a puzzled silence. Finally when they'd got to the point of whether it was a good thing to have all publishing come through New York Saxon gets up and says (looking very fat and well massaged) "New York has treated some of us mighty well and I for one don't believe in biting the hand that's feeding you." Bradford felt called on to make a speech too then so he said that a good story was a good story anywhere and he didn't know what they were talking about anyhow.

Mrs. Bradford in the rear could be heard audibly observing that she had worked in a publisher's office for five years and it was all a matter of making the right contacts. "Just a talk over a cocktail in a speak easy." Any speak easy (I swear this is what she said) would do. The New Orleans Times Picayune who are against Huey of course reported that Allen looked like the Little Colonel and that Bradford brought the light of cold common sense to the matter. John Bishop, straddling the fence, as usual, was also reported as speaking sensibly—I think they just trusted him on instinct.

For me the highlight of the convention was a limerick. Red says it's the only necrophilic limerick he knows of. Well, anyhow Bishop and some other gents having got the women off to New Orleans were reciting limericks. This is the only version I've been able to get but it gives you the idea:

> There was an old fellow named Dave
> Who kept a dead whore in a cave
> He said I admit   (God knows what these
> I'm a bit of a nit   lines really are)
> But look at the money I save.

. . . .

I suppose it's nearly summer at Wrightsville Beach—it's really heavenly here now. The leaves are still in that tender green stage and roses in bloom everywhere—even in the backyard of the Hamburger house. We are dying to get back to Benfolly—I don't know whether we could stand summer school—it would keep us here till July first—still I suppose we may have to.

Allen has his book of essays almost in shape to send to a publisher. I have The Cup of Fury pretty well planned out—every day I think I'll get the opening sentences. I'm afraid to force them. Lovat Dickson[5] has decided to call my book "The Pastimes of Aleck Maury" which seems odd when the book was written mostly to prove that sport is not a pastime. Still I don't suppose it makes much difference. I finished the story with Buckingham and it was a beaut. The agent said perfect Sat. Eve. Post. The

Post said not quite. Collier's has it now. The agent says they can surely sell it and urges me to write more. But I don't know whether I can or not. It put me in bed for weeks. I've just got over it.

No real news here. Ariadne is really going to have kittens. We're all disgusted with her, including Theseus. Do write and let us know the minute you finish the book. It will be almost as much of a relief to me as to you. I think one reason I'm so down on it is that your writing has become so good in the last few years that I hate to see it wasted on nonfiction.

Love . . . . .

C.

[added as a postscript]

Fletcher, of course, appeared at Baton Rouge, armed to the teeth. After telling us that he was through with us and could never be friends again he wrote saying he'd like to drive down there with us. I wrote back that his place in the car was now filled by Ford. He writes back that Ford being an Englishman has no right to be at the conference or to appear in the new magazine they're starting and that he'll fight him and me to the death. I was going to suggest pistols and coffee for him and Ford under the duelling oaks but Allen said let him ride. When he got there he was as mild as milk and was particularly nice to Ford. I really think the man is mad.

1. James Rorty had married Winifred Raushenbush, and it was on account of my previous connection with the family that he was acquainted with the Tates.
2. President of Southwestern College at Memphis.
3. Huey Long, governor of Louisiana (1928–1931) and U.S. senator (1931–1935).
4. American writer (1891–1946), author of *Old Louisiana* (1929) and *Children of Strangers* (1937).
5. British publisher of *Aleck Maury*.

Memphis, June 2, 1935
To S. W. in Rochester

Dear Sally:

I had been wondering just what had become of you.

. . . .

Well, thank God the manuscript is off.[1] When I finished Aleck

Maury I had the persistent delusion that I was a baseball and was just about to whiz over the fence. The trip to New Orleans with Manson driving cured the delusion. Maybe getting married will have the same salutary effect in your case. I hope your family does not take it all very hard. Don't call it off now you've got this far. Allen, by the way, is working on your wedding present this afternoon and he will be sad if there is no occasion to send the present which he secretly thinks is very fine.

We have just been down town sweating over the question of trading the Memphis gas stove and ice box for an oil stove to be used at Benfolly. It is very exhausting because if I get a stove here my grandmother may give me one after I get to Clarksville. There is also the matter of transporting Ariadne and Theseus—I mention all this just to show you that everybody has problems. We expect to get away from here, bag and baggage, Wednesday morning. Rosy suddenly decided this morning that she would go with us which sheds quite a glow on the proceedings. Last year's cook has got married and I had no idea where to get another one.

Childe Jones has departed for Oxford, escaping exams by some sort of hocus pocus and arousing great envy in the breasts of the rest of the faculty. The year is really drawing to a close. Tomorrow the poor devils have to hear two sermons. Sam Monk suggests that we make a trip to Arkansas for liquor—you can get it across the bridge now, thank God—and all get very drunk which I think we—at least I—will do.

I have written three chapters of The Cup of Fury. It doesn't seem to go very well when you examine it in detail. I can only hope it will be impressive in the mass. Anyhow I am going to barge through, paying very little attention to the writing of it.

No real news and I'm too hot and tired to write it if there were. Do write as soon as you are able. My felicitations to Larry and love for you from all of us,

c.

1. My manuscript—"The Education of Nancy Calkins."

Larry and I finally decided to marry, and since he had a fairly large practice in Rochester and also taught at the medical school, this had to be considered a more or less public event. In those days doctors still made house calls and dealt with emergencies at night and on weekends. Larry was far from thinking of his wife

as being solely domestic. His mother had been an M.D. in the early nineties—
that was the kind of companionship he wanted from a woman.

At the idea of my getting married, Allen Tate shook his head and said I
would never get over being a gypsy. He was wrong. Clifton Fadiman, whom I
saw after submitting my "Education of Nancy Calkins," which he finally re-
fused, said that I would never write anything in Rochester. He was wrong too.

Clarksville, June 15, 1935
To S. W. in Rochester

Dearest Sally:

I was just wondering whether I ought not after all to write letters
this morning instead of trying to work on my novel when the mail came
with the lovely velvet coat. I can see you going over things and saying
Caroline really ought to have this and then heaving yourself together for
the superhuman effort of getting it off. It really is a superhuman effort
and it was sweet of you to think of me. It is lovely. I am due to have a
new evening dress next winter and I shall have a white one to go with it.

Well, we are now what you might call settled at Benfolly only it
doesn't really seem like Benfolly. We have worked steadily since our arrival
a week ago and as a result the place is cleaner, things more in order than
we have ever had them. I wish you could see Benfolly clean and in order
just once. It really looks quite nice. Allen is still on a debauch of painting
but I have got so bored with waxing and polishing and taking things upstairs and downstairs that I have washed my hands of the whole business.
The house has got all the attention out of me that it will get this whole
summer. Rosy decided to come with us, after all, and is grimly carrying
on downstairs. God knows it is a comfort not to have to break a new one
in. We found things in very good order, really. The yard greener than it
has ever been and the whole hill blooming with larkspur. Daisy Miller
doesn't like larkspur but she ate up all the hollyhocks. The cats had had to
go out and forage but they are all straggling back, Tri-Couleur came in
day before yesterday so weak she could hardly work her jaws to eat. We
now have only Colonel Crockett, Blue Tato, Tri-Couleur, Theseus,
Ariadne and a stray cat who is not going to be named as I am going to
chloroform her.

The usual flow of company has set in; Ford and Janice to our surprise telegraphed that they would come tomorrow and stay two weeks, and Sam Monk and Ted Johnson arrive tomorrow too on their way north. Sam's friends the McGhees[1] have taken a house in Tory Valley about a mile from where we used to live. Little May is at Guthrie—her aunt May is quite ill. She wanted us to drive to Meridian to Dicky's[2] wedding which we might have done if we'd still been in Memphis but couldn't think of doing now. She seems highly pleased with her daughter-in-law. Hope it'll last. Well, May is easily pleased.

I wish you would write us some definite news about your own plans. Whether you're going to get married or whether you ain't. If you ain't it is time to start a new book. But God knows it's always time to start a new book. I've written three chapters of mine.

I wish, my girl, that you could cast your eye on Merry Mont. I almost fainted on the threshold when we arrived. Never was there such a transformation. Everybody had told me about it but descriptions pale beside the actuality. They haven't painted the house yet but that's all they have left undone. Uncle Doc's room is the jewel—it should have a little fence at the door and be put on exhibit with admission charged, I think. A tester mahogany bed with a rose satin quilted canopy is the piece de resistance but there are always cigarettes on the night stand by the bed—it didn't really seem right. Ma looks like a cat that has swallowed two canaries. They have used miracles of tact in handling her, letting her keep both her winter and summer bedroom and letting her fool with the milk all day long just as of old. I only hope the poor children can stick it out. But Bill has always had the secret of handling her. When she gets peevish he leans down from his great height, slaps her on the shoulder and says "Why, Ma, you know I've always been your favorite grandson."

Emily Mallon has been quite ill, had peritonitis and still has some pelvic infection left over. Both the Mallons seem rather depressed. They are all coming out Saturday night and we aim to play charades in the old time way. I am going to try to get Ted Johnson drunk.

I wish you were making your visit now instead of during that horrible spell in February. I believe that time is ghastly anywhere except positively tropical places though God knows the furnace doesn't need to choose just that time to quit working.

It has rained for weeks here and the country is miraculously green. All our little trees are living which gives us a very opulent feeling. Of course they may die during the August drouth but it is nice to see them now. My zinnias are just coming up but the roses just over so I'm dependent on wild flowers for the house.

Please write. Love and thanks for the lovely coat. I shall enjoy wearing it very much,

as ever,

c.

1. The McGhees were also friends of mine, as was Sam Monk. Paul McGhee came from Rochester, where his wife, Elizabeth, studied music at the Eastman School. Paul developed New York University's adult education program and became a dean. Sam Monk and I were godparents to Paul and Elizabeth's two sons.
2. Little May and Sherman Morse's son.

Louisville, Kentucky, July, 1935
To S. W. in Rochester

Dearest Sally:

It now seems to be the end of July and I now realize that you were married on June 29. Well, I reckon you've realized it too by this time. Do write and tell us where you are living and how. Did you have the wedding the day after you mailed the manuscript or did you rest up a few days?

We are now in Louisville. We have hardly been at Benfolly all summer. I don't know exactly how it happens. As Andrew says he and I have not been of this world for many weeks now. Oh yes, we closed Benfolly, sent Rosy to Memphis, bought a lot of clothes I could ill afford and set off for Michigan to a school of creative writing[1] because Joseph Brewer, the president of said school had promised us each fifty dollars a week and living expenses. Allen with his rare presence of mind had thought to leave a forwarding address at the Western Union so Mr. B.'s telegram caught us in Louisville. He said that being as only two pupils had turned up for the school he thought it best to call it off. Being all packed up and having forgot in the mad rush to get Rosy's address in Memphis we decided to move on to Cornsilk for our annual visit. And a good thing, too, it proved.

I never saw such a place for work as Cornsilk. The first morning I was there I walked as in a trance into a secluded corner of the dining room. I dug myself out a spot by removing several bushels of peanuts, a

mediaeval cuirass, three or four demijohns of cherry bounce etc., set up a
card table in the spot thus cleared and almost without thinking began to
write steadily. Having carried your ms. all over the United States you will
understand what a phenomenon this was. And the strange thing was that
this spot—it's about two by four—this spot which proved such a wonderful place, I couldn't even see it at first for the peanuts and things. Well,
God moves in a mysterious way . . . . . Writing there I produced fifteen
thousand words in one week. I could say twenty thousand but I wish to
make a conservative estimate. Why, I am almost through the first section
of The Cup. If I can only get back to Cornsilk I will start on the war part
next week. The war part will be very simple. Style something like this:
"Waving his bloody right hand high above his head he charged into the
battle. 'My God, men,' he screamed, 'will you see them kill your general
before your eyes?'" (Wyeth's Life of Forrest. I am just lifting sentences
like these from every place I find them.)

It is too bad you didn't land at Cornsilk during your peregrinations
with your book. I am convinced that you would not have had to expend
so much moral energy getting it written. I think it is the spectacle of Andrew's father's unbridled energy. As A. says he begins the world new every
morning. This sounds annoying in a person but it isn't in him. Running
half a dozen farms doesn't satisfy him—he specializes in making fancy
desserts for dinner. Comes in from the field around eleven o'clock attended by two field hands, shouts for a quart of whipped cream and starts
in and makes something marvelous for dinner. We had Jesse Sparks' First
Wife's Roman Punch for dinner the other night and all wished she could
have been there to taste it. (Mr. L. rejects the second wife's recipes, says
she was no housekeeper. He uses only a Murfreesboro cookbook.)

Andrew doesn't find all these goings on as stimulating as I do. He
has had to retire to the woods to write. It's the turkeys. There are four
hundred and A. says it is hard enough to reject the world and the flesh
without having to reject the turkey world anew every morning. We are
neck and neck on our books and hope to finish in time for a debauch in
New Orleans at Christmas. You and Larry better come join us. Of course
I may not be there. I don't see how I can make it. But Perkins has put the
fear of God into me by practically promising to make it the leader on
Scribner's list if I get it in for spring publication. I think the reason is that
all of their big shots have just published a book and they're actually look-

ing around for a leader—it may never happen again, God knows, and I'm certainly going to try to make it.

We came up here a few days ago to visit the Agars. Allen couldn't stand the Cornsilk pace. He's right torn in his mind, is Allen. As an overworked professor he ought to rest all summer but as a writer with four overdue contracts he can't relish the rest much. Slowly but surely he's being forced to the wall—he'll have to work during August.

The Alcestis Press are bringing Allen's poems out this summer in a most deluxe edition.[2] I can hardly wait to see it.

Lovat Dickson is advertising Aleck Maury in England as a book full of clean thinking and healthful living. The only clipping I've had commented: "Truly, publishers are odd cards."

Dr. Sanborn is giving us a dachshund puppy. I think a dachshund puppy will suit Nancy's style, don't you?

Now that I'm getting so much work done we've decided to visit the rest of the summer and are returning to Cornsilk in a few days. I never realized before how much work you could get done visiting. We work till five every day, then we swim in the lake then we wrestle with the problem of which cocktail we'll have—you can make a marvelous vermouth cassis with cherry bounce—then we eat an enormous dinner and fall into bed. I always go to sleep on the front porch right after dinner. I feel rather guilty, somehow, not being at Benfolly and visiting instead of being visited but it's grand. I like it. Of course the system wouldn't work with anybody but Mr. Lytle. He is a man who revels all day long in his own aesthetic pleasures so he's indulgent to other people.

I do wish you would write. You can see that a letter from me will hardly be worth receiving—me being in a sort of submerged condition till I finish this book. But I do want to hear all your news. I wish we could all have a bat in New Orleans Christmas.

Much love and felicitations to Larry. Allen has a record of one of his poems for you. I believe it's "The Mediterranean." It's very interesting making records of poems. He's been making a good many this summer but few turn out well. The Ode to the Confederate Dead he's tried several times. The voice sounds like a politician.

[added as a postscript]
Mr. Lytle has a Fidus Achates,[3] a "white" man named George.

George has a farm of his own but he prefers to live with Mr. Lytle because life is so much more exciting there. One day George and I were there alone for several hours. He kept coming back in every now and then to try to tell me what kind of man Mr. Lytle was, his Napoleonic talents and his noble nature. Finally with his face working he said "Why, that man, if he liked you he wouldn't think nothing of killing a calf for you." Two nights later we had home killed veal for supper. George looked at me with triumph in his eye.

1. Olivet College in Michigan.
2. *The Mediterranean and Other Poems* (1936), twelve copies printed for Ben Tate.
3. The prototype of the faithful friend in Virgil's *Aeneid*.

Guntersville, August 8, 1935
To Sally Wood, now Mrs. Lawrence Kohn of Rochester and not so free to make journeys

---

Dearest Sally:

Your letter describing the wedding has just come and was much enjoyed. I knew the ceremonies attendant would be an ordeal in a way—I am glad they turned out to have some pleasant spots. They sound swell to me. I am sure Mikey and Hugh[1] were very grateful to you for giving them such a swell time.

No, we didn't go to Michigan—I realize that I have had a letter to you written and lying around for weeks. The reason I haven't mailed it is not just orneriness either but we've been in one of those recurrent periods of waiting for a check to come in so I just let the letters accumulate till the check does come in. Seems strange to be broke and living as I consider myself doing in the lap of luxury. This life at Cornsilk gets better every day, at least for anybody writing a book. The routine—we speak of it now as "THE" routine is almost inflexible. Andrew and I did allow ourselves to get drawn into an argument last night by some visitors and got the blood up into our heads instead of being down at our feet where it should have been at such an hour and consequently were a little late going to sleep and were afraid we might be stale this morning. We weren't, though, just started right off to work like two clocks. THE routine is breakfast, work, lunch, short nap, work, swim from five to six thirty, cocktail (one) supper, bed. Sleep like hell. Get up and go at it again. Even Allen wrote two pages this morning.

Your wedding present, by the way, is a record of one of Allen's poems. He vacillates as to which one it is to be. We made a good many. Some were duds but those that are successful are very lifelike, almost weird effect. It's lots of fun. You realize you don't really know the poems till you've heard them that way. I was making you what I thought were going to be some handsome table mats, double hemstitched till they look lacy but I got preoccupied and put in some pretty dreadful stitching and I begin to fear now they won't do. Will send the record, though, tout de suite.

By the way next summer we may accept that invitation to Rochester! Letter from Mark Van Doren says he has made arrangements for Allen to give five lectures at Columbia for the sum of four hundred bucks! Imagine emerging from the year at Memphis with enough money to live on during the summer. This means that I can certainly finish The Cup of Fury before another year rolls around, Deo Volente, as Dad says.

The wedding present notes must be awful.

Must get to work.

Love,
C.

---

1. The reception was in my sister's garden. My little nephews ate quantities of cakes unobserved and enjoyed throwing rose petals.

Letters were lost here.

Larry and I had been trout fishing in Canada with his father. Fortunately, I had been brought up to fish. Then I had been getting to know the medical world in Rochester, which I enjoyed. It was close knit and noncompetitive. As Larry said, "We have one common enemy, disease."

The Tates had had to move back to Memphis where Allen could teach. Their writing had not produced enough money to live at Benfolly.

Memphis, October 27, 1935
To S. W. in Rochester

Dear Sally:

I was writing a business letter yesterday. Allen said I ought to date it. I knew the day of the month but I had to ask him the year.

With me it is September 18, 19th, 20th, 1863—just starting on the battle of Chickamauga, having returned from a scout on Stone's river. I am, you will see, a poor correspondent, and likely to be that way till I finish this book. Scribner's hold out promises if I will only finish it by December 1. I can't do it but I have to try.

. . . .

We are established for the winter in a bungalow on the other, the leafy end of Forest avenue. Allen calls it our gold oaken nest and it is pretty full of g. o. But there is a heavenly work room glassed-in sun parlor at the back of the house which we both enjoy.

Allen is getting the ms. of his essays off to the publisher.[1] Nancy strained a muscle in her knee yesterday trying to kick the back of her head in dancing class but it seems to be all right now. She is going to Mrs. Jett's school this year—Mrs. J made such handsome offers we couldn't resist—and likes it very much. Only eight in a class where there were twenty eight at the public school. She has dancing along with the other frills you will be glad to know and is accumulating a small, carefully selected French vocabulary—she will not allow us to add a word to it— "Mama, we don't have words like that"—continues very fat and healthy. Colonel David Crockett alone of all the cats accompanied us here from Benfolly. It is pretty sad. He was the bully of Benfolly but the Memphis cats have got him licked.

The colors in the park are gorgeous but I don't see much of them. I have been working till ten and eleven every night.

I have been pursuing some by ways in the literature of the civil war period. One book has the adventures of a Union woman, spy, prostitute, psalm singer and I think nymphomaniac who seems to have had the time of her life during the war. There is one strange affair with a dying Confederate soldier. "Strange how attractive disease is" says she. I have also discovered a Confederate Cranford. Three old maiden ladies in South Carolina who were tyrannized over by their servants. They had a butler who was so indolent that he burst into tears when they told him company was coming to tea. Their coachman, a confirmed drunkard, drove right over them hoop skirts and all when he came to fetch them home from the theatre. They preserved the skirts with the print of the horses' shoes to show how kind Providence had been to preserve them. Another story I want to write some day is an altercation over the virginity of a battery. "No Rebel's hand had ever been laid on that gun" one of these Union gunners insists, "We had always been proud of her virginity. Colonel So and So is mistaken when he says so and so . . . . ." I shall resist the temptation to call the gun "Lady Lil" though there was one gun called "Lady Davis." And Cousin Kitty, the old lady at Eupedon,[2] had a gun named for her: "The Kitty Tutwiler."

But I spare you. Nancy said very crossly last night "Mama, I don't care what those Confederate soldiers ate." She and Allen were complaining of their dinner and it seemed to me so unreasonable when I had just been reading about men picking blackberries as they went into line of battle.

If Larry would write to Nash Buckingham, Box 720, Memphis he would get the very best advice possible about a dog. Nash Buckingham in that line is the most learned man of my acquaintance. Larry is sweet to like Aleck. Well, I got the royalty report on him from England the other day. Seems I owe the publisher thirty pounds.

By the way Larry might like the story Nash Buckingham and I have in I think the December Scribner's.[3] The story, faked by me, is no good but the dope, all got from Nash is really swell.

Do write, even if I am such an unsatisfactory correspondent. I hope to get out of this press of work before the winter is over.

Love,

c.

[added as a postscript]

I repeat I am the worst adviser in the world. If you take this group of people and fill your story with the light and warmth of Sunday Morning Breakfast—and that I think is what you'd do—you'd have something. The mother in there with her stretched skirts and belt buckle is grand.

1. *Reactionary Essays on Poetry and Ideas* (New York: Scribner's, 1936).
2. Another Meriwether plantation.
3. "B from Bull's Foot."

Memphis, January 8, 1936
To S. W. in Rochester

Dear Sally:

I do not think that Nancy is going to be a writer. She certainly writes very laconic letters at any rate.

She loved the little dress and it looks sweet on her. . . . . I suppose, if the cold snap was as general as we were told you can imagine how cold Benfolly was at Christmas. I thought I would die the first day but it was rather fun after we got fires going—and after our blood thickened up a little.

We have just got back to the Memphis bungalow after a rather confusing holiday. We'd invited a lot of people to Benfolly but as the days went on and they didn't telegraph or write we got tired of waiting for them and went off to Louisville to visit the Agars. They all came while we were gone, of course. Some of them were pretty bitter. Andrew was wandering around middle Tennessee with a twenty-five pound turkey for days (not bitter, of course. He never gets bitter.) We all finally met, including turkey, at James Waller's in Nashville. Had a fine time there though it was rather funny. James' mother had been away in New York visiting her daughter. She arrived on an early morning train, was considerate enough to take a taxi out. When she entered her house she was greeted by a long howl from the basement—Vili, our dog, was shut up there. Poor Mrs. W. thought at first that somebody had left a baby on her doorstep she says. She rushed from bedroom to bedroom and found a strange head on every pillow. Finally, the heads all being fathoms deep in sleep she retired to the first floor and gave us quite a shock when we came down to breakfast.

I suppose the worst contretemps of the festive season was the Warrens' Christmas Eve which they spent in the servants' room at Benfolly with Rose and the Normans.[1] They had never written a word about it but it seemed they expected to spend Christmas with us. We, of course, had gone out to Merry Mont and were at that moment keeping Miss Carrie company. Cinina was pretty mad.

Well, I'm glad it's all over and I am back in the bungalow, even with the prospect of work to face. I think Andrew and Polly are coming down soon for an indefinite stay. Andrew is halfway through his novel[2] but as he confessed to me in a dangerous psychical condition. He's arrived at the civil war part and says he feels cold to it. We all agree that something ought to be done when Andrew is cold to the civil war so we've decided to spend the next few months together and try to whoop each other on. Their movements at present, however, are rather embarrassed by the number of animals they've collected during three months' stay at Monteagle.

There's a horse, a Russian wolfhound, a mongrel bitch with seven pups and a turkey. The turkey is the worst as she cannot bear to be alone. Andrew's grandmother let her roost for several nights on the headboard of Andrew's bed but I don't think the old lady will keep that up long. The furniture in that house is all teakwood or rosewood or something carved in great obscene excrescences—must have been a funny sight.

Please don't ever pay any attention to anything I say about novels or short stories, in fact about writing in general. I have just read half of Andrew's novel. Everything he's done I'd have said couldn't be pulled off (and it's true there are some pretty bad spots) but somehow he's contrived to turn out some tremendous stuff—it may be a sort of Wuthering Heights.

Well, I, in turn, must get to work. I hope you and Larry had a good Christmas—my idea of a good Christmas, really, is staying in bed and reading an omnibus of crime—well, anyhow, I hope you didn't drink too much.[3] Do write and let us know how you are and what you're doing. This incoherent note is the first I've written. My brain was congealed for several days and I'm just testing it out.

Love—and thanks for the lovely sweater. The dog, by the way, is a dachshund and so nervous that he jumps if you look at him. He is sweet, though, and reluctantly I've grown very fond of him.

Caroline

. . . .

[added as a postscript]

Vili, the dachshund, has one parlor trick. It is to do a "Temple Drake."[4] It isn't really much of a trick for him. He skitters from room to room in exactly the way Temple did—I begin to think Popeye is a misunderstood character in fiction. That skittering would provoke to almost any crime. He is getting over it a little but he can't bear anybody but me which is a disappointment as we got him for Nancy's dog. He does love his mother, though, in fact he always speaks of her as his sainted mother. He spoke only German when we got him but now he speaks the vernacular mostly. We left him—and the unfortunate Rosy—alone at Benfolly while we went to Louisville. He wrecked the dining room, ripped the curtains to shreds and, quite a feat I thought for such a short dog, tore the curtain rods off. I am proud to state, however, that during his stay at

Mrs. Waller's he did not commit one single nuisance except for a few scratches on her bathroom which I hope she'll never notice. He loves Benfolly—I had him off the leash there for the first time and we had some splendid walks in the snow. I think in time he will be quite a dog. Dr. Sanborn, who breeds this strain, says that one dog he gave away took a year to get used to his new owners—pleasant prospect.

Vili did bite Sam Monk, Sam's fault, of course. He insisted on holding Vili in his lap and talking German to him. Vili stood it until Sam made a sudden movement when he automatically sank his teeth in his arm. But as I told Sam all his own fault. I'd warned him not to make a sudden movement. Vili just can't bear them. Anyhow, it was the inspiration for a good charade Christmas time. Will Lamp, a very solemn Dutchman enacting the role of Sam, Nancy as Vili. Will was smarter than Sam. He whispered in Nancy's ear before he sat down that she was not to bite him really.

1. Tenant farmers.
2. *The Long Night* (1936).
3. Little did Caroline know of a medical Christmas. It is one of a doctor's busiest days.
4. A character in Faulkner's *Sanctuary*.

After the college term was over the Tates still did not have enough money to return to Benfolly. In Rochester, Larry and I were busy buying a house. It had to be within one traffic light of his office.

Allen had resigned from his teaching position at Southwestern. After giving the Phi Beta Kappa address at the University of Virginia, he had turned to the writing of his novel, The Fathers *(1938). He was jointly editing* Who owns America? *with Herbert Agar.*

Monteagle, Tennessee, September 10, 1936
To S. W. in Rochester

Dear Sally:

Allen just came back from the village with your letter. I was just getting ready to get drunk in preparation to calling on Mrs. Waller, an old lady here on the mountain—desperate situation, this call. Have to go. Will kill us to do it. Polly and I decided it was better to go drunk than not at all—well, I will write you a brief note before hitting the bottle.

We are at Monteagle, in Andrew's log cabin. We have been here
two weeks during which two weeks I have mastered details of life in
Camps Chase, Douglas, Johnson's Island and Fort Lafayette. I have also
written nine thousand words. I have twenty more thousand to write, including the Battle of Brice's Cross Roads, the technical details of the
strategy of which I have not yet studied out. When I get these thirty thousand words done I shall be through with my Civil war novel, entitled
"The Cup of Fury"—and hasn't it been one? One reason I haven't written
to you or anybody else has been that until the middle of June I was working all day and all night on said novel. I am nearly dead. However, I am
usually nearly dead so let that pass. Where was I? Oh, at Andrew's cabin.
Well, we came up here because we like to live with Andrew and also
because we can live here so much more cheaply than at Benfolly. We will
probably never open Benfolly again till one of us writes a best seller.

Before coming here to this mountain we looked at a great many
other mountains, including the Smokies and the Green mountains, also
hills in Michigan. We left Memphis in June and rapidly traversed twelve
states, stopping off in Michigan (Olivet) for two weeks where we offici-
ated at a writer's conference. We were—and the conference was—a great
success. The middle westerners are lovely, kind people. They were crazy
about the conference and the staff. They admired us so and we worked so
hard with them that it drained us all of our vitality. Alfred Kreymborg[1]
used to get up in the morning and say "Don't come near me. I've stored
up some vitality. I can't waste it on you." By the way we almost came to
see you. We went to—God knows what town—anyhow where you take a
boat on a lake, probably Lake Erie. Allen worked it out; I couldn't take in
the details, too exhausted. We were going to get on the boat with the car
and get off at another town, probably Buffalo. Then we were going to
drive by Rochester but we got there twenty minutes late and they
wouldn't let us on the boat. Then Allen said we had to go another way—
he was already almost late for his lectures at Columbia. He lectured at Columbia and we stayed in New York a while—ate too much, drank too
much. We also went to Connecticut and other places. Then we came
home. While I was in New York I saw my publisher who said The C[up]
of F[ury] was all right so far as it went but he would like to know what
became of some of the minor characters. He also complained that I killed
too many young men. I came here, settled down and have killed one more
young man, besides giving one chronic diarrhea and the other a gangre-

nous foot. I don't care whether he likes it or not. Margaret Mitchell has got all the trade, damn her. They say it took her ten years to write that novel. Why couldn't it have taken her twelve? Andrew's book of Vengeance[2] is off to a fine start. Bobbs-Merrill are simply splitting themselves over it. He may make some money.

I am glad you have got a house. It sounds nice, specially the rose-bush. Canada sounds fine too. Hope to do some walking up here if I can get caught up on my work.

I am now going out to get that drink. I wasn't writing today because I was too exhausted, after knocking out two thousand words yesterday before lunch. It's a mean trick to write anybody a letter when you're in that state but it was now or never. I am going to have to stick to it every minute in order to get through by the eighth of October which is the last day Scribner allows me on revision.

                                          Love,
                                          c.

1. American playwright, poet, and critic (1883–1966).
2. *The Long Night.*

Monteagle, January 8, 1937
To S. W. in Rochester

_____

Dear Sally:

Nancy's handkerchiefs—and won't she get a thrill out of them!—were awaiting us when we got back from a hellish trip to Richmond and points east. The letter you mentioned in your Christmas card has never come. Maybe it went to Andrew who is now in Monteagle.

We started out from here weeks ago and ricocheted between Chattanooga, Merry Mont, Nashville and Washington until I thought I would go mad. However it is over now and we are back in the log cabin and damn glad to be here. We had Christmas eve and Christmas day with Nancy in Chattanooga then sandwiched in a visit to Merry Mont and went on to Richmond where Allen read a paper on poetry at the Modern Language Association. The program was all Fugitives except Mark Van Doren who came down from New York for a day and night. Lots of talking and drinking in hotel bedrooms. Miss Ellen Glasgow gave an eggnog party which I got through nicely by collaring the first man I saw and saying Bring me a whiskey and soda. After Richmond we went on to Washington to meet Seward Collins and his bride, Seward and Allen conferring about the American Review. The bride, Dorothea Brande, the Wake up and Live lady[1] woke up and found that her mink coat had been stolen from her suite together with other valuables. What it is to be rich. We leave our door open for hours and nothing is ever stolen. We felt bad about the mink coat as they had come down to meet us. (The papers had it that they had come to attend Mrs. Evalyn Walsh McLean's New Year's eve blowout. Quite a contrast between Mrs. McLean and Allen whom they'd really come to see.) Dorothea said she had bought the mink coat to impress clubwomen who treat visiting lecturers like hired help unless they have mink coats and it was a judgment on her as she really hated mink coats. Hope she gets it back but the detectives seemed very dumb to me. We all, being ardent detective story readers, cautioned those detectives about smearing the finger prints on the door knobs etc but they went right on smearing them.

Next year—if I have the cash—I am going into a hospital two weeks before Christmas and emerge only when it is safely over. I believe I hate it worse every year. Nancy, however, had a grand time. She had set her heart on a sapphire ring and other trinkets and Santa came across with all of them. She will adore the little handkerchiefs. She is living in the house with a sixteen year old cousin who is pretty snooty to Nancy. Those monograms will put quite a crimp in Moggy.

I forgot to report on Merry Mont—I would not spare you any detail of my sufferings. My aunt, Loulie (surely you know that noble woman, the one who made the immortal remark about the menopause. "I saw it was all foolishness so I just stopped it.") Well she is now at Merry Mont taking care of Miss Carrie. Being so benevolent Loulie always has a few lame ducks to exercise her benevolence on. The two she has now are Little May's mother, Cousin Mag and another Cousin, Kitty. Cousin Mag except for that persistent delusion that she is a pea that has rolled into a crack in the floor is quite sound on practically every subject, including the King and Mrs. Simpson. Cousin Kitty wrings her hands and mutters and paces the floor all day. Her conversation goes like this. "Lord have mercy on me . . . . . Don't that dog have short legs . . . . . Lord have mercy on me . . . . . I told Loulie not to do that . . . . . Lord have mercy on

me . . . . ." Allen as he sank to rest that night murmured "I'm not afraid
of Cousin Mag but I am afraid of Cousin Kitty" and gets up and puts a
chair against the door. My grandmother is in high feather. She and Loulie
wage continual war. Ma: "If I didn't have any better memory than you
have I'd offer myself to an institution." Loulie: "I would if I weren't
already the head of one." All pretty grisly yet they managed to have quite
a little Christmas spirit with eggnog before breakfast and all the other
ritual observances. I felt ten years older when I emerged from the fray,
however . . . . . Yes, I'm going to write a novel about them. It will be
pretty Russian. I think I'll call it "The Women on the Porch."[2] The two
lunatics will furnish the chorus. I'll try to restrain myself when it comes to
those lunatics but they are tempting.

By the way, if my generally unsound advice is of any help on your
current opus it, the said advice, is at your service. I just haven't been any
good on anything like that for the last two years. That Civil war novel
kept my nose closer to the grindstone than I thought a nose could go and
not be pared off. And now that it's all over I realize dismally that the book
doesn't come off.[3] I could have done it too if I could have had just a little
more time but I was still writing extra chapters up to a few weeks ago.
And of course Margaret Mitchell has taken all the trade. I think I might
have made some money but for her. But how can people go on reading
about the civil war forever? I sold my book in England the other day, to
Constable. The British government takes over half of the advance and I
suppose they'll take as much out of the royalties if there are any.

Allen is developing some kodak prints. I enclose some. Tell Uncle
Bud to take a good look at the Herr Baron Vili von Isarthal. The Herr
Baron is like Abraham Lincoln. He says that all that he is or hopes to be
he owes to his sainted mother. He still growls at Allen when he makes a
sudden movement or sometimes he just sits and looks at him emitting a
thoughtful growl. He thinks the typewriter is my voice or rather that it is
I who emit those constant clickings. When I go away he mopes and will
not eat but they can always lure him into a room by typing rapidly. The
white poodle dog in the picture of the log cagin is the Duke of Cornsilk.
He is a self made man. Used to belong to the bootlegger but decided he'd
rather belong to us. The baron thinks he is pretty silly.

Speaking of Uncle Bud whom should we run into in Richmond
but Thomas Wolfe. He was drunk and dumb and extremely amiable. He

kept looking at me and blubbering "Mrs. Gordon, Max Perkins thinks you're wonderful." He is so dumb that he can hardly follow a conversation. We were talking about the wonderful whore house scene in Sanctuary. Wolfe assured us solemnly that he had intimate acquaintance with whore houses in many places and that whore house wasn't true to life.

Must go to bed and catch up on some of the sleep Christmas deprived me of. Christmas really is awful. I can't say I hope you had a good time. You couldn't have. Hope only that it wasn't too fatiguing.

Love,
Caroline

1. Dorothea Brande (1893–1948) was on the editorial staff of the *American Review*. She wrote the book *Wake Up and Live* (New York, 1930).
2. She did it. The three women became the three Fates.
3. This was just the usual writer's fatigue after finishing a book. The book contains some extraordinary descriptions of battles.

Clarksville, May, 1937
To S. W. in Rochester

Dear Sally:

. . . .

We are back at Benfolly after two years' absence. It has taken us two weeks to brush off the debris and drag the furniture up and downstairs but today for the first time we feel settled and are able each of us to sit down at our desks and assume at least the attitude of one about to write something. I have the servant's room for study—having a cook who sleeps out, thank God—and Allen is sitting this moment at a most elegant desk, a combination book case and desk which he has built into that dank corner of the dining room where the plaster had all fallen off. It is positively elegant—he admits it is his masterpiece. Until this morning he said nobly that he was going to turn it over to Ford but he just said "I can't do it. I've got to have it myself."

Ford and Janice arrive Tuesday, by car, bus or train we know not—but eighty pounds of Janice's pictures are already at the express office waiting to be brought out. I am hoping that this year they will reconcile themselves to not having French cooking. Last time Janice was quite bitter about that but if she could spend a day with the cook I now have she

might understand. I spent yesterday going through the motions necessary
to get one simple dinner of roast lamb, green peas, rice, asparagus with
mayonnaise and cream pie. (I have discovered after forty years of dealing
with negroes that you can never tell them anything but they can always
imitate motions. God, the time I have wasted telling them when I should
have been showing them!) This one is named Ida and often goes upstairs
here when she means to go downstairs—she says this house baffles her—
as it has me these many years. She was telling me of a neighbor who spent
the winter in Florida and has now gone off "to a new place. I fergits what
they call it . . . . . Europe, that's what they calls it." I told her you had to
get to it in a boat and she says it must be a sight to be seen.

Benfolly, you will see, is running in the same old way, except that
the Normans have not had a baby for three years. Dorothy Caroline (I
was the midwife at her birth hence the honor) is walking and talking. Mr.
Norman said a few years ago he for one would be glad when "it" was all
over. I have hopes that it is all over for Mr. Norman and that henceforth
he can keep his thoughts only on heaven.

Staying away from Benfolly really seems to help it. Our hill is
greener than I have ever seen it, thick turf over the whole sweep and even
a few flowers—pale blue iris blooming. The locust trees are all blooming
too this year and smell heavenly. I was sorry Janice missed the dogwood.
She might have done something nice with it. Occasionally flowers bring
out her best talents. I am curious to see how she has progressed in the
years since I've seen any of her work. I hope to God, too, that she is less
pretentious about it. Manson reports that she is miraculously well behaved. (He says he does not believe she exists, that Ford 'took pleasure in
creating her out of his head.') She was certainly not well behaved last time
she visited us, a hellion, in fact, but maybe we bring out the worst in her.

I am trying to finish a novel called "The Garden of Adonis" (see
The Golden Bough) in time for fall publication. Such announcements are
getting monotonous—I know people are tired of hearing them. I think
it's absurd for me to get out another novel so soon but Scribner's insist
that the iron is hot and must be struck quickly. NSB[1] has sold about ten
thousand. That gives us enough money to live on—frugally—for a year
irrespective of what comes in from England. It is a wonderful feeling. Of
course I don't get any of it until October. However having a year provided for is good enough.

Allen is halfway through his novel.[2] It is going to be good too. I didn't think he had that particular kind of writing in him.

Have you read Djuna Barnes' "Nightwood"? It is a remarkable thing—the doctor's bedroom is one of the finest scenes I know anywhere —but I don't on the whole agree with Eliot about it.

Well, must get to work. No news from us you see except of books trying to get written and domestic chores. Is there any chance of you two ever coming to see us?

> *Love,*
> *caroline*

[added as a postscript]

I cannot remember whether I have reported on Merry Mont recently. It is now in the final stages of decay, and this winter was in strange and lurid bloom. Loulie was there taking care of Ma and with her several insane cousins, two, in fact but they so filled the house one had the illusion of many. One, Little May's mother, is placid and gentle, the other, Cousin Kitty, walks the floor, muttering "Lord have mercy on me." She keeps this refrain going continually and interpolates her comments on everyday matters: "Lord have mercy on me . . . . . You reckon Nick is going to milk tonight? . . . . . Lord have mercy on me . . . . . Where is that nigger going with that mule? . . . . . Lord have mercy on me . . . . ." Ma took them all very calmly. Her comment on Kitty was a reference to Jane Eyre: "Reminds me of Mr. Rochester's wife" says Ma.

My next novel is to be a study of Merry Mont. I am going to call it "The Women on the Porch." I hope the title sounds sinister. It's meant to be.

One thing, I don't have to worry about the old figure these days. Down to 126. Benfolly took four pounds off in four days.

Second Installment

Had this letter written several days ago but couldn't get around to mailing it. Your letter came this morning. I can't see why Scribner's should have sent it back—they make a point of sending on dozens of tiresome letters. You didn't mention your eye again so I suppose it was nothing serious. Glad you're over flu—and glad you liked the book. I think it has some merit but am still uncertain whether a book can be written using that scheme. The Brothers Karamazov which hinges on the fact that each of the brothers is morally guilty of his father's death does not really come off as I found by re-reading it last year. Comforting to think about that. I am inclined, I know, to have too rigid a scheme. I think Lucy ought to have been allowed to have a little more life in order to be stricken down more convincingly but I wrote the damn thing at top speed. One thing I really succeeded with, I believe: each battle, it seemed to me had to be treated in a different way or you'd get monotony—some people complained as it was. I treated Fort Donelson in Plutarchian style, reserving my impressionism for Chickamauga. I was worried about that but now after some months believe it works out all right. Main fault in the book is that I didn't devote enough space to the people's private lives. Oh, well . . . . . After one month's rest (January) I am finishing up another. I think it will deal a sad blow to what little reputation I have but needs must when the devil keeps driving.

It is so lovely here today I really shouldn't be complaining of the devil. The wistaria is in full bloom on the portico, my two lemon lilies bloomed this morning, the peas in the garden are in bloom and the lettuce will be ready to eat in a few days. I really think we're going to have a garden this year.

The Fords arrived last Wednesday and we've shaken down into a routine—but not without strife. I took Janice by the horns last night before she'd had time to get really obnoxious and explained to her that while I seemed very feckless I had in my way a system and that it didn't include French cooking by a Tennessee negro or by me either. We had for dinner yesterday spring lamb, home grown strawberries, new potatoes and cauliflower with Hollandaise sauce. A damn good dinner I call it; I knocked off work at ten to cook it. Janice said if I'd only had [*sic*] told her in time we could have had the cauliflower Polonaise. "No, we wouldn't," says I, "we like it better Hollandaise." It's dreadful to feel that way about a guest but I knew she would run me nuts and ruin my book if I didn't smack her paws off the bat.[3] When I think of all the people I've had here, feeding them on a shoe string (financially if not literally)—you, I suppose, were the most patient and long suffering, but none of them ever really complained. I just made up my mind I wouldn't take any of her damn nonsense . . . . . She takes a spanking well, is extremely amiable this morning and resolved to be good.

Further note on life at Benfolly: The other day we had what I believe is the strangest visitation we ever had. Allen and I were standing in the circle admiring the lemon lilies when a car drove up to the gate and a young man got out. He stopped down there by the post box and answered the calls of Nature then ascended the slope. We stood there eyeing him sternly and were on the point of shouting "defense d'uriner" when he came up to Allen, regarded him fixedly and muttered something about Ford. Something made us treat him more gently and ask him into the house. He is a young man named Lowell from Massachusetts who heard Ford lecture in Boston and as he wasn't getting on well at Harvard decided to come south to learn how to write. We kept him overnight and sent him on to Nashville to learn further about writing. I think Ford really rescued him from a bad situation. His family decided he was crazy because he wants to be a poet and had him in a psychopathic sanitarium. He does have a queer eye on him but is very well behaved and affable, but imagine a Lowell (yes, the poor boy's mother is a Cabot)—imagine one coming all the way from Boston to sit at Southern feet.[4]

Must get to work. Nancy arrives the twenty second. She wrote us a long letter the other day saying "I hope the Fords won't stay long. I can't have any company while they're there, can I?" There is a little girl she wants to have visit her. "Her mama is a clubwoman, though" which I thought the most pathetic note. I've given her the way upstairs bedroom and have fixed it up a bit and am determined that she shall have her company, Fords or no Fords.

We do wish you and Larry could come down.

> *Love,*
> *caroline*

[added as another postscript]
The Fords brought with them Janice's sister-in-law who is acting as Ford's secretary—no I don't think he's making any passes at her. She is a pretty, modest child (one of those half dozen typical Jewish faces you see so often in New York). A rabid Communist she asked me shyly the other day "How wise would it be to have the Daily Worker sent to me here? I can't live without it?" I think she thought she might be ridden off of Benfolly on a rail if caught with a copy of the Worker. It would be too impossible if she were at all like Janice but she is really a sweet child and very

agreeable. Wife of Janice's brother, Jack, whom I can live a long time without meeting.[5]

Allen who has always taken a gloomy view of the Janice question says he thinks Ford is about to shake her off—and insists that he will leave her with us!///xcc***. I verily believe I would drop her in the river with less compunction than if she were a puppy or kitten. But I believe Ford knows he couldn't get away with that.

1. *None Shall Look Back*.
2. *The Fathers*.
3. Ford had trained Janice in French cooking. It was his influence really, but he understood Caroline's difficulties and Janice did not.
4. The young man, Robert Lowell, did not go on to Nashville, or if he did, he came back. Caroline said airily, "I'm sorry. There's no place to put you unless we put up a tent on the lawn." The next day they were amazed to see a tent there. Lowell wrote an account of his visit in the *Sewanee Review* (Fall, 1959), in which he dates his arrival in April. The episode at the mailbox is transformed into smashing it with the bumper of his car, and he remembers bringing the tent only on his third visit.
5. Jack Tworkov, a famous painter, who lived in Provincetown.

Clarksville, July 10, 1937
To S. W. in Rochester

Dearest Sally:

First (I know it grows monotonous but so many facts are monotonous: I have four days in which to finish my novel, collect clothes for Olivet etc. etc.) This remark in case the letter following sounds more than usually crazy. (I've done the cooking for six or eight people all summer besides writing the novel.) Have a negro girl who washes dishes but can't clean up because there is somebody writing a book in every room in the house. Anyhow we have lived through the summer and the Fords, too, are still breathing though a little wan. We've really got through beautifully but you can imagine how it's been. Ford has had insomnia, indigestion and gout to boot and many days is confined to the middle floor. I don't think I'd have had the courage to ask them to come if I'd known about the indigestion. His diet is difficult as it is. But enough of that.

We go to Michigan July 15 for one of those schools of writing. (It is like being put under glass and having all the air pumped out of your lungs). We return here August 1 and after that we will be very much at home—lonely, doubtless since all the captains and kings will have departed. (Ford and Janice go on to the coast and sail from there for France.)

Much as I want you and Larry to visit us I wouldn't have cared to have you these last two months. The grandnephew of James Russell Lowell lives in an umbrella tent on the lawn. Ford saw him in Boston and told him to go south young man and learn how to write. He promptly came. Ford was so enraged at being taken literally that he doesn't speak to him at the table. He's such a nice boy. Drives me out to Merry Mont to haul in buttermilk etc., flits the dining room—the handiest boy I ever knew, in fact. When he isn't doing errands he retires to his tent whence a low bumble emerges—Robert reading Andrew Marvell aloud to get the scansion. I've given Ford hell about not speaking to him and he now addresses him as "Young man." I develop my paragraphs poorly—the point is that one can only have a certain number of guests not speaking to each other . . . . . and I hate to have guests suffer more than the ordinary pains.

Can't you come down some time after August first? And if Rem is in the south can't he come? You know—and I trust he knows—that we'd love to have him. We really will have the coast clear by August. And I am taking a rest when I finish this book. I've got to. I can't keep this up. I write more and more like the late John Galsworthy.

Larry sounds so nice I'm glad to know he has a few failings—like getting ridiculous ideas. Heavens! Well, I can't develop that paragraph properly either. You do it for me.

I have fallen off to 124 pounds, thank God.

Nancy is still fat but extremely pretty.

I should have waited till I had time to write a real letter but I wanted to get this note off to you.

Again, if there's *any* chance of any of the Woods or Kohns coming to see us *any*time (after August 1) this summer we shall be immensely pleased. If I *have* given you up it's along with a lot of other things. I'd like to hang on to you. I have just been under such a grind the last four years that everything had to go. It was mean of Scribner's to make me turn out another book so soon.

Harper's Bazaar has just bought one of my inferior stories called "The Brilliant Leaves." Collier's wired for a story the other day and I had none to send them.

I will take your story to Olivet with me and read it there. Dipped into it and saw some felicitous phrases. The only trouble with you as a writer is that you haven't *had* to write enough. The chief trouble with me as a writer from now on is going to be that I've had to write too much. Too bad we can't strike a happy medium.

Ford in his old age is slaving at hack work. It makes one sad. God knows what is going to become of him.

Must return to Ote Mortimer who is about to commit a murder. "The Garden of Adonis" is from a quotation of Sir James Frazer. About the vegetation rites for the god, Adonis. The women put earth in pots and planted fennel, wheat, barley etc. The plants shot up but not being planted in the earth itself withered and after the eighth day were carried out and cast into the sea . . . . . Not a new theme for me. But I have got more character into it this time. It's all about people. Four or five illicit love affairs all going on at once.

Must quit. Love and don't write us off as a total loss,

> *as ever,*
> *caroline*

. . . .

[added as a postscript]

Aleck Maury is being remaindered in England at fourteen cents a copy. I am getting fifty copies and will give you some when you come— but if you wanted to invest in some copies for yourself I am vain enough to believe that it would not be a bad speculation. Address my agent, Alan C. Collins, Curtis Brown, Ltd., 18 East Forty Eighth street, New York. But for heaven's sake don't do it because I told you to. I just really think the copies will be valuable some day. Naive of me, I know.

I was entranced with the medical life as practiced by my husband. Being a Hopkins man, he had acquired the Aequanimitas *Sir William Osler recommended for a doctor. He could leave a New Year's Eve party to attend a dying patient, talk with the relatives, and return with the full burden of sympathy for the dying and yet recover the pleasure of living. It was sometimes a little slow—the recovery. I usually knew what had happened, and he knew that I knew.*

I was still writing, but slowly. A serious novel that I had begun soon

*after our marriage stopped when we adopted a little boy, aged 7½. We had
planned this as soon as we had a house to put him in. He took up so much of my
time at first that I just wrote a detective story—easy to get in and out of. It was*
The Murder of a Novelist, *published by Simon and Schuster in 1941.*

*I did not intend to go on with this sort of thing and only wrote one more.
Quite a lot of nursing had turned up unofficially in my life and that was my
first love. Writing became a sort of* violon d'Ingres. *Needless to say, Caroline
did not approve.*

Clarksville, October 16, 1937
To S. W. in Rochester

Dear Sally:

Lovat Dickson, the English publisher of Aleck Maury, is undoubtedly the stupidest man living. He has just pulled some sort of stupid trick
about those remaindered copies of Aleck Maury. I can't quite make out
what it is—but fear that he simply billed you for twenty five copies. This
because I mentioned your name as one who might be interested in getting
some copies.[1] I was vain enough to think that at fourteen cents a copy
they would make nice Christmas presents—but I didn't want you held up.
I am sorry.

I sent you a few days ago a package from Scribner's which I was
morally certain contained my photograph. It was done up so nicely I
didn't want to go into it. It comes over me now that it may be a contract
or God knows what. So if it doesn't contain said photograph just write it
off as another error—mine, this time, not the publishers.

Me, I am always mortified by my errors but publishers always seem
to think theirs are just acts of God.

Nancy is having her tonsils out tomorrow. We are both scared to
death, of course. After twelve years of phenomenal health she has suddenly developed bad tonsils and she also has a pretty bad astigmatism and
is now fitted with reading glasses which give her a deceptively scholarly
appearance. She also has to have in the near future a basal-metabolism
test. I have been trying for years to get doctors interested in her excessive
plumpness and finally struck one who said off hand that she undoubtedly
had some disturbance of the thyro-pituitary. He says, though, that those
things are still in an experimental stage. It may not be necessary to do

anything about it but it's just as well to have the test. Nancy is resigned to all these doctorings. She looked in the glass the other day and found a small bump on her really very fair complexion. "Those adolescent pimples," says she with a snicker.

By the way she is doing very well in dancing this year. I do not note much progress in her other studies.

I had intended long ere this to write you about your story. It seems to me that it is about as well done as it could be. You are evidently able to handle anything you want to handle. The only defect in the story for me—of course I must always go for defects—is the long stretches of time involved. The time necessary for the boy and girl to grow up and become persons themselves. I dislike to see that much time handled in a short story. For a short story, its seems to me is a mushroom affair, grows up overnight. The characterization is awfully good, though, skillful and done with great economy.

Are you writing anything now?

Allen has one hundred and fifty pages done on his novel. A little more than half through.

I have been extremely busy for three months recovering from the Ford visit. I was simply flat when they left. By taking two naps a day for several weeks and reading many detectives stories I managed to recover my moral health about three weeks ago. It is certainly grand to feel like a human being again.

Katherine Anne stayed with us five weeks but went to New Orleans about a month ago. She couldn't write here—life was so distracting, what with the cats and all the fruits of the earth needing to be preserved, pickled or made into wine. She made mint liqueur, preserved peaches whole, made five gallons of elderberry wine, brandied peaches and would have brandied and preserved bushels more if I had provided her with them. All this, of course, partly out of domestic passions, partly out of charitable concern for our welfare and a good part I wickedly believe just to get out of work. She has to sever every earthly tie she has before she can do any work, go off to a hotel somewhere usually.[2] I wonder what will happen if she finds herself without any ties to sever. Will she be able to work then? Just now she is busy getting rid of a husband, who to her great surprise has acted exactly the way her husbands always act. He does have one new dodge, though. When she told him she was leaving him he refused to believe it and all the time she has been away he writes her pleasant letters, saying he does miss her but he wouldn't for worlds cut her visit short. These letters cause her to simply tear her hair.

. . . The country is simply lovely now, that October haze over everything, helped out a bit by the smoke from the tobacco barns curling up everywhere. I have undertaken to rake the whole yard for the sake of my figure—Ford had me down to one hundred and twenty four but I speedily took on five pounds as soon as he left.

Nancy has a beautiful sorrel pony. She was as ridiculous as a city child about riding at first but now she has gotten very horsy, jumped the pasture bars on Brownie the other day and sometimes rides without bridle or saddle just for the hell of it. I'm sending you some pictures if I can lay hands on them. My study is in its usual mess, me just having finished up a lousy short story.

I wish you and the doctor could take a vacation and come to see us. Wish we weren't so far away. Can't you stop by on your way to Florida[3] . . . . . no, I suppose there's no use in going to Florida if you have to freeze yourself first at Benfolly. I could keep you in the cellar bedroom with roaring fires going. We haven't been here in the winter for several years now and are really looking forward to it. October is the best month, of course. The summer is always so hectic. Don't you think you might risk a stopover on your way south—I take it for granted that you'll be going when the bad weather sets in.

Found the picture I was looking for. The cow is your old friend, Daisy Miller, the calf is her bull calf, Uncle Andrew. He is not destined for veal but has gone to the next farm to have, we trust, a brilliant career as a bull.

Must get out and do some raking. I also tote manure from one place to the place where I think it will do the most good—a very soothing occupation after writing fiction.

> *Love and do write,*
> *as ever,*
> *caroline*

1. Larry was a fly fisherman, who doted on these books and sent them to fishing friends.

2. When we had a maid and no young children in the house, I used to board a bus with my typewriter and small suitcase and go to a country hotel. Unlike Katherine Anne, I always came back. When country hotels disappeared, I even went to a motel a few times.

3. With a small child on my hands and a husband very busy in the winter, I was destined to forego Florida and the South for many years. Caroline and I met in New York, Princeton, and Rochester, instead.

Epilogue

The marriage of Allen and Caroline had never been one of just two people involved with each other. They had always had dependents. Though Caroline's mother had taken Nancy soon after her birth, the baby had been replaced almost immediately by a much more difficult member of the household, Hart Crane. He had seemed in a desperate situation, and once the Tates had figured out how to have a roof over their heads, it was in the nature of both, as southerners and writers, to offer him a place under it. As it turned out, he found himself in possession of more money than they had and took a bigger share of the roof. But in spite of the ensuing uproar, Allen felt responsible, not for Hart's shelter, but for his gifts, and he helped him with *The Bridge*. This was the kind of thing that constantly happened to them. Bringing up Nancy, when they eventually retrieved her, was child's play compared to the dependence of many friends and even strangers who constantly flocked around them.

Of course, they enjoyed it. The most literary people of their time were constantly coming through their doorway, often bowed down with problems they hoped to shake off and deposit with the Tates. Very often the miracle happened. There was such a degree of unity—as Robert Lowell said, "Both stately and Bohemian"—about this pair that it steadied many a wavering course in others.

The responsibility, however, was great, always mixed as it was with their desire to get away from it all and do their own writing. The first years at Benfolly were the ones when everything worked. Allen was making enough money—helped, one supposes, to some extent by his brother—to keep the grocery bills just about paid. Caroline felt the support of her ancestral acres and helpful aunts and her indomitable grandmother. Allen was in the company of the Fugitives, and naturally, Benfolly became the center that they clustered around.

The degree of help people gave to each other was extraordinary. As far away as New York or San Francisco, other writers spoke of Benfolly with awe and planned to visit there as if making a pilgrimage. It was a milieu where writers influenced each other. Encouragement and criticism were equally expected. Even detachment had its place. One can think of no other creative center like it ever having existed in America. In France, of course, it had; and though one thinks of Bloomsbury, that was a place where private lives tangled with each other as much as or more than did talent.

The multiple pressures—not the least of which was poverty when Allen struck a noncreative period—took their toll. And of course, Allen was also depressed by the long dry spell.

He was forced to turn to teaching in the wake of Robert Penn Warren. Although they thought their first try at it, in Memphis, would be only temporary, it proved to be the most reliable way of making a living. At times their surroundings were disagreeable. Caroline began to teach also. Since they had both published books by then, they were a rather new spectacle on the academic scene. They were people without Ph.D.s or special courses who taught writing because they could actually do it.

This is a familiar feature in college life now; it was not in the 1930s. There was sometimes resentment among the purely academic faculty, but more often, especially in Allen's case, pleasure in his evident scholarship and ease of manner and freedom of conversation. The Tates, wherever they were, could not help being conspicuously social and hospitable. They carried with them, at the least, those strands of the Confederate flag—hard as it was in foreign parts to keep hold of the habits of more leisured centuries. Even Ford Madox Ford, so productive of conflict elsewhere, could not make a dent in the iron-clad good manners of the South, outnumbered as he was there.

They made a sort of spiritual home for me between my two marriages, as they did for others who needed one. Even to think of them during their years at Benfolly was a pleasure. We were only the beginning of several lost generations, but the Tates seemed to have escaped the *mal du siècle* and lived in a combination of the past and a hopeful future.

When life became too unrewarding, the Tates talked of separating. But

Caroline would say, "I don't think we could ever be to people separately what we are to them together."

History must decide. It is difficult because one whole generation knew them together; then another knew them apart. They did not separate for good until old Mr. Gordon died and Nancy was married. Before that they spent many years in Princeton. They had become acquainted with Jacques and Raissa Maritain.[1] Caroline became a Catholic convert, and Allen eventually did also.

1. Jacques Maritain (1882–1973), a visiting professor at Princeton, was a French philosopher and follower of Saint Thomas Aquinas who converted to Roman Catholicism in 1906. He played a leading role in the Catholic renaissance in France.